HE ALMOST CHANGED THE WORLD

HE ALMOST
CHANGED THE WORLD

The Life and Times of Thomas Riley Marshall

David J. Bennett

Bloomington, IN  Milton Keynes, UK

authorHOUSE®

AuthorHouse™
1663 Liberty Drive, Suite 200
Bloomington, IN 47403
www.authorhouse.com
Phone: 1-800-839-8640

AuthorHouse™ UK Ltd.
500 Avebury Boulevard
Central Milton Keynes, MK9 2BE
www.authorhouse.co.uk
Phone: 08001974150

First published by AuthorHouse 1/23/2007

ISBN: 978-1-4259-6562-4 (sc)

Library of Congress Control Number: 2006908883

Printed in the United States of America
Bloomington, Indiana

This book is printed on acid-free paper.

CONTENTS

October 2, 1919

On the morning of October 2, 1919, President Woodrow Wilson awoke in his bedroom at the White House. The temperature outside was a mild fifty-seven degrees, but the weather was wet, as an inch-and-a-half of rain would fall in Washington on that day.

The President's thoughts on that dreary morning are unknown, but the cessation of hostilities in Europe did not bring an end to Wilson's worries. The German peace treaty had not yet been ratified by the Senate, and, more importantly to Wilson, a recalcitrant group of Senators, led by Henry Cabot Lodge of Massachusetts, was opposing United States participation in the League of Nations. King Albert I of Belgium, the first reigning monarch in Europe to visit the United States, was scheduled to arrive in New York later that day, but Wilson had asked his Vice President, Thomas Riley Marshall, and his wife, Lois, to greet the visiting royalty.

Domestically, labor unrest was on the rise, and a steelworkers strike in Gary, Indiana had turned violent. Thousands of returning soldiers were trying to reassimilate themselves back into their families, their jobs and the lives they had before the war. But he knew discontentment with his Democratic Party was growing. The elections of 1918 had gone badly, and Republicans now controlled both Houses of Congress. Unless he produced a decisive victory soon, 1920 would continue the electoral momentum gained by the G.O.P. He might have had his mind on less weighty matters, as on the previous day the Cincinnati Reds had defeated the Chicago White Sox 9-1 in the first game of the World Series.

We don't know what Wilson was thinking that morning. What we do know is that, a few minutes after eight o'clock that morning, the President suffered a severe thrombosis of the middle cerebral artery of the right hemisphere of his brain. He lost consciousness, and fell from the bathroom stool, striking his head on the side of the bathtub and opening a gash across the bridge of his nose. He lay on the floor, unconscious and undetected, for nearly thirty minutes, until he was discovered by his wife who, with the help of the President's personal physician, moved Wilson to his bed. When he regained consciousness, the President's left leg and left arm were completely paralyzed, as was the lower half of the left side of his face. Further complicating this severe organic hemiplegia was Wilson's greatly diminished ability to both see and speak.

The President was, by any reasonable analysis, disabled not only from a medical perspective but from a constitutional perspective, as well. Yet Vice President Thomas Riley Marshall did not assume the powers of the presidency. Marshall spent the remaining year-and-a-half of the Wilson presidency much as he had the first six years – in the background, far from policy-making discussions, a humorous but largely ignored second-in-command. He greeted diplomats, traveled to public appearances and presided when the Senate was in session, but even with a disabled President the Vice President had little impact on public policy.

In hindsight, however, Marshall's inaction meant that he was unable to influence the extraordinarily important and far-reaching policy decisions that were made in the last two years of Wilson's second term. At Paris, Wilson's arrogance and self-confidence, combined with that of his counterparts in Great Britain, France and Italy, had crafted an armistice treaty that not only led to another tragic world conflagration within twenty years, but would also spawn regional conflicts which still simmer nearly one hundred years later. And the world organization that could have served as a vehicle to mediate these disputes – the League of Nations – was doomed by the intransigence of its two great protagonists – Wilson and Henry Cabot Lodge. "I have sometimes thought", Marshall wrote in his memoirs, "that great men are the bane of civilization; that they are the real cause of all the bitterness and contention which amounts to anything in the world."[1]

By many yardsticks, Thomas Riley Marshall was not a great man of his generation. An only child in a family of privilege as a doctor's son, Marshall had the advantages of a stable home environment in a family viewed as leaders in their small community in Indiana. Politics often dominated dinner table conversation, but he did not successfully run for office until well past the age of fifty. His academic work was superior but not outstanding. He was educated at one of the finer colleges in the Midwest, and graduated to a career in law where he was respected in the small community in Northeast Indiana that he called home.

But the untimely death of his fiancé, and other unknown personal demons, resulted in crippling alcoholism. For much of his early adulthood he gained the titles and status befitting an attorney from a prominent local family, while those who knew him or saw him in the courtroom were aware that Marshall would be incapacitated for days at a time due to his alcohol addiction. Close friends looked the other way; those opposed to his drinking privately grumbled but said little.

With the love and support of a caring wife, however, Marshall overcame his addiction and rebuilt his reputation, both in his community and throughout the State. He emerged from his decade-and-a-half of drink-induced squalor with a sincere and genuine set of principles that would guide him through the rest of his life. He cherished his wife and was unerringly faithful to her. He sought and nurtured genuine friendships, and was loyal and committed to those who befriended him. And Marshall was scrupulously honest, even to the point of frustrating party bosses and political partisans. While many would consider Woodrow Wilson to be a great president, he could claim few of the attributes of personal integrity held by Marshall.

Marshall served ably in his one term as Indiana governor, from 1909 to 1913. His most notable – but ultimately unsuccessful – policy initiative was the rewriting of the State's constitution. The Marshall Constitution, as it came to be called, was flawed, but it contained many forward-thinking ideas, such as initiative and referendum and a line-item veto for the Governor. These reforms, adopted by many states during the Progressive Era, have yet to be adopted in the Hoosier State.

The Marshall Constitution was voided by the courts, but the issue brought him to national prominence. Three forces combined at the Democratic Convention in Baltimore in 1912 to swing the Vice Presidency to Marshall. First, the Indiana delegation was led by Thomas Taggart, who would use his considerable influence among prominent Democrats nationwide to support Indiana's native son (as Taggart had done four years earlier at the Indiana state convention to earn Marshall the gubernatorial nomination). In addition, Marshall's stature was boosted by Wilson's inability to emerge in early balloting as the leading candidate. Wilson, Champ Clark of Missouri and perennial nominee William Jennings Bryan slugged it out for ballot after ballot, giving Taggart a chance to broker a compromise that elevated Marshall to the second spot on the ticket. Finally, Indiana was a key swing state, and provided geographic balance for the candidate at the top of the ticket from New Jersey.

In the election of 1912, Teddy Roosevelt's Bull Moose Party split the Republican vote and ensured a Wilson victory. The next four years would cement Wilson's place in history, as he forged an alliance with key Democratic supporters and Republican progressives to enact a far-reaching domestic policy agenda. Enactment of an income tax, reduction of tariffs, implementing new commerce regulation, and creating the Federal Reserve were some of the landmark legislation enacted in a remarkable period between 1913 and 1916. Through it all, Marshall played a role common to Vice Presidents – supportive, but hardly crucial. Part of the team, but riding near the back of the bus.

The gathering of war clouds in Europe was mirrored by clouds over the Wilson presidency. The death of his wife Ellen in June 1916 was a tremendous personal loss, and many of the miscues over the next four years could be traced directly to his ambitious second wife, Edith. Edith also convinced Woodrow to turn his back on his friends and personal advisors, Colonel Edward House and Joseph Tumulty, just at the time when the President needed their advice and counsel the most.

The high mark of the Wilson presidency probably came on April 2, 1917. After months of negotiations and indecision, the emergence of unlimited submarine warfare and the disclosure of the Zimmerman Telegram led Wilson to ask, on that date, for a declaration of war. His speech to a joint session of Congress ranks as one of the finest in presidential history.

While American doughboys were bringing World War I to a close, Wilson was blundering domestically. His call for a Democratic victory in the elections of 1918 resulted in just the opposite, and when Congress convened in 1919 both the Senate and House were controlled by Democrats.

Blind to domestic political realities and supremely confident of his own vision and abilities, Wilson led a delegation to the Paris Peace negotiations devoid of meaningful Republican participation. Wilson set forth his philosophy of the world order after the War to End All Wars in his Fourteen Points, causing one sage to remark wryly, "Moses only needed ten." Crafting treaty terms and drawing national borders like he was playing chess at his seaside home in Seagirt, Wilson advocated for peace terms which avoided resolution of many critical regional issues – issues which he was confident could be resolved by the newly-proposed League of Nations.

But opponents of the League, led by Henry Cabot Lodge (now Chairman of the Senate Foreign Relations Committee thanks to the election of 1918), were concerned about elements of the plan, particularly those which seemed to commit the United States to what George Washington had termed "entangling alliances". Rather than compromising with those who favored passage with reservations, Wilson embarked on a nationwide tour that he hoped would galvanize public opinion and force the Senate to agree to the League as proposed.

It was at this juncture in history – even prior to Wilson's most serious stroke – where Marshall's ability to forge coalitions among competing viewpoints could have salvaged support for the League of Nations and passage of the Treaty of Versailles. But by 1919 Woodrow Wilson had supreme self-confidence in his own wisdom. With House and Tumulty out of favor, Wilson sought advice either from his physician, Cary Grayson, or more commonly from Edith, who was poorly prepared for strategic decision-making and was far more confident in her own ability than was warranted. With Wilson's debilitating stroke on October 2, 1919, decision-making in the executive office of the most powerful nation on earth was largely in the hands of a self-centered, boorish and poorly educated widow of a jewelry storeowner. While the world order for the next generation was being established, Edith Wilson maintained the reins of government with one eye on her husband's health and the other on his legacy.

A stronger man than Thomas Riley Marshall might have fought harder to take the reins of power and carry on the stricken president's vision, crafting a compromise that could have been approved by the Senate. But the results of such an action are pure speculation. Marshall thought such a step could have led to a darker outcome. "I could take this country into civil war", he told Lois, "but I won't."

Wilson's biographer, Arthur Link, understood the consequences of the futile battle over the League of Nations. "In a world with the United States playing a responsible, active role, "Link said, "the possibilities of preventing the rise of Hitler were limitless."[2]

Thomas Marshall triumphed over his personal adversities, and emerged with a pragmatic view of world events and the importance of relationships, integrity and the art of compromise in the world of politics. Wilson's background of academia and privilege failed to instill in him the realities of the political process and the limits of presidential power. If both men had taken the opportunity to learn from the other, the world today might be a very different place.

CHAPTER ONE:

I Liked the Tall Man

(1854-1878)

In the decades after the young United States gained independence from England, the territories on the Western frontier beckoned with opportunity for ambitious settlers. Kentucky, Ohio and Tennessee began to fill with tenacious adventurers who, often with their families, staked their claim on small parcels of fertile farmland. The first years always led to hard work and more often than not disappointment. Forests were cleared, cabins built, fields tilled and wells dug. Some years, the weather cooperated with moist springs, sunny summers and mild winters. But uncooperative weather could test the endurance of a pioneering family, either through a summer drought or bitterly cold winter.

In the early years of the eighteenth century, an area roughly bounded by Fort Dearborn (present-day Chicago) and Fort Detroit to the north and the Ohio River to the south came to be known as the Indiana Territory. The name derived from the large number of Indian tribes known to reside there.

Along with the vagaries of the weather, then, early settlers to the Indiana Territory had to manage their relations with the Indian tribes that usually occupied the best farmland. The largest tribes in the northern Indiana territory in the early 1800s included the Miamis, Delawares and Shawnees.

The largest was the Miamis, who controlled the area from Fort Wayne to Lafayette and everything in between. The Delawares migrated from the Chesapeake Bay area, settled in Ohio and Pennsylvania during the early eighteenth century, and finally established villages in the Indiana Territory between the Ohio and White Rivers. The highest concentration of Delawares could be found on the upper west fork of the White River in present-day

Hamilton, Madison, and Delaware Counties. Another migrating tribe that settled in Indiana was the Shawnee. At the invitation of the resident Delawares, the Shawnees relations between the three tribes alternated between cordial and hostile as they positioned themselves for the most fertile land and best hunting grounds. They viewed each other with general distrust until the arrival of a common enemy – the white settlers – and the emergence of strong leadership.

A Shawnee medicine man, Tenskwatawa, known to the whites as the "Shawnee Prophet," emerged as a leader among the tribes in fighting against white settlers. He called on Indians to return to the ways of their ancestors and to forgo the white ways. The native Indian tribes would often follow a pattern of at first welcoming the occasional trapper, growing cautious as they observed large bands of hunters, and finally massacring villages of settlers who demanded increasing amounts of land.

Tensions rose on the frontier and the federal government sent General William Henry Harrison to clear the area of hostile Indians. Harrison defeated The Prophet and his brother, Tecumseh, in the Battle of Tippecanoe in 1811, clearing the way for both unlimited white settlement and his nomination for the Presidency.

Riley Marshall, Thomas's grandfather, grew up in Greenbriar County, Virginia – that part of the state that was to split off in 1863 to become West Virginia. Little is known of Riley Marshall's early years, but he made the decision in 1817 to travel west to the Indiana territory. The Miamis, Delawares and Shawnees who lived in the northern third of Indiana territory valued their land for the good and plentiful hunting, rivers for navigation, and a mild climate for farming. It is likely that Riley was aware of Harrison's victory and was attracted by the lure of prime farmland now free from Indian threat. By the time that Harrison had cleared the way for Riley Marshall and other settlers to move to the new State of Indiana, the land was made valuable by the same three factors.

Crossing Virginia and Ohio in six weeks, he first settled in Randolph County for a few years before moving north to Grant County, where he began farming on 640 acres near Marion, Indiana.[3]

My grandfather was one of the pioneers and pathfinders. He came to Indiana when it was a primeval forest. He had only youth, a stout heart, a sharp ax, a young wife and courage. He lived before the day of congressional appropriations. It took him six weeks to get here from Virginia. How foolish he was not to have waited until now![4]

The invention of the steam engine would soon put riches into Riley's lap far beyond what he could earn with his hunting rifle and plow. The grandfather of Thomas Riley Marshall had located his farm over one of the largest and richest oil and gas deposits discovered up to that time in the Midwest. Within ten years of making the fateful decision of traveling to the Western frontier, Riley sold a portion of his property for $25,000 – a princely sum in those days. Though it was not in a way he could have anticipated, he had achieved his goal. Riley Marshall was a rich man.

Riley's wealth helped him to rise in prominence within the Democratic Party, and he served as the first clerk of the circuit court in Grant County from 1832 to 1838. His family grew to include nine children, including Daniel M. Marshall, born in 1823.

Daniel studied medicine, and, while in training, met Martha Patterson, who had emigrated from Ohio and come to live with her sister in Marion after the death of her parents.

I never knew my grandparents on my mother's side. She and they were Pennsylvania born, and her humorous side led her to tell me that they trekked across the Alleghany Mountains and settled in Ohio for the reason that the county in Pennsylvania in which they lived had only four families and they were intermarrying until there was a danger that some man would have an imbecile for an ancestor. My mother's parents died in Ohio, the victims of the medical ignorance of the times. They had bilious fever. The doctor refused to permit them to drink water, and they literally burned to death. My mother came to Marion, Indiana to visit a sister, and there she and my father were married.[5]

After their marriage in 1848, Dr. Daniel Marshall began his medical practice in North Manchester, Indiana – thirty miles northwest of Marion.

My grandfather became the first clerk of Grant County, Indiana, and the courts were held in his house for several years. School facilities were meager; opportunities for educational improvement were few. My father grew to manhood in this environment and then, because he met with an accident, turned to the study of medicine. In this science he was fortunate enough to obtain as good an education as that age afforded.[6]

The Marshalls were living in North Manchester when their son, Thomas Riley, was born on March 14, 1854. He would be the only surviving child of Daniel and Martha, as another child, a daughter, died in infancy.[7]

Because of his father's activity in politics, Dr. Marshall certainly would have had numerous political conversations in his family while growing up and it can be presumed that a man of his intelligence would have thoroughly understood the political upheaval in Kansas in the years before the civil war.

During the time that Daniel and Martha lived in North Manchester, the nation became more divided over the question of the expansion of slavery. Most of the territory west of the Mississippi River was yet to be carved into states. Anti-slavery forces, mostly from the northern states, opposed permitting slavery in the newly created western states. Pro-slavery forces from southern states sought to expand slavery to at least some of the new western states.

The Marshall family was traditionally allied with the Democratic Party, but that party itself was split over the slavery question. On February 28, 1854, just two weeks before Thomas's birth, a group meeting in Ripon, Wisconsin formed a new political party opposed to slavery. They called their new political party the Republican Party.

෯ ෯ ෯ ෯ ෯

Not long after Thomas's birth, Martha was diagnosed with tuberculosis, and the family spent the next four years traveling from state to state in search of a climate more favorable to Martha's condition. The family traveled by covered wagon to Champaign, Illinois.[8]

Despite Dr. Marshall's professional training, his treatment of Martha's condition seemed grounded more in folklore than established medical practice.

Thomas asked his father what had led him to try fresh air, raw eggs and milk in treating his mother's illness. Dr. Marshall answered that he had once read a statement that six hundred years before the Christian era the Greeks took their weak-lunged patients up into the mountains, let them sleep out of doors, and gave them goat's milk, raw eggs and wine.[9]

While the Marshalls were in Illinois, Abraham Lincoln challenged Stephen Douglas for election as United States Senator from Illinois. Their debates helped to frame the slavery question over the next few crucial years.

Lincoln carried the banner of the newly created Republican Party, and its anti-slavery sentiment:

A house divided against itself cannot stand. I believe this government cannot endure, permanently half slave and half free. I do not expect the Union to be dissolved – I do not expect the house to fall – but I do expect it will cease to be divided. It will become all one thing, or all the other. Either the opponents of slavery will arrest the further spread of it, and place it where the public mind shall rest in the belief that it is in the course of ultimate extinction; or its advocates will push it forward, till it shall become alike lawful in all the states, old as well as new – North as well as South.

While in Illinois, Thomas's father took him to one of the debates in Freeport, Illinois and created a memory that would last throughout his lifetime. During the debate, 4-year-old Thomas sat on Lincoln's lap while Douglas was speaking and on Douglas's lap while Lincoln talked. "One was tall, ungainly; the other, small and animated," Marshall later remembered. "I think I have a recollection that I liked the tall man." As Marshall noted in his autobiography, it pleased him "to think that perhaps in a small way something of the love of Lincoln and of Douglas for the Union, the constitution and the rights of the common man flowed into my childish veins."

From Champaign, the family moved once again, to Ossawatomie, Kansas in 1858. Kansas was not a friendly environment for people with strong political convictions like Daniel Marshall. The state was embroiled in violent clashes between pro-slavery and anti-slavery forces. Gangs of men, armed with the latest technology in armed warfare, the breech loading Sharps rifle, roamed the Kansas countryside and terrorized those opposed to their viewpoint. Most were opposed to slavery, including a fanatic named John Brown, who killed a number of innocent people at the "Pottawatomie massacre".[10]

The Marshalls did not stay in Kansas long. Dr. Marshall was vocal in his support of popular sovereignty, but local harassment caused the family to move to Lagrange, Missouri, where Tom's father resumed both his medical practice and his activity in the Democratic Party.

Slavery had been prohibited in Missouri by the Missouri Compromise of 1820. Dred Scott was a slave who had been taken by his master, an army officer, first to Illinois, then to unincorporated territory and finally to Missouri. Scott sued for his freedom, arguing that the time he had spent in areas that prohibited slavery should make him a free man.

The United States Supreme Court ruled otherwise. Their ruling, in March 1857, said that Scott, as a Negro, was not a citizen of the United States and therefore had no right to sue in a federal court. In addition, the Court's ruling said that, even though Scott has spent time in areas declared free of slavery due to the Missouri Compromise, Congress had no right to deprive citizens of their property without due process of law. The Missouri Compromise, which had controlled the slavery question for 36 years, was unconstitutional and void.[11]

John Brown, who was responsible for much of the violence in Kansas, moved his band of followers to the other side of what was then the settled United States. On the evening of October 16, 1859, attempting to establish a republic of fugitive slaves in the Appalachians, he led a band of eighteen men in a siege of the federal arsenal at Harper's Ferry. They killed the mayor and seize a number of town leaders as prisoners.

A band of marines, led by Colonel Robert E. Lee, captured Brown and the five members of the raiding party that were still alive. Just two weeks after the raid, Brown was convicted of murder and treason. Brown was hung and denounced by most Northern leaders, but became a hero to those who advocated violence to end slavery.[12]

The nation was sharply divided as it entered the presidential election of 1860. That election in many ways mirrored the one that was to come 52 years later, in 1912. Both elections witnessed a schism in the predominant party (The Democrats split in 1860; in 1912, it was the Republican Party that was fractured), and the emergence of new political parties (Republican in 1860; Bull Moose in 1912). Democrats even held their convention in the same city both years, Baltimore.

Democrat Stephen Douglas could have united moderate proslavery and antislavery forces and perhaps avoided the coming secession. Douglas advocated a policy that would have preserved a union of free northern and slave southern states. "If each state will only agree to mind its own business," Douglas said, "This republic can exist forever divided into free and slave states, as our fathers made it and the people of each state had decided."

This viewpoint found wide acceptance among many northerners, including Daniel Marshall. When the presidential candidates made appearances in Fort Wayne, a large urban center just east of Pierceton, the town fathers were so impressed by one of the contenders that they renamed a street after him – and it is still known as Douglas Street.

Douglas, however, lost his support in the South due to his actions in the dispute over Kansas. Proslavery and antislavery forces had each drafted separate constitutions for Kansas, and asked the Senate to choose one. The Senate voted to accept the proslavery constitution, but Douglas, adhering to the principal of self-determination, was successful in putting both constitutions before a vote of the people of Kansas. When they voted overwhelmingly against the proslavery constitution, Douglas was branded as a "traitor to the South".

Douglas knew his actions were morally justified but harmful to his political ambitions. Nevertheless, he stood for what he felt was right – and it eventually cost him the presidential election. Tom Marshall never forgot the decision Douglas made, and often referred back to Douglas's courage and moral standards.

After the Democrats had rejected a proslavery platform and nominated Douglas, eight southern states held a separate convention in Charleston and nominated John Breckenridge of Kentucky.

Republicans saw their chance to divide the Democrats. They adopted a platform that called for no slavery in the new territories, but no interference with slavery in states where it currently existed. They chose as their nominee

Abraham Lincoln, who they knew could carry the key states of Indiana and Illinois.

The emotionally charged atmosphere forced the Marshalls to move again. Dr. Marshall

> *Became involved in a violent political controversy one day in October, 1860, with Duff Green, who later became a Confederate officer. Dr. Marshall's relatives wisely advised that he should flee to Illinois that evening, since they knew that Duff Green was already the leader of a body of irregular followers. Thomas remembered to the last years of his life how he had watched the setting sun as they took the boat that evening for Quincy, Illinois.*[13]

The Marshalls stayed in Quincy, Illinois only a short time. Their next move would be back to their homeland in Indiana, and they returned to northeast Indiana and settled in Pierceton, Indiana on November 6, 1860 – as Thomas Marshall would recall, "the very day on which Abraham Lincoln was elected President of the United States."[14]

Lincoln won the election with over 1.8 million votes, and 180 of 303 votes in the electoral college. Douglas and Breckenridge together garnered over 2.2 million votes, but the split between the two meant they finished second and third, respectively. For the southern states, the election of the Republican nominee as their President moved the slavery and states rights question to the point where they felt they needed to take decisive action. By the time of Lincoln's inauguration, eight southern states had seceded from the union.

The election of 1860 was also the start of a generation of Republican domination of the presidency. From the election of 1860 until 1912 – when Marshall was on the ticket – Republicans would win every presidential election, with the exception when Grover Cleveland was the candidate.

❧ ❧ ❧ ❧ ❧

Daniel and Martha would remain in Pierceton for the next 14 years. A small town just north of North Manchester, Marshall's birthplace, Pierceton is

the second largest town in Whitley County, Indiana, whose county seat is
Columbia City.

From the age of six until he entered Wabash College, Tom Marshall
enjoyed the life of a small town boy in Pierceton. Pierceton at that time was
a small community with a central business district ringed by wood-frame
homes. The central part of the Town is bisected by railroad tracks, below
which underpasses were constructed using stone shaped in a Roman arch to
accommodate Second and Third streets. The western part of town would in
time become home to several thriving industries. Just south of the commercial
district is the Carnegie Library, built in 1912.

Thomas was a precocious child, comfortable in an academic setting and
advanced well beyond children his age in maturity. While his spelling and
grammar reflected his young age, he shows maturity well beyond that of most
nine-year-old boys in this letter written from Pierceton to his Cousin Lizzie
in March, 1864:

> I thought I would write you a few lines to get an invitation to
> your wedding. We received a letter from there stating that you
> and Callie were both getting married and would like when you
> and Callie get married to make us a visit. Ma says when you
> get married you get a major who will feed you potliquour. ...
> I suppose you have heard the sad news of grandfather's death.
> ... We supposed that there was something the matter that you
> did not write. I am at exchange of currencies in my arithmetic.
> I believe I have told you all the news as you are going to be
> married. How I send their love to all. I remain your cousin.[15]

While world events are often beyond the grasp of young boys, it is
noticeable that Tom's "newsie" letter says nothing of the Civil War – a conflict
that was certainly on the minds of Cousin Lizzie and her fiancée Callie. By
the time of Thomas's tenth birthday, Americans were intimately familiar with
the bloody battlefields of Manassas, Shiloh, and Antietam, and later that
summer the two armies would meet in the climatic battle near Gettysburg,
Pennsylvania. But young Tom spent each day playing with friends, watching
the trains go by or just passing time. Marshall recalls a time when he attempted
to record his events for posterity:

My father thought it would be a good thing for me to keep a record each night of the things that impressed me during the day, so when I was about ten years of age he gave me a diary. I remember that on the evening of the first of January, after carefully pondering over my day, I recorded the fact that we had buckwheat cakes and sausage for breakfast, roast turkey, cranberry sauce and sweet potatoes for dinner. With this record I was compelled to stop, for there seemed to be nothing else in the day that was worth recording for future generations. [16]

From all indications, Tom was a good student. In 1865, his teacher presented him with the book *The Boat Club* by Oliver Optic, with the inscription "As A Reward for Good Lessons". In 1866, he attended higher school in Warsaw, Indiana. Two years later, at the age of 14, Marshall moved on to Fort Wayne High School, thirty miles east of Pierceton. Students at that time studied the classics: Virgil's *Aeneid* and Homer's *Iliad*, as well as science books such as *Anatomy, Physiology and Hygiene*.

As Thomas's interest in national affairs grew, he began to take greater interest in the news, particularly political news. The presidential election of 1868 drew his attention, in part because Hoosier Schuyler Colfax was teamed as the running mate of war hero General Ulysses S. Grant. This would be the first presidential election to be held since the impeachment of Andrew Johnson. During his tenure, white Southerners fought aggressively against Reconstruction policies. Reformers from Northern states, termed "carpetbaggers", controlled the local governments, including the educational systems. The reforms were financed by high real estate taxes, which became more burdensome when agricultural prices plunged in the Panic of 1873.

White Southerners fought back with a campaign of violence and terror. Leading the mayhem was a group of secret societies, the most famous of which was the Ku Klux Klan. Led by former Confederate military commanders such as Nathan Bedford Forest, the K.K.K. terrorized Negroes and their white supporters. In one Florida county in 1871, the Klan was responsible for the murder of 163 Negroes. [17]

Government officials reacted with predictable outrage to the actions of the K.K.K., and in some southern states the Klan was formally disbanded. But the attitudes that led to the creation of the Ku Klux Klan remained, and their brand of violence did not disappear in the South, or in Indiana. Racial hatred would continue to plague Indiana, where the Ku Klux Klan would find strength well into the next century.

❧ ❧ ❧ ❧ ❧

As Marshall entered his teenage years, he would read about two milestones in transportation would occur which would dramatically alter transportation – and, as a result, the fates of nations – forever. On May 10, 1869, near Salt Lake City, Utah, the final spike was laid connecting the Union Pacific railroad from the east with the Central Pacific railroad out of Sacramento. For the first time, cargo and passengers could travel from the Mississippi to California by rail. Soon, three other rail lines were opened. The Northern Pacific stretched from Lake Superior to Portland, Oregon; the Southern Pacific, from New Orleans to Los Angeles; and the Santa Fe linked Atchison, Kansas with San Diego. A trip by horse or covered wagon that took weeks could now be covered in just a few days. Finally, the western states were open for expansion.

Barely a year later, half way around the world, a team of French workers completed the 105-mile Suez Canal linking the Mediterranean with the Indian Ocean. A trip from Europe to India was shorted by 5,800 miles, and the Middle East would once again become the crossroads of world trade.

But some, on hearing of the Transcontinental Railroad and the Suez Canal, dreamed of a day when the distance between the seaports of the eastern and southern states could be brought dramatically closer to California and Asia. In the 1870s, travel by ship between New York and San Francisco took several months to cover the thirteen thousand-mile journey. A canal between the Atlantic and Pacific would shorten that journey by eight thousand miles. While many would dream of such a canal, the world would have to wait another generation before such an idea was realized.

❧ ❧ ❧ ❧ ❧

Daniel and Martha Marshall were determined to have their only child continue his education beyond high school.

> *My people chose to send me to Wabash College, at Crawfordsville,*
> *Indiana. It was staid, as it is yet. An old-fashioned institution,*
> *founded for the purpose, if possible, of giving a young man what*
> *I am pleased to call a cultural education: that is, to train him*
> *in those studies and direct his mind along those lines which will*
> *give to him powers to reason accurately, or practically so, upon*
> *the great problems of life, and to be philosophic under all the*
> *misfortune that may come to him. About it I venture to say what*
> *Webster said of Dartmouth, in the great cause wherein he won*
> *his fame, that a charter is a contract, that it is a small college,*
> *but there are those of us who love it.*[18]

Marshall developed a deep and abiding love for Wabash College, and would one day serve on its Board of Trustees. Perhaps it was because, as he noted, Wabash trained him to "reason accurately ... upon the great problems of life." Or, more ominously, to be "philosophic under all the misfortune that may come to him." Tom would be faced with both challenges, and he remained loyal to the institution which gave him the knowledge and courage to be a thoughtful and farsighted leader.

At Wabash, Marshall developed a deep respect for the faculty, and also a profound appreciation for the joys of knowledge. Of his instructors, he wrote:

> *They cared not for riches and less for preferment, but they were*
> *intensely moved with the spirit of implanting the principles in*
> *which they believed in the minds of the young men who came*
> *under their charge. They were what much of the educational*
> *world has now lost – great teachers – and their satisfaction came*
> *not from the worldly goods with which they could surround*
> *themselves but from the impetus they could give to high thinking*
> *and right living and the additions they thus could make to the*
> *wealth of civil and religious liberty which the Republic then*
> *possessed.*[19]

Marshall's career at Wabash was not without controversy, and one incident proved to be quite traumatic for young Tom. As it happens, it brought together three great men in Hoosier history.

While working for the school newspaper, *The Geyser*, Marshall wrote an article about a visiting woman lecturer in which he made disparaging remarks about her virtue. Marshall had written that the woman was caught flirting under the table with the boys at her boarding house.[20]

The woman sued and her attorney, Civil War general and *Ben Hur* author Lew Wallace, asked $20,000 in compensation. From the historical record, it is likely the woman was trying to take liberties with the young men at the college. Furthermore, it would be entirely uncharacteristic of Marshall to fabricate the story and publish it. But it would be impossible for Marshall to support the facts of the story.

Marshall traveled to Indianapolis to ask help from General Benjamin Harrison.

> *After much difficulty I found myself in his presence, submitted the article to him and asked him if it was libelous. He read it carefully and then looked up and said: "Young man, if I had an enemy that I wanted to libel and could hire you to look after the job, I would not hunt further".*[21]

After some legal maneuvering, the case was dismissed. The much-relieved Marshall went to Harrison to ask him what he owed him. "Not a cent", said Harrison.

> *"I wouldn't think of taking anything from you. You have been foolish boys and this will be a great lesson to you. Never hereafter in life charge anybody with wrongdoing or crime that you do not have in your hands undoubted proof that it is true before you make the charge, and even then don't make it unless you are quite satisfied that by making of it you are either defending yourself or performing some real public service."*[22]

"It was a great lesson to me," Marshall wrote, "And I have never again been sued for either slander or libel."[23]

At Wabash, Marshall's interest in politics only deepened. "The real amusement of those earlier days was not golf or mah jong." wrote Marshall, "It was local politics. It was played by everybody with the zest of a confirmed gambler".[24] Due to the fiercely partisan Democratic views of his father and grandfather, it is hardly surprising that Marshall embraced that party's philosophy. Daniel Marshall had supported Douglas over Lincoln in their senatorial race in Illinois in 1858. During the Civil War, Tom's grandfather maintained his loyalty to the Democratic Party, even though the local Methodist minister threatened to expel him from the church. His grandfather replied that he was willing to take his chance on Hell but never on the Republican Party.[25]

Marshall became active in Democratic politics while at Wabash. During the campaign of 1872, he organized the Democratic Club of Wabash College. "I have forgotten how many members we had," Marshall wrote, "whether there were seven or eight. But I know we had only one voter, and I was not he".[26]

During the Civil War, "greenback" currency had been issued to finance the purchase of military supplies and personnel. With the end of the war, Congress wrestled with the question of redeeming the currency for gold or letting it remain in circulation. In September 1869, Jay Gould and Jim Fisk, two New York financiers, took advantage of a tip given them by an official in the Grant administration and cornered the market in gold. On "Black Friday", September 24, 1869, the price of gold soared and dozens of Wall Street firms were ruined.

Many blamed the President Grant for the debacle. In the election of 1872, the Republicans renominated Grant, while the Democrats, after a bitter fight, backed Horace Greeley, who had been the editor of the New York *Tribune* for over thirty years.

While the Democrats had Horace Greeley at the top of the ticket in 1872, in the election for Indiana's governor from that year they nominated Thomas Hendricks.

Thomas Hendricks was born on a farm near Zanesville, Ohio, on September 7, 1819. At an early age he moved to Indiana where his uncle, William Hendricks, would become governor. After attending Hanover College, he attended law school in Pennsylvania and returned to open a practice in Shelbyville, Indiana. He married in 1845 but the couple would have no grown children as their only child died at age three.

Before he was age 30, he was elected to the Indiana House of Representatives and two years later won a seat in the U.S. House of Representatives. Like Tom Marshall's father, he became an admirer of Senator Stephen Douglas and supported Douglas' controversial Kansas-Nebraska Act. That law repealed the Missouri Compromise and permitted residents of the territories to determine whether or not to permit slavery. Hendricks firmly believed that citizens of the new states should have the right to determine their own destiny, but abolitionists were strongly opposed to even the possibility of expansion of slavery.

Daniel Marshall and Thomas Hendricks both paid a price for their belief in self-determination for the territories. For the Marshall family, which moved to Kansas as it entered statehood, their political beliefs would force them to leave under cover of darkness to avoid a violent confrontation with radical anti-slavery forces. Hendricks paid a political price, as he was defeated for reelection in 1854.

After losing his seat in Congress, Hendricks accepted an appointment from President Franklin Pierce in the Interior Department in Washington. Still eager to return to political office, he returned to Indiana to run for governor in 1860. He was defeated in that race, and soon afterward the Democratic Party faced a schism that would split its members for a generation. Some Democrats —such as Hendricks – supported the war efforts and worked to provide assistance for Union forces. A smaller but significant faction of the party, however, opposed the war and even went so far as to support the Confederate army.

One such "Peace Democrat" was Jesse Bright, the president pro tempore of the U.S. Senate. Bright's opposition to the war was well known, but when it was discovered that Bright had offered rifles to the Confederates from an Indiana company his colleagues felt he had gone too far. Bright was expelled from the Senate in February of 1862, and after the appointment of an interim successor the Indiana Legislature voted to put Thomas Hendricks in the U.S. Senate.

The fractured Congress of the Civil War years was heavily Republican. When Hendricks took office he was one of only ten Democrats facing thirty-three Republicans. He gained a reputation as a partisan but fair lawmaker, and while he advocated fiercely for his party and its positions he also showed the ability to work effectively with legislators from both sides of the aisle.

Hendricks visited Abraham Lincoln just four weeks before he was assassinated. "We have differed in politics," Lincoln told him, "but you have uniformly treated my administration with fairness."

The end of the war brought a substantially weakened Democratic party. Many leading Democrats had been labeled as Copperheads, or southern sympathizers, and it was a stigma that neither they nor their party would be able to shake so long as Union war veterans were alive. But Hendricks was clearly not a Copperhead, and, as such, became a leader of the Party both in Indiana and nationally.

Hendricks had been considered for the 1868 Democratic presidential nomination, but when he lost that bid he returned to Indiana to run for Governor. But the first post-war presidential election proved the strength of the Republican Party, and Democrats across the board, including Hendricks, were defeated. Four years later, however, when Horace Greeley was soundly defeated on the national ticket, Hendricks proved his popularity among Hoosiers and was elected governor.

The Wabash Democratic Club had the honor of escorting Thomas Hendricks through Crawfordsville as he campaigned for Governor that year. Another night, Marshall participated in a rally in support of Hendricks. Marshall's recollection shows that he understood that the angle of a story often depended on the viewpoint of those doing the telling.

> In the morning the Democratic newspaper, in giving an account of the political meeting, announced that it was the greatest torch-light procession that had ever marched in the City of Crawfordsville; that it was so large it took two hours to pass a given point. The evening Republican paper quoted this statement, confessed it was true, and then added that the given point was Mike Mulholland's saloon.[27]

The Club also provided Marshall the opportunity to make his first political speech, as he gave an impromptu oration lauding Horace Greeley when that candidate stopped in Indianapolis. Though the crowd was not large, Marshall was naturally nervous and went through with the speech only with the prodding of some of his classmates who had accompanied him. Newspaper accounts do not record what he said in support of Greeley, but

Marshall learned two important lessons from speaking to the crowd on that day. He loved talking to crowds. And, he was very good at it.

Despite the scandals of the Grant administration, Greeley was no match for the battle-hardened general. Greeley was a man of unquestioned personal integrity, but the nation was not ready for his brand of liberalism. During the campaign he supported such ideas as socialism, temperance and women's rights. In a choice between a war hero and a liberal journalist, Grant won all but six states.

Greeley was exhausted and broken-hearted by the campaign. In the weeks following the election, at age sixty-one, he went out of his mind and died before the end of November.[28]

Marshall's political viewpoint became apparent in classroom discussions, and he didn't hesitate to disagree with classmate or even faculty during discussions of current events. One classmate recalls:

> *Dr. Joseph Tuttle taught us Political Economy from a free trade textbook but he inoculated the principles of the protective tariff. But Marshall, the only Democrat in the class, steadfastly stood firm against him and all of us, claiming it was the granting of special privileges to some, was unconstitutional and would lead to an unequal distribution of wealth.*

❧ ❧ ❧ ❧ ❧

Academic success also came to Marshall. He was not only bright, but well organized and punctual. As one classmate recalled:

> *One could almost set his watch accurately by the promptness with which [Marshall left his] room three or four minutes before the recitation began, and hurried to the classroom.*

Marshall's experience at Wabash College proved to have an influence on his success throughout his life. His classmates and other Wabash connections played a key role in his gubernatorial campaign. Though his class was small, they remained life-ling friends and provided mutual support as each rose in their respective careers.

The class of 1873 was noted for its unity. The class motto was "one heart – one way". It is said that they always stood together. One of them has written that "driven by fate and adverse winds they were scattered from Persia to Japan, and letters of hope and encouragement followed them. In financial entanglements they opened and used checkbooks for each other. In political conventions they led the voting delegates to the rescue of each other. They invaded the adverse lines of political conventions to strengthen the cause of old classmates. At the ballot box they supported each other regardless of party lines, believing that while party fealty was sweet, the elbow touch of classmates was sweeter."[29]

While at Wabash, Marshall developed an interest in the study of law. As graduation approached, he sat in on court sessions, and also nurtured relationships with members of the Indiana bar.

While I was yet a college boy I had made up my mind that I should like to practice law and, if possible, to become a lawyer. As a sequence of this determination I spent most of my Saturdays in the courtroom in Crawfordsville. There I watched men as they practiced the law, and I had an opportunity to form ... an acquaintance with ... President Harrison and Vice President Hendricks ... and others.[30]

By the time of his graduation, Marshall had made up his mind to reunite with his parents, now in Columbia City, and become an attorney. He also saw the move as the chance to seek his own political career.

Marshall received the highest possible mark in fourteen of the thirty-seven courses he completed, and won election to Phi Beta Kappa. In June, 1873, Marshall received his degree during a ceremony that included a speech by each of the 21 graduating students.

At last the four years at college came to an end. I spoke my piece, got my diploma, put it away (where I have not, to my knowledge, ever seen it since), regretfully bade farewell to those good, gray-haired gentlemen and to my classmates, and started out to conquer the world, bolster up the Constitution of the United States, which was then in a falling condition, and restore the Republic to the Democratic Party.[31]

In the late nineteenth century, students of the law could become attorneys either by attending a law school (of which there were relatively few in the Midwest in 1873), or by developing a close, learning relationship with a practicing attorney. Until 1925, the only requirement for admission to the Indiana bar was the filing of an affidavit of good moral character by another member of the bar. Tom Marshall loved to tweak the egos of some of his more learned colleagues from the legal profession regarding the priorities for training attorneys in the Hoosier state.

Much amusement has been afforded the lawyers of America over the fact that the Constitution of the State of Indiana contains a provision that any man of good moral character may be admitted to the practice of law. Sometimes when gentlemen of other jurisdictions have trumped too harshly upon our toes about this provision it has pleased some of us to answer that it is far better to have less learning and more moral character in the practice of the law than it is to have great learning and no morals.[32]

Marshall chose not to attend law school, and came to Columbia City to study with a practicing attorney. As a well-educated, articulate man from a good family, Marshall had no trouble receiving offers from prominent local law firms. He accepted an offer from the firm of Hooper & Olds.

Adam Hooper was one of the first lawyers to settle in Columbia City. He became law partner with Walter Olds in 1869, and built the firm into one of the most prominent law practices in that part of the state. (Olds, whose wife was a cousin of Thomas Marshall's mother, eventually became a judge in the Indiana Supreme Court.)

That the strongly Republican Hooper would bring the fiercely Democratic Marshall into the firm is perhaps a testament to the high regard for the

Marshall family. Hooper had been appointed Postmaster of Columbia City by President Fillmore. In 1852, he represented Whitley and Noble in the Indiana House of Representatives; was elected County Auditor in 1854, and in 1868 served in the Indiana State Senate.

Adam Hooper died in March, 1875, and Olds brought in Isaac Sickafoose as a new partner. Under the tutelage of Olds and Sickafoose, as the firm was now called, Marshall studied law for two years. Walter Olds filed his affidavit that Marshall was of good moral character. After Marshall took the oath "to support the Constitution of the United States and the Constitution of the State of Indiana and that he will faithfully demean himself as an attorney of this court", he was appointed an attorney of the Whitley County Circuit Court in April, 1875, at the age of 21.[33]

Marshall's connection with Adam Hooper also brought another partnership, of sorts. Marshall became acquainted with Hooper's youngest daughter, Catherine. Kate was described as someone "fitted … to shine in society, yet she sought no social distinction and lived retired from the eye of the world, contented to make all happy around the family hearthstone."

The Marshall and Hooper homes were only a block apart, and Thomas and Kate began to see each other frequently. Eventually, they became engaged.

Thomas Marshall may have looked with assurance at the world that lay before him. College degree in hand, his reputation as a first-rate lawyer growing, secure as a member of a prominent local family and about to marry into another well-respected household, Thomas seemed ready to launch a fruitful legal practice, successful political career, and loving marriage.

But fate would not be kind to young Thomas Marshall, and within a few years his dreams would be shattered and his happiness gone.

❧ ❧ ❧ ❧ ❧

As an attorney in a small town, Marshall's law cases reflected a broad range of litigation. Mortgage foreclosures, drainage cases, the drawing of deeds, administering probate and minor criminal trials were some examples of his early legal work.

As the son of the local doctor, Thomas was well known and well-liked, which was an asset during the early years of his law practice as he worked to add to his growing list of clients. Despite his popularity, he was still nervous speaking before the court in front of judges, attorneys and clients much older than he was. He recalls his first speech in court.

> *When I arose … the world went black, I saw nobody, and my voice sounded as though it were in the neighborhood of Chicago. I was about to give it up … I said, "I'll do this thing if it kills me". I proceeded to talk – perhaps not intelligently, certainly not logically and assuredly not wisely, but nearer and nearer my voice came back to me as I proceeded and one after another the faces of the jurors came out as faces upon a photographic plate in the bath in a dark room. I said all I had to say and a good deal more. This has been the result of that experience: I have addressed kings, colleges, universities, Doctors of Divinity, scientists and plain citizens: I have made some of the worst speeches that ever were perpetrated upon the American people, but I have never been afraid since then to face an American audience.*

At times he found the work bordered on the mundane, and financial success was slow in coming. "We felt that it had been a rather dull and stupid Saturday unless we had a half dozen assault and battery cases to try before the local justice of the peace … for a long while I eked out a precarious existence with these … cases."[34]

But Marshall did not live on assault cases borne out of fist fights for long.

> *Scarcely had we reached the point where these fist fights ceased, and it looked as though I might be compelled to seek some other calling than the law, when the railroads began to cut off arms and legs and opened up a new source of revenue. There is hardly a good lawyer of the ancient days of northern Indiana who did not build himself an atrocious brick house out of the contingent fees which he collected from lawsuits prosecuted against railroad companies for mutilating and killing our citizens.*[35]

As a young attorney, Tom sought to use his rich educational background to improve the quality of his legal work. At times, though, he may have underestimated the challenge of applying a liberal arts education to the work of a practicing attorney, as the following story shows:

> *I never appreciated more in my life the usefulness of the language of diplomacy than I did during the attempt to act as host to this distinguished body of Frenchmen. I, of course, had in the days long ago what is known as college French. I read the language with facility. I even kept up, after I went into the law, my study of it by subscribing for and actually reading a French newspaper. I really imagined that I was a French scholar until one day in court a Frenchman, who could speak no word of English, presented himself as a witness. With that rashness of youth which is quite sure it can do all things, I tendered myself as an interpreter and was duly sworn. After fifteen minutes' vain effort to understand my French and for me to understand his replies, it was given up as a bad job, and I was the butt of the humor of the gum-booted lawyers of my bar. This so incensed me that I went home, threw everything French I had into the fire, cancelled my subscription to the newspaper and demanded from that time forward that the head waiter tell me in English what the menu card is all about.*[36]

The law practice continued to grow, and within a few years Tom had become a well-respected attorney with a growing list of clients. He opened his own practice, and brought in as a partner William F. McNagny. McNagny had grown up in Whitley County, and in 1872 became a station agent for the Pennsylvania Railroad. During his spare time McNagny read law, and was admitted to the bar in Kosciusko County, just west of Whitley County.[37]

❦ ❦ ❦ ❦ ❦

Tom Marshall began not only the practice of law in Columbia City, but he also became more active in Democratic politics. He volunteered for the campaign of a man who was close to Marshall both geographically and politically, fellow Hoosier Thomas Hendricks.

Due to the scandals of the Grant administration, a Democratic victory seemed certain in the Presidential Election of 1876. The Democratic nominee was New York Governor Samuel J. Tilden, a wealthy attorney from Albany. Tilden had fought against the corruption of Boss Tweed and the Tammany Hall gang. Coming from the most populous state, and with his impeccable integrity, Tilden was considered a strong favorite.

The Republicans nominated Rutherford B. Hayes, a brigadier in the Union army who had served three terms as governor of Ohio. After New York, Ohio was also a key political state. This dual strategy of combining geographic strength with war experience proved effective for a generation. The Republican strategy was to "wave the bloody shirt". "Every man that shot Union soldiers was a Democrat," went the Republican message. Five of the seven Presidents between 1869 and 1901 – Grant, Hayes, Garfield, Harrison and McKinley – were both Ohio natives and former Union officers in the Civil War.[38] The Republican Vice Presidential nomination in 1876 was awarded to Thomas Hendricks.

Democrats, also, knew that geographic balance was important in presidential elections, and Indiana had emerged as an important swing state. In addition, Hendricks had personally become an advocate for the farmers in his state through the use of "soft money", or the expansion of the currency through the issuance of greenbacks or the minting of silver currency. His geographic home base and his monetary viewpoint led to his first vice presidential nomination. When the Democrats nominated Samuel Tilden, a hard-money supporter from the East, Hendricks provided an attractive geographic and political counterpoint and he was asked to serve as Tilden's running mate.

Marshall campaigned hard for Tilden and Hendricks, who won Indiana. When the votes were counted nationwide, though, questions were raised over the results in three Southern states and Oregon. Without those states, Tilden would have only 184 electoral votes to 185 for Hayes.

In South Carolina, Florida and Louisiana, thousands of Democratic votes had been thrown out. Two sets of results were submitted – one showing Hayes the winner, the other Tilden. Marshall wrote:

I was enthusiastically for Tilden. When the well-known troubles in the South began, we were all anxious for Mr. Tilden to announce that he had been elected president and intended to be inaugurated. [39]

Congress set up an electoral commission made up of eight Republicans and five Democrats to investigate. At the time, Southern Democrats were strongly opposed to Fifteenth Amendment of the Constitution guaranteeing civil rights to freed slaves. In return for Southern Democratic support in the election, Republicans promised to withdraw federal troops from the south, and avoid enforcing the Fifteenth Amendment. No attempt was made by the federal government to enforce the Fifteenth Amendment until John Kennedy became president.

Passions ran high over the election. Marshall became a member of "Tilden's Guards", a group committed to ensuring that Tilden became president. "If all communities had been such as was ours," Marshall said, "Samuel J. Tilden could have plunged us again into a fratricidal war, for we were foolish enough to have met secretly and to have declared that we would purchase guns and go to Washington to help inaugurate him."[40]

When Hayes was declared President, Marshall was livid. He never forgot the injustice of the stolen election, and remained committed to his chosen candidates, even in defeat. "Tilden and Douglas were my idols," Marshall wrote, "They are the two men in all American history who when the peace and good order of their country were at stake cast aside every hope of personal preferment for the sake of the Republic they loved so well."[41]

For the rest of his life, Marshall contended that Tilden, not Hayes, was the true choice of the voters in 1876. In a letter he wrote in July, 1912, Marshall was trumpeting the ability of Hoosier voters to side with the winner in the presidential election. Indiana voters

Have voted twenty-three times for President of the United States. Nineteen times her choice has been inaugurated. She voted for Jackson when John Quincy Adams was elected by the House of Representatives and she voted for Tilden. I claim, therefore, that twenty-one times she voted for the choice of the Union.[42]

ᴔ᷼ ᴔ᷼ ᴔ᷼ ᴔ᷼ ᴔ᷼

One Monday morning in late 1878 a small article appeared in the Columbia City newspaper, which read: "It is with great sadness that we report to you the death of Catherine Hooper, who died Saturday, September 21, 1878 at the age of 21." The record suggests that the death was not a complete surprise. "For years she was the victim of a disease that she knew was fatal", wrote the local newspaper, "yet that knowledge did not sour her disposition or oppress her with fear."[43]

CHAPTER TWO:

The Hour of Man's Redemption

(1879-1907)

After the death of his fiancé Tom Marshall's alcoholism came to the surface. Little is known of his drinking habits prior to this time, but if Wabash College was like most institutions of higher education drinking was acceptable, if not officially condoned. Marshall might have developed a drinking problem while in college; if so, Walter Olds may have been unaware of it prior to hiring Marshall, or he knew of it and chose to ignore it.

After Kate Hooper's death, however, Marshall's drinking problem was more pronounced. He was the type of drinker whose behavior deteriorated after the first drink, and he admitted that he was seldom able to stop after one drink. In his own words he "wanted a barrel (of whiskey), not a drink". "The first drink improved his sparkling wit and humor," wrote Charles Thomas, his biographer, "but successive ones blunted his witticisms and sometimes put him under the table".[44]

Marshall's drinking put him at odds with his family, and would have certainly been well known in a town as small as Columbia City. Dr. Daniel Marshall was the president of the local temperance organization and often asked his son to speak at rallies and meetings; he had to know that Thomas was not practicing the advice he was giving. Tom Marshall still lived with his parents, and it must have caused them pain to see their son consumed by alcohol abuse.

There is no question that Marshall was well liked in Columbia City, and his oratory skills were in high demand. He spoke at rallies and picnics, commencements and luncheons. In 1877 he was chosen as the secretary of the Whitley County Joint Stock Agricultural Association, which gave him the responsibility for organizing the annual county fair.[45]

✌ ✌ ✌ ✌ ✌

In the election of 1880, Indiana began to emerge as a pivotal state in presidential elections. Part of the reason for this would hold true for the next forty years – the mathematics of the electoral college.

By the end of the nineteenth century, the states that were formerly in the Confederacy had emerged as a solid block for the Democratic party. Of the 188 electoral college votes needed to win the presidency, in 1880 the Solid South accounted for 138 votes. The Democratic Party, then, need only win an additional fifty votes to win the election.

Indiana's fifteen electoral votes were highly prized by both parties. Another factor that overemphasized Indiana's prominence was the rare Hoosier October election day. In future elections voters would cast their ballot on the first Tuesday after the first Monday in November, but from 1851 to 1880 voters in Indiana would vote in October – and those results would be known nationwide. "If we carry Indiana in October the rest is comparatively easy," wrote the Republican candidate, James A. Garfield. "We shall make a fatal mistake if we do not throw all our available strength into that state."[46]

Both parties poured prominent speakers and financial resources into Indiana in the election of 1880. The Democrats considered making Hoosier Thomas Hendricks the presidential nominee, but eventually settled on Civil War General Winfield Scott Hancock. To try to win the state, however, William H. English, a wealthy Indianapolis banker, was nominated for Vice President.

The Republicans pressed the advantage they felt they had in advocating for a protective tariff. When the Democrats failed to respond with strong tariffs of their own, two prominent Indiana businessmen – John Studebaker and Washington DePauw – renounced their membership in the Democratic party to vote for the Republican ticket.[47]

Marshall felt his party had made a mistake by not being more aggressive on the tariff issue in 1880 – as well as what he felt was the stolen election four years earlier.

The campaign of 1880 might have contained some hope for the Democratic party if it had been fought on the tariff question and the rectification of the wrong which in the judgement of so many of us had been done Mr. Tilden. But the campaign of 1880 drifted away to the question: Who saved the Union – the Democratic or the Republican party of the North?[48]

At the Whitley county convention of 1880, Marshall was nominated as the candidate for prosecuting attorney. The Democratic County Chairman, Eli Brown, was a friend of the Marshall family and asked Thomas to run. While Whitley County was traditionally Democratic, other adjacent counties – such as Kosciusko, immediately to the west of Whitley – had strong Republican majorities.

Marshall campaigned vigorously, and the local newspaper was optimistic prior to the vote. The final tally, however, showed that Marshall had lost by a vote of 5,023 to 5,594. He won Whitley County by 315 votes, but this was offset by Republican majorities in other counties.

Republicans in Indiana won almost the entire ticket in the 1880 election, supporting not only Garfield but also Albert G. Porter for Governor with a plurality of nearly seven thousand votes. The election was also marred by accusations of vote-buying by both parties. In the political climate of the time, Vice President-Elect Chester Arthur hinted at the use of illegal payoffs during a dinner at a New York restaurant. "Indiana was really, I suppose, a Democratic State", Arthur reportedly said, "It had been put on the books always as a State that might be carried by close and perfect organization and a great deal of …. (laughter, and cries of 'soap!'). I see the reporters are present, and therefore I will simply say that everybody showed a great deal of interest in the occasion and distributed tracts and political documents throughout the state"

After the bitter disappointment of the election of 1876, the loss of his beloved Kate in 1878, and his own political defeat in 1880, Marshall tried to press on. He continued his law practice and his Sunday school teaching, and he began to become more active with the local Masonic temple. Yet at times, he would appear in court so inebriated that he was unable to conduct his business.[49] Columbia City in the late 19th century was, however, a forgiving community. Whether it was through ignorance or, more likely, by the accepted social custom to ignore alcohol abuse, Tom Marshall entered a phase of his life devoid of ambition and clouded by abusive drinking.

Whether saddened by his losses, or simply consumed too much by his drinking, the election of 1880 marked the beginning of a dark period in Marshall's life. Enduring love would elude him for more than a decade, and Tom would not seek elected office again for 28 years.

❧ ❧ ❧ ❧ ❧

Marshall became active in the local Presbyterian church. He did not proselytize or try to spread his faith to non-believers; nevertheless, he was a fundamentalist who believed in the literal truth of the Bible. "I should probably be called a fundamentalist", Marshall wrote, "I take my bible from kiver to kiver, Jonah, whale and all."[50] Until the day he died (in fact, even at the moment of his death) he regularly read from the Bible.

Marshall attended church regularly, including two services on Sunday (one on the morning and one in the evening). He gave generously to church offerings, and served for many years on the governing board of the church.

Marshall did not try to impose his religious beliefs on others. During World War I, a Presbyterian chaplain expressed concern to Marshall that he would be unfrocked for administering extreme unction to non-Presbyterians on the battlefield. "We'll go out of the church together, if it be necessary", he replied.[51]

It was also at this time that Marshall became active in the local Masonic order. After joining in 1881, he rose steadily through the ranks and earned his Thirty-Third Degree distinction in 1898. Even while Vice President, he continued to be active, serving on several Masonic boards and committees.

❧ ❧ ❧ ❧ ❧

Though he did not seek elected office in the years between 1880 and 1908, Marshall reputation as a powerful orator grew. His speeches were fiercely partisan, but also carried the common theme of strict adherence to the Constitution. One of his more prominent speeches during this time was delivered before the Democratic Editorial Association in June of 1884.

The speech was Marshall's comparison of the Democratic and Republican parties. In it, he contrasted the typical Democrat who is "filled with a large love for this country, venerating and worshiping her Constitution and her founders, with the Republican who

> *Believed the Constitution was only a paper platform which it was bound to respect when it could be made to subserve the interest of bigotry and intolerance, and, in casting it aside upon all other occasions*[52]

Marshall reflected his family's affiliation with Douglas Democrats when he railed during the speech against the Republicans whose "fondest boast" was "the insulting, spitting upon and mocking of manhood because it dwelt South of Mason and Dixon's line."

Marshall's words were blatantly partisan, but what also emerges is his reverence for the Constitution as the highest law of the land. He praised "the refulgent splendor of Tilden and Hendricks" and other Democrats who, "like young Achilles standing picket guard" are "heroes of an hundred hard fought battles for Constitutional rights – battles as all important to the world as Runnymede."[53]

Marshall would, one day, face a decision pitting personal ambition against the Constitution. Unlike many of the leaders of his time or now, he chose a course of action consistent with his political rhetoric.

ᰍ ᰍ ᰍ ᰍ ᰍ

The national Democratic Party was split going into their Chicago presidential convention in 1884. Over the objections of Tammany Hall, New York Governor Grover Cleveland won the nomination, and once again the party was looking for a strong candidate from the Midwest to balance the ticket. They turned again to Thomas Hendricks.

Hendricks had been in poor health since his last campaign, as he had suffered a stroke and walked with a pronounced limp. But knowing that Cleveland could realistically become the first Democratic president in a quarter of a century, he campaigned with renewed vigor.

Marshall campaigned for Hendricks. Hendricks knew of Marshall's political skills, and sought his support. During the campaign, Hendricks wrote to Marshall

> *In many public addresses during this canvass I have urged the democracy of Indiana generally to make an earnest and determined struggle for success at the approaching election. But believing, as I do, that much depends upon the activity of individual Democrats on election day I am induced to address you and some more of my brother Democrats personally.*
>
> *The request that I have to make is that you do everything in your power to effect a thorough organization before Election Day, and that you be present at your precinct early on the 4th of November, and devote a full day to the cause. I have an earnest belief that the best interests of the country are deeply involved in that days struggle, and that our cause is the cause of the country. I hope you will see to it, as far as you possibly can, that every democratic vote in your precinct is deposited in the ballot box at the earliest hour practicable.*[54]

Republican nominee James G. Blaine of Maine cut into his opponent's support by publicizing Cleveland's illegitimate child. During the 1884 presidential election, supporters of the Republican candidate, James G. Blaine, discovered that Cleveland (a bachelor at the time) had fathered a son by Mrs. Maria Crofts Halpin, an attractive widow who had been on friendly terms with several politicians. Republicans promptly distributed handbills depicting a baby labeled "One more vote for Cleveland" and arranged for paraders to mockingly repeat the chant: "Ma, Ma, where's my pa? Gone to the White House, Ha, Ha, Ha!"

But Cleveland's reputation as a reformer brought him victory, and he won Indiana by 6,500 votes. Cleveland's margin of victory was also enough to sweep Democrat Isaac P. Gray into the Governor's office.

After finally achieving his goal of election to national office, Hendricks served as Vice President for less than a year. While returning for a visit to his home in Indianapolis, Thomas Hendricks died in his sleep on November 25, 1885. His death called into question, not for the first time, the issue of the order of presidential succession. If Cleveland should die, who would become president? The Presidential Succession Act of 1792 provided that the Senate's president pro tempore and the Speaker of the House, in that order, should succeed. Furthermore, the Constitution contained no provision for filling the vacancy of the Vice President between elections.

But opponents argued that this order of succession was flawed. Of primary concern was the idea that, while under the method of electing a president the Vice President was always of the same party, congressional leaders could easily be of a different party. A presidential death without the availability of a vice president could lead not only to a change in leadership but a change in party power, as well. In addition, some argued that cabinet responsibilities provided better experience for the presidency than time of service in congress.

As a result, Congress in 1886 adopted a law that made the Secretary of State third in line for presidential succession, rather than congressional officers. This system, then, was in place until 1947, when the president pro tempore of the Senate and the Speaker of the House were again put in the line of presidential succession after the Vice President. The ability of the President and Congress to fill a vacancy in the office of vice president would not be enacted until 1967.

The new order of presidential succession would also lead to intrigue for Thomas Marshall. Farsighted political strategists knew that the 1886 succession law replaced elected officials with an appointed position, as the Secretary of State now stood in the line of succession behind the Vice President. This would mean, then, that president could, with the acquiescence of his running mate, effectively appoint the new president naming a Secretary of State and then implementing the simultaneous resignation of a President and Vice President. While some might have dismissed the tactic as the stuff of suspense novels, later events would prove, once again, that at times pragmatic truth can be stranger than imaginative fiction.

❧ ❧ ❧ ❧ ❧

After their loss in 1884, by 1888 the Republicans had developed a strategy to counter the Democrats, who gave Grover Cleveland their nomination again. Knowing the importance of Indiana and New York, the GOP nominated Hoosier Benjamin Harrison as their Presidential candidate, with New Yorker

Levi P. Morton as his running mate. Republicans knew they could not break the Democrat's grip on the southern states, but their strategy was to keep the Democrats from winning any significant states outside the south.

Accusations of illegal vote buying continued during the campaign. Both parties worked to garner the votes of so-called "floaters", who shifted political allegiances regularly depending on who was offering the best deal. In late October, an Indianapolis newspaper printed a front page story under the headline, "The Plot to Buy Indiana", and released a letter from the treasurer of the Republican national committee purporting to outline a plan to buy the "floaters". "Divide the floaters into blocks of five," the letter stated, "and put a trusted man with necessary funds in charge of these five, and make him responsible that none get away and that all vote our ticket."[55]

The election should have been won easily by Harrison, but the vote-buying stories made it close. Harrison won the state by 2,300 votes, and Republican Alvin P. Hovey became Governor by even less. Nevertheless, Democrats saw their electoral gains of 1884 in both the Presidency and governorships disappear.

In the period after the Civil War, the voting process in Indiana was generally felt to be corrupt and subject to widespread voter fraud. Under the State's election laws, the political parties themselves provided the ballots, which naturally contained the names of only the party's candidates. Balloting was not done in secret, so a party worker could watch a voter from the time he received the ballot until when it was dropped into the ballot box. Party workers could buy votes from floaters for amounts ranging from two to twenty dollars.

One observer noted in 1886:

> *If Nathaniel Hawthorne's magic bugle were to summon into line – clothed in proper raiment of horizontal stripes -- all the rascals who bribed voter, or who took bribes for their votes, who corrupted election officers, or falsified election returns, who swore in illegal votes, who colonized voters, who voted twice, or voted double tickets, who tampered with ballots after they were cast, who consorted with or encouraged repeaters or ballot-box stuffers, or who were accessory to their escape from the just penalties of the violated law, it would be, I fear, a large*

procession, in which we should see both parties represented, and in which we might discover men of good repute, as the phrase goes, and some who have had and now have official preferment mainly because they had earned a place in that procession.[56]

Marshall was aware of Indiana's reputation for vote buying, and he wove this theme into one of his homespun stories.

There is an ancient story told in Indiana, of the good old days when ballots were hawked around the election precincts and votes were purchased with impunity. A somewhat impecunious citizen, with four boys, came to the polling place. They stood around most of the day without voting, waiting for the price of ballots to go up. They finally agreed to vote the Democratic ticket for ten dollars. After receiving the money they still delayed, and as the contest waxed warmer the Republicans paid them twenty-five dollars for their votes. Then they voted. On being upbraided for their conduct by the Democrat who had originally bought them the old man replied: "Well, we voted the Democratic ticket anyway." And on being asked how that was, he said that the family, after due consultation, thought they ought to vote the Democratic ticket, it being the "less corrupter" of the two.[57]

Those interested in reforming the election process became advocates for a system of voting known as the Australian ballot. With this system, the government was responsible for printing and distributing ballots to voters. Each polling place, then, provided an area for voters to mark their ballot in secret.

Thanks, in part, to widespread charges of vote buying, during the 1889 session of the Indiana legislature, reformers were successful in enacting the Australian Ballot system in Indiana.

❧ ❧ ❧ ❧ ❧

Thomas Taggart was born November 17, 1856, in Amyvale, County Monaghan, Ireland. The sixth child in a family that would eventually number seven children, in 1861 young Tom immigrated with his family to the United States. They settled in Xenia, Ohio.[58]

Tom's father worked as a baggage master at the local railroad station. The family had little money, so Tom left high school after one year to work in the lunchroom at the train depot. Due to his outgoing personality and popularity with the customers he was quickly promoted. When a new hotel was opened near the railroad station in Garrett, Indiana, about an hour northwest of Xenia, Tom jumped at the promotion.

Just eighteen years old and by now and American citizen, Tom built the DeKalb House Hotel into a profitable venture for the company he worked for. Success also came in his personal life, for while in Garrett he met Eva Bryant. Eva, who was three years older than Tom, had been raised by her aunt and uncle, who operated local store.

After just one year in Garrett, Tom's business success led his company to offer him a position in the restaurant at one of the largest train stations in the Midwest – Union Depot in Indianapolis. The relationship between Tom and Eva continued, however, despite the 150 miles that separated Garrett from Indianapolis. In the late spring of 1878, Eva discovered she was pregnant.

Thomas Taggart and Eva Bryant were married on Monday, June 17, 1878 in Mount Vernon, Ohio, with Eva eschewing a white bridal gown in favor of a burgundy red silk dress. After a brief honeymoon in Cincinnati they returned to Indianapolis.

Florence Eva Taggart was born October 4, 1878. She would be the first of six children born to Tom and Eva. The growing family needed more room, and in 1882 they moved into an apartment in the train station.

Tom Taggart's personality and ability to make friends easily attracted the attention of local political leaders. In 1884 the local Democratic party asked him to run for the office of township trustee. He declined the offer, not because he was uninterested in politics but because his canny business sense told him to wait for a better offer.

That better offer came two years later, when the Democratic Party asked him to run for Marion County Auditor. But the Democratic nomination by no means meant that Taggart would be victorious in the general election. In fact, Marion County was strongly Republican, and in 1886 Marion County had never been won a Democratic presidential candidate. But Tom proved to be a popular campaigner, and won the election by 1,700 votes. Four years later he won reelection by an even larger margin.

To be the Auditor – the chief financial officer – for an urbanized county like Marion (which contained the City of Indianapolis) could be a lucrative position for someone with ambition. Indiana law allowed an office holder to keep a portion of the fees paid for government services. In addition, of course, the powers of the office allowed for other payments not described by law.

Estimates place Tom Taggart's annual income for the eight years he held the office of County Auditor at between $20,000 and $50,000 per year – an enormous sum in the years before the turn of the century. (It would be nearly thirty years before Henry Ford would shock the business world by paying his workers the unheard-of pay of $5 a day.) In 1895 the local newspaper published a listing of the wealthiest property owners in the county. Thomas and Eva Taggart were near the top of the list—no far behind Colonel Eli Lilly. Taggart had also acquired enough wealth to buy the hotel and restaurant at Union Station where he worked.

Tom Taggart's electoral successes in a Republican county line Marion brought him further opportunities. In 1888, the Democratic County Chairman had been convicted of altering voting tally sheets. Taggart was asked to take his place and organize the party for the presidential election of that year.

The challenge must have certainly seemed daunting. Not only was Taggart expected to with the County for the Democratic presidential nominee, but he had to do so with Indianapolis attorney Benjamin Harrison leading the Republican ticket. Taggart's organizational skills carried Marion County for Cleveland over Harrison – the first time in Indiana History that the Democratic presidential nominee had won Marion County. Harrison's margins in the rest of the state, however, were enough to give the Republican a victory.

⁓ ⁓ ⁓ ⁓ ⁓

In the presidential election of 1892, both Harrison and Cleveland easily won renomination from their respective parties. Thomas Hendricks had died during Cleveland's first term in office, and while efforts were made to put former Indiana Governor Isaac Gray in the Vice President's spot, the Democrats instead chose Adlai Stevenson of Illinois (whose grandson, Adlai Stevenson III, would challenge Dwight Eisenhower for the Presidency in 1956).

Because of his success in organizing Marion County in 1888, Tom Taggart was named chairman of the Indiana Democratic Party in January, 1892. He again implemented his political organizational skills, but this time he had the advantage of trying to defeat an incumbent who had performed poorly while in office.

President Benjamin Harrison's term had proved a disappointment for many Republicans. Manufacturers who made campaign donations were rewarded with high tariffs to protect their products, and Harrison put little effort into civil service reform. While the Republicans felt compelled to renominate the incumbent president, they delivered a lackluster campaign. The long illness and eventual death of Harrison's wife kept him from actively campaigning, as well.

The result was a sweeping victory for the Democrats at both the national and state levels. Cleveland won the presidency and carried Indiana by over seven thousand votes. Democrat Claude Matthews was elected Governor, defeating Ira Chase, the former lieutenant governor who had become Governor on the death of Alvin Hovey in 1891.

With the election, Tom Taggart's reputation as a powerful political boss was now secure. Taggart would control Democratic politics in Indiana for a generation, and would be a formidable power broker at the national level as well. The Democratic Party, it seemed, had overcome the Republican Bloody Shirt strategy and was poised to regain the power that had eluded them since before the Civil War.

But it is often said that, in politics, timing is everything, and the Democrats had the misfortune of coming to power just prior to the most significant economic collapse in a generation.

෴ ෴ ෴ ෴ ෴

To comprehend the passion that surrounded the debates over monetary policy in the United States in the late nineteenth century, it is important to understand how economics influenced political alliances.

It is well known that inflation helps people who have borrowed money, and hurts those who have loaned money. After someone – perhaps, a farmer – has borrowed money, inflation means that the borrower can repay that loan using "cheaper" dollars. That is, if the farmer borrowed money when wheat was sold for $2.00 a bushel, and inflation pushes the price of wheat to $2.50 a bushel, the farmer needs to use fewer bushels of wheat to repay the loan.

Another important economic concept can be traced to Milton Friedman's famous dictum: "Inflation is always and everywhere a monetary phenomenon."[59] By that, Friedman asserted that inflation rises when the money supply expands rapidly. When the money supply is steady or declines, prices will be stable or tend to fall – termed "deflation".

How do governments control the growth of the money supply to prevent inflation? Today, most governments have created central banks that are given the authority to control the growth of the money supply. In the late nineteenth century, however, the concept of a central bank controlling the money supply had not yet been adopted.

In the period after the Civil War, those who advocated slower growth in the money supply – and low inflation – sought to tie the growth of money to the supply of gold. The supply of gold was relatively stable, as even in periods of significant gold discoveries the overall gold supply total changed very little.

The politics of the money supply in the period prior beginning of the twentieth century pitted debtors – generally farmers and small business owners – against creditors, often located in New York and other urban centers. Bankers, financiers and other lenders advocated for tying the supply of money to the supply of gold. As a result, in 1879 the United States adopted the "Gold Standard" meaning that each dollar of currency could be redeemed for a dollar of gold.

By the late 1880s, however, powerful political forces began to clamor for expanding the "acceptable" metals that could back up the money supply to include silver. This "bimetallism" would mean that the money supply could expand more quickly – hopefully, from the perspective of the farmers, causing inflation and allowing the debtor farmers to pay back their loans with cheaper dollars.

Joining with the farmers were representatives from several Western states that were silver producers. Tying the money supply to silver would increase the demand for the metal and, therefore, raise the price of silver.

These political forces came together in the summer of 1890. Legislators from Western states agreed to support the higher tariffs advocated by the industrial Eastern states in return for their support for legislation supporting bimetallism. The result was the Sherman Silver Purchase Act of 1890.

The Act stipulated that the United States Treasury purchase 4.5 million ounces of silver each month, payment of which would be made using newly-issued currency. The new currency would be redeemable for either gold or silver.

The weakness of this arrangement was that in the rest of the world, most notably Europe, currencies were backed by gold alone and not silver. That made those currencies more stable, and more attractive for wealthy investors who wanted to invest in countries with a stable currency, not in countries like the United States, where the new bimetallism would, it was believed, lead to inflation.

For European investors, the solution was simple. They could sell their silver – which was not tied to their own national currency – to the United States Government and receive, in turn, the new currency that would be redeemed for gold. When economies were strong and business conditions robust, investors would be willing to hold some of their wealth in the currencies of other countries – including the United States dollar. In periods of uncertainty, however, investors wanted to hold their wealth in gold, which was less subject to fluctuating value. As world economies weakened in the early 1890s, it became a common sight to see ships in New York harbors being loaded with gold bullion bound for Europe.

As a result of this exodus, the U.S. Treasury's gold reserves dipped from $190 million in 1890 to $95 million in 1893. When reserves dipped below the government's self-proclaimed "floor" of $100 million, the flight of gold accelerated.

President Cleveland had proposed that the government issue long-term bonds, and use the proceeds to purchase gold and restore the reserves. But this action would require the approval of Congress, and there Cleveland was fought by a coalition of Republicans who opposed him on partisan grounds and Democrats from states which supported bimetallism.

J. Pierpont Morgan was the head of a financial powerhouse known as J.P. Morgan and Company. In the late nineteenth century governments around the world had little financial strength, and privately held banks such as J.P. Morgan and Company in the United States and one owned by the Rothschild family in Europe exerted enormous influence over global financial matters.

Andrew Jackson had vetoed the second Bank of the United States in 1832, and the United States government would not have meaningful financial tools until the Federal Reserve Act of 1913. So powerful was J. Pierpont Morgan that journalist Lincoln Steffens called him the "Boss of the United States". His power extended throughout the globe. As Peter Finley Dunne's character Mr. Dooley put it:

> *Pierpont Morgan call in wan iv his office boys, th' prisident iv a national bank, an' says he, 'James', he says, 'take some change out iv th' damper an' r-run out an' buy Europe f'r me. I intind to reorganize it an' put it on a paying basis'.*[60]

Gold reserves were near exhaustion when Morgan came to the White House to meet with Cleveland in February of 1895. Congress was debating legislation to permit a public bond issue that could be used to purchase additional gold. Morgan, with his vast wealth, had the ability to issue his own bonds to purchase the gold – a move that would not require Congressional approval.

Morgan knew that if the United States exhausted its gold supply the result would be financial chaos. He traveled to Washington and met with Cleveland, who was reluctant to have Morgan use his power to calm the crisis. Such a move would only highlight the financial weakness of the government, he felt, and it would provide his opponents with ammunition in the next election.

As Morgan and Cleveland spoke, a messenger informed the President that only $9 million in gold remained in government vaults. Morgan said that he was aware of a $10 million gold purchase that was about to be requested. "If that $10 million draft is presented", said Morgan, "You can't meet it. It will be all over before 3 o'clock".

Cleveland had no choice but to allow the private bankers to bail out the United States treasury. A syndicate led by Morgan issued the bonds and the crisis was averted.

The crisis of the gold supply was over, but the effects of the economic slump lingered. Prices remained low, and the ranks of the unemployed swelled. In this environment labor unrest was encouraged. In the spring of 1894 employees working on Pullman railroad cars struck, and other unions left their jobs in sympathy. Cleveland ordered soldiers to Chicago to maintain order, and violence ensued. Eventually the strike was settled, but Cleveland's reputation never recovered, particularly among the growing number of members of organized labor.

Cleveland's actions also split the Democratic Party. His supporters called for sound money (currency backed only by gold), forceful action against strikers, and stronger central government. But populism was growing across the country, as exemplified by a thirty-six-year-old congressman from Nebraska. "You shall not press down upon the brow of labor this cross of thorns", said young William Jennings Bryan, "You shall not crucify mankind upon a cross of gold."[61]

✺ ✺ ✺ ✺ ✺

William Jennings Bryan was born in Salem, Illinois, on 19th March, 1860. He graduated from Illinois College in 1881 and, after studying law, moved to Lincoln, Nebraska. At the time, Lincoln was very much a frontier town. Nebraska had become a state in 1867, and its largest town, with 40,000 inhabitants by the late 1880s, was named after the fallen President.

Bryan's law practice began to grow, but he had also developed strong political views on the economic issues that faced Americans in the post-Civil War era. Witnessing the effects of tariffs and conservative monetary policy on farmers and their families, Bryan became an advocate for free trade with lower tariffs and looser monetary policy. He began speaking about the issues at political gatherings, social clubs, and any other opportunity to try to persuade an audience.

Williams Jennings Bryan was one of the most compelling public speakers in American history. He learned early in his career that he had the ability to move large groups of people with his oratory. After one speech in which he spoke for two-and-a-half hours yet left the crowd demanding more, he wrote his wife:

> *I have had a strange experience. Last night, I found that I had power over the audience. I could move them as I chose. I have more than unusual power as a speaker. I know it. God grant that I may use it wisely.*[62]

Good speaking skills were critical to a successful political in America. Marshall and Bryan were both blessed with extraordinary oratorical skills, but their methods of engaging theirs listeners were quite different.

Marshall's oratory was conversational. He would engage those in attendance with folksy stories and clever witticisms. Much like Franklin Delano Roosevelt's fireside chats of a later generation, Marshall's audience was encouraged to relax, pull up a chair, and enjoy Marshall's historical references – sometimes reaching back into ancient history – or clever analogies. This style was partly forced by Marshall's speaking voice, which was often described as "high pitched" and would not carry in rooms with very large crowds. He was most effective when his audience numbered dozens or hundreds, but not thousands.

Had Marshall been a politician in the modern political era, he would have provided ample ten second sound bites for the evening television news. He could take a complex issue and turn it into a clever or pithy phrase. In the process, he convinced his listeners that he was in touch with them, the common man, and understood their everyday lives.

Bryan also clearly made a connection with the common man, but his audiences were not encouraged to relax and enjoy a witty, folksy speech. Bryan's booming voice and the animated way in which he gesticulated with his arms motivated his listeners to action. He appealed to their passions, their hopes, and their dreams of a better future. He railed against injustice, big business, wealthy tycoons, and anything else that stood in the way of a better life for farmers and working families. Bryan combined the passion of a revivalist preacher with the compassion of a benevolent leader. He roused his audiences with a fury that moved them to follow this tall, handsome man from America's western frontier.

During one of William Jennings Bryan's numerous presidential campaigns, he was invited to speak to a large crowd assembled in a field. Bryan climbed onto the manure spreader that had been enlisted to double as an impromptu stage. "This is the first time I have ever spoken," Bryan wryly observed, "from a Republican platform."

Bryan became the advocate for the large portion of Americans who were left behind in the economic boom of America in the Gilded Age. In 1889, in a leading magazine of the day called *The Forum*, author Thomas Shearman had written an article entitled "The Owners of America." In it, Shearman pointed out that America's richest families owned a significant percentage of the nation's wealth. He listed seventy of the wealthiest: Astor, Vanderbilt, Armour, Rockefeller, Morgan, and others – and calculated that these seventy families had wealth of $2.7 billion, or nearly $40 million per family. Half of the nation's wealth, he calculated, was concentrated in the hands of just 50,000 families. At the time, eighty percent of American families had annual incomes of less than $500.[63]

Shearman concluded that America's system of taxation perpetuated these differences in wealth among families. Federal government revenues in the 1880s were derived from tariffs on imported goods. The tariffs were justified as protection against the importation of cheaper products that would put American manufacturers out of business. Thanks to years of intensive lobbying by the different manufacturing trusts in Washington, nearly every manufacturer had successfully argued that their products were deserving of tariff protection. As a result, tariffs represented, on average, about half the cost of a product. Imported goods cost more due to the tariff; domestically produced goods could be sold at a higher price because the imported competing product cost more.

Bryan touched a nerve in the electorate by railing against the inequity of the tariff. "When you buy $1 worth of starch," he told his audiences, "you pay sixty cents for the starch and forty cents for the trust and tariff."[64] It was a theme that resulted in his election to the House of Representatives in 1890.

◆ ◆ ◆ ◆ ◆

After he had proven his political management skills in the elections of 1888 and 1892, and given his newly-acquired wealth from two terms as County Auditor, Tom Taggart chose to run for Mayor of Indianapolis in 1895 – the year his second term as Auditor would expire. He easily outdistanced his Republican opponent, winning by the largest margin of any mayoral race up to that time.[65]

From the early days of his term as Mayor, Taggart's methods put him at cross purposes with government reformers. In these early days of the progressive movement, civic-minded associations had sprung up which focused on reforming the practices of municipal government. These groups advocated for competitive bidding on contracts, requiring that meetings of town and county councils be open to the public and, most importantly, civil service reform.

The efforts by government reformers were encouraged by leading journalists of the day. In 1899 Scribner's Magazine published a series of articles by Jacob Riis which would eventually result in the publication of *How the Other Half Lives*. In that book Riis documented – both with stories and photographs – the abject poverty of many city dwellers. He also showed how corrupt and mismanaged municipal governments were aggravating the problem through poor sanitation, lax enforcement of safety laws, and police departments filled with ineffective political appointees.

But Tom Taggart had little sympathy for government reformers. One of his first actions as Mayor was to fire all of the Republican policemen and firemen, and replace them with political appointees. Eyebrows were raised further when Tom Colbert, who worked for a brewing company, was named Chief of Police. Three months after Taggart took office, an investigation by the *Indianapolis News* found that twenty-two of twenty-five saloons it surveyed were open on Sunday, in violation of the law.

During Taggart's term, the park system in the City of Indianapolis expanded significantly. In addition, he oversaw the completion in 1902 of the 284-foot Soldiers and Sailors Monument that now stands in the center of the City. But even though Elwood Haynes in 1894, had invented the automobile in Kokomo, just north of Indianapolis, most city streets were still dusty dirt roads in dry weather and piles of mud when it rained.

Despite the enmity of municipal reformers, voters favored Taggart. He ran twice for re-election to two-year terms. His margin of victory in 1897 was even larger than his win two years earlier.

On December 6, 1898, Taggart's eldest daughter, Florence, set out by boat on a trip from Louisville, Kentucky to Clearwater, Florida via the Mississippi River and Gulf of Mexico. Joining three other friends on a yacht, by early 1899 the party had made its way to New Orleans, and set out from that City for Clearwater on January 3.

The boat never arrived. Search parties were dispatched, but found no sign of the ship. Taggart spend nearly five months looking for any clues to what happened to the ship or his daughter. Articles of debris from the vessel would periodically be found washed up on shore, but most felt that it was unlikely that the remains of any of the passengers would be recovered from the hostile environment of the Gulf of Mexico. By May of 1899 Taggart had all but given up when word came that a body had, in fact, been discovered near Venice, Florida. Taggart traveled to that city and confirmed that it was, indeed, his daughter. Her remains were returned to Indianapolis for burial.

Taggart turned his attention, once more, to his mayoral position. He ran for reelection again later that year, but his daughter's death sapped enthusiasm from his campaign. In addition, "good government" advocates had been able to significantly erode his base of support. He won reelection in 1899 by just 347 votes. Taggart would serve out the remaining two years of his term, and then turned his attention once again to his business interests.

    ❦ ❦ ❦ ❦ ❦

By the early 1890s, as the memories of the carnage of the Civil war faded, enthusiasm built in America for both a celebration of the changes brought by the Industrial Revolution and the optimism as the country faced the dawn of a new century. Those who looked to the future saw a nation not of agriculture but of industrialism, and the idea was raised to celebrate the four-hundredth anniversary of the voyage of Christopher Columbus.

The World's Columbian Exposition was held in Chicago in 1893, and proved to be immensely popular, drawing over 27 million visitors. The official goals of the Fair were to provide stability in the face of great change, to encourage American unity, to celebrate technology and commerce, and to encourage popular education. In addition, the Exposition celebrated different cultures from around the world, and was used to introduce such new consumer products as Juicy Fruit Gum, Pabst Blue Ribbon beer, Aunt Jemima syrup and Shredded Wheat cereal. Visitors of the Fair were also introduced to two permanent additions to America's cultural landscape: Picture post cards, and hamburgers.

The Exposition provided the United States with a new holiday, Columbus Day, and a new method for schoolchildren to show their patriotism -- the Pledge of Allegiance. Darkness and night would soon be transformed across the country with the widespread use of electricity, but in 1893 electricity was a frightening and overpowering symbol of technological change. Fairgoers, however, were treated to many demonstrations of the benefits of electricity in running motors and moving trains, as well as lumination. After the Columbian

Exposition, Americans embraced the technological changes that were coming into their home and workplace.

The Columbian Exposition in Chicago marked a period of revival for the nation. After the bleak days surrounding the Panic of 1893, the Exposition can be seen as the start of a new and robust period for the United States. Over the next twenty years, foreign policy successes would lead to a triumph over Spain and territorial expansion, the creation of a strong navy, and the opening of the Panama Canal. Domestically, the two decades after the Exposition saw the rise of the automobile and birth of the airplane.

Thomas Marshall also experienced a rebirth at this time. Despite its close proximity there is no indication that he visited Chicago in 1893. Possibly his alcohol addiction prevented him from travel too far from home. His mother Martha, with whom he had lived since graduating from Wabash more than twenty years earlier, suffered from failing health at about this time. She died in 1894, two weeks before Christmas.

> *I think back through the years, the lean and the fat, the good and the bad ones, to my earliest recollection: I see a woman with an eye that flashes swift as an archangel's wing and a mouth that breaks with laughter and hardens at the sight of wrong, singing lullabies; a woman who, with her hand grasping the Unseen Hand, walks the briar-bordered paths of life unashamed, unafraid, unharmed … She brings me no longer drums and fifes. But she still brings me the vision of my mother and the music of that angelic chorus which sang at creation's dawn and at the hour of man's redemption.*[66]

In his early forties and now living alone, Thomas must have looked sadly on what he had become: A fine legal mind clouded by alcohol, an unsuccessful politician, and a lonely man growing old with only a shot of whiskey as his close companion.

But in 1893, Marshall was appointed as the special judge for a case in Lagrange County. While on that assignment, Thomas met Lois Kimsey, who was serving as deputy in the office of her father, the county clerk. By the time the trial was over, Tom and Lois were engaged, and they married on October 2, 1895, when he was 41 and she was just 23.

From all indications, Lois became the driving force in Tom's life. Her first task was to cure him of his alcohol addiction. In 1898 Tom took a course of treatments as a cure. Lois had acquired some drugs from a facility in Illinois. Under the supervision of medical specialists, Lois locked herself up with Thomas for two weeks to help him through his alcoholic illness.[67]

Marshall never forgot the sacrifices made by Lois. After that time the record shows that, despite political campaigns and the social nature of Indianapolis and Washington, he never had a drop of alcohol again. Theirs was a close marriage, and, though they were never blessed with their own children, they were affectionate and inseparable. Through state and national campaigns, through four years as governor and eight years as Vice President, they were separated only two nights in their 30-year marriage.

℔ ℔ ℔ ℔ ℔

The schism that split the national Democratic Party in 1896 also fractured the party in Indiana. Two state conventions were held that year. Those who wished to maintain the gold standard nominated their slate of candidates, but "free silver" advocates dominated and they nominated Congressman Benjamin Franklin Shively of South Bend for Governor. The Democratic platform called "the immediate restoration of bimetallism by the free and unrestricted coinage both silver and gold, as primary money".

More conservative members of the party, known as "Gold Democrats", actively opposed the election of William Jennings Bryan, the Democratic nominee for president. Bryan himself made five campaign appearances in Indiana, electrifying the crowds with his powerful oratory.

The split in the Democratic Party was felt deeply by Marshall.

> *That campaign of 1896, when I was a member of the Democratic State Central Committee, was perhaps the most disheartening of my life. We had no money; disloyalty was everywhere apparent in state and local organizations. I could not get a notice inserted in the papers without paying for it out of my own pocket, in advance.*

Republicans in 1896 nominated William McKinley of Ohio. Knowing that his charisma and speaking skills paled compared to his opponent, McKinley's campaign manager, Mark Hanna, chose to keep McKinley in his Ohio home and use surrogate campaigners to stump for votes. It was during this time that younger Republicans – Albert Beveridge, Charles Warren Fairbanks, James Hanly and James Watson, for example – came into prominence.[68]

Hanna's strategy came to be called the "Front Porch Campaign" because of the unique way in which the voters came to the candidate – rather than the other way around. McKinley stayed at his home in Canton, Ohio as, from across the country, people came by the thousands to visit him on his front porch. When the trains (with special low-cost fares, since the railroads were strong supporters) would pull into the station, visitors were greeted by marching bands and welcoming officials on horseback. They would make their way a short distance down North Market Street, past banners, gateways and posters, and arrive at McKinley's front lawn.

After a few minutes, the candidate would emerge to the cheers of the crowd. Similar cheers marked the arrival of his elderly mother, as well as the reclusive Mrs. McKinley, who never fully recovered from the death of their infant daughter.

McKinley's talks with the crowd – they could hardly be called speeches – would be long on a cordial welcome and short on substance. He would take his place in a chair on the porch next to his wife and his mother McKinley, say a few words on the issues of the day, and then make an effort to shake the hand of everyone who made the trip.

For visitors, it was a thrill to ride a train, be warmly welcomed, and then get the chance to shake the hand of a presidential candidate. Each of them became McKinley disciples, returning to their home towns and telling, over and over again, about they day they met William McKinley.

Mark Hanna's strategy worked. He carried Indiana by over 18,000 votes, as did the Republican candidate for Governor, James Mount.

Marshall recognized that the furor over "sound money" or "free silver" was a proxy for other issues. "Like most of the great things of life", he wrote, "the fight was made over a false issue."

The campaign of 1896, regardless of what the wise men may say about it, was not fought over the free and unlimited coinage of silver at the ratio of sixteen to one. It was a question of banking, and the election disclosed it to be such, for every state that had sound and responsible banking institutions, and where people did their business by check and not by cash, went for McKinley, while all the states where the banks were wild-cat and irresponsible, and where men carried in their pockets currency with which to pay their debts, went for Bryan.

An analysis of the vote suggests that 1896 was a turning point for partisan politics in Indiana. Prior to that year, Hoosier voters could be characterized as rural farmers who felt closer politically to southern Democrats and western Radicals. A more conservative viewpoint emerges in the election of 1896, which was more attracted to sound money and urban industrial growth. Also important was the growing population in northern Indiana – traditionally less Democratic than their southern neighbors.

Indiana would continue to play a prominent role in national politics for another generation, but the children and grandchildren of the voters in the election of 1896 would gradually embrace a political viewpoint that was more conservative, more opposed to radical reforms and more Republican. In the twentieth century, Indiana voted for a Democratic President just four times. Hoosiers support Franklin Roosevelt the first two times he ran for president (but not for his third and fourth terms), supported Lyndon Johnson in 1964, and went for Wilson and Marshall in 1912. In every other election, the Republican presidential candidate won Indiana.

❧ ❧ ❧ ❧ ❧

With the loving hand of Lois to guide him, Tom Marshall over the next ten years developed a philosophy that would find him in accord with the ideas and beliefs of much of the electorate. On the one hand, Marshall began to embrace a view of the role of government in society that has come to be known as Progressivism. On the other, he remained grounded by his fundamental religious beliefs in a respect for tradition and deference to institutions such as the church and the family. For this reason, Marshall was referred to as "a progressive with the brakes on."

In a very real sense, the Progressive movement combined the Judeo-Christian teachings of the interconnectedness of mankind and the biblical call to be our brother's keeper with a more activist view of the role of government in society.

Marshall knew the dangers of a government that was too intrusive in the lives of citizens, or tried to create legislation to address matters that were beyond the scope of lawmakers. As an example of the latter, he needed to look no further than an attempt by the Indiana General Assembly to legislate the value of *Pi*.

The number *Pi* is a numerical constant that represents the ratio of a circle's circumference to its diameter on a flat plane surface. The value is the same regardless of the size of the circle.

For several thousand years, mathematicians around the globe have labored to uncover more precise measures of *Pi*. The number was known by the Egyptians, who calculated it to be approximately 3.1604. The earliest known reference to *Pi* occurs in a Middle Kingdom papyrus scroll, written around 1650 BC. Towards the end of the scroll, which is composed of various mathematical problems and their solutions, the area of a circle is found using a rough sort of *Pi*.

Around 200 BC, Archimedes wrote a book regarding the measurement of a circle in which he estimated that the ratio of a circle's circumference to its diameter was a constant number that was about 3.14. The first person to use the Greek letter *Pi* for the number was William Jones, an English mathematician, who coined it in 1706.

Pi is an irrational number. It cannot be precisely defined as the ratio of any two whole numbers. Thus, its decimal expansion has no pattern and never ends. Using computers of today, *Pi* can be calculated very precisely.

In 1897, a the request of a constituent, Edward J. Goodwin, a physician and an amateur mathematician, Representative Taylor I. Record of Posey County introduced legislation in the Indiana House of Representatives.

> *A bill for an act introducing a new mathematical truth and offered as a contribution to education to be used only by the State of Indiana free of cost by paying any royalties whatever on the same, provided it is accepted and adopted by the official action of the legislature of 1897.*

Be it enacted by the General Assembly of the State of Indiana:
It has been found that a circular area is to the square on a line
equal to the quadrant of the circumference, as the area of an
equilateral rectangle is to the square on one side.

Bill #246 was initially sent to the Committee on Swamp Lands, but was later referred to the Committee on Education. The latter committee gave the bill a "pass" recommendation and sent it on to the full House, which approved it unanimously, 67 to 0.

In the state Senate, the bill was referred to the Committee on Temperance. It passed first reading, but that's as far as it got. It happened that soon before the bill was to be referred to committee, a professor of mathematics at Purdue was visiting the legislative chambers. A member of the legislature asked the professor to read the bill, and then offered to introduce him to the bill's author. The declined the offer, remarking that "he was acquainted with as many crazy people as he cared to know."[69] The bill went no further through the legislative process.

❧ ❧ ❧ ❧ ❧

As America approached the end of the nineteenth century, those who advocated a more aggressive foreign policy – including Theodore Roosevelt and Henry Cabot Lodge – began speaking of a long-term strategy which would eventually lead to the annexation (or at least the colonization) of Cuba. Not only was the island just a short boat ride away, it also held strategic importance as the gateway to the Caribbean and also to the planned canal linking the Atlantic and the Pacific.

In addition, the Cuban people had been suppressed by a series of ruthless dictatorial leaders appointed by the Spanish government. Cubans fought for their independence in a variety of short-lived insurrections, but the suppression tactics used by Spain in 1895 were especially brutal. Spanish forces destroyed not only sugar cane fields and factors, but homes and other businesses as well. Many were herded into fortified areas surrounded by barbed wire and armed guards, and thousands died of disease and starvation.

President William McKinley preferred diplomacy to war, and the ruling government in Spain did take some steps to grant limited self-government to the Cuban people. As a show of support to the rebels, McKinley dispatched the battleship *Maine* to Havana, hoping also to use the ship to evacuate Americans should hostilities break out again. On the evening of February 15, 1898, the *Maine* exploded, killing 260 crew members. While the cause of the explosion has never been fully resolved, for those advocating war with Spain there was no doubt that the Spanish were the cause of the disaster.

Marshall supported America's involvement in the Spanish-American war. He viewed it not as retribution for the *Maine* disaster, but to provide freedom for an oppressed people.

> *The Spanish-American War was not fought because the Maine was sunk in the harbor at Havana, although that was the ostensible reason given to the people. The real reason was that the soul of America had been so long outraged by Spanish misrule in Cuba that it could no longer keep silent.*[70]

In 1897, McKinley had appointed a young politician from New York named Theodore Roosevelt as Assistant Secretary of the Navy. Thomas Marshall was four years older than Theodore Roosevelt, and though they shared some common experiences they were vastly different in temperament, physical build and ambition. But the choices Roosevelt would make would lead directly to the election of Thomas Marshall as Vice President.

Both Marshall and Roosevelt were born into well-respected families led by politically outspoken fathers. Roosevelt's father, also named Theodore, was an outspoken advocate for political reform, much as Daniel Marshall advocated against slavery. The two were well educated (Marshall at Wabash; Roosevelt at Harvard), and developed an interest in politics while still young men.

Both also faced tragedy at an early age; Marshall when Kate Hooper died just prior to their wedding, and Roosevelt when his wife died after giving birth to their first child on the same day that his mother passed away from typhoid fever. Like Thomas after the death of his fiancé, Roosevelt was shattered by his double tragedy. Roosevelt's diary entry for the day reads simply, "The light has gone out of my life."[71]

But while Marshall eased the pain of tragedy with liquor, Roosevelt found a different method of escape. Though sickly as a youth, Roosevelt had become a young man of considerable strength and capacity for physical exertion. He became a rancher in North Dakota, and when he returned to New York City gained a reputation as an indefatigable advocate for municipal reform and good government. In part because the political bosses in New York were anxious to rid themselves of Roosevelt's zeal for honesty and integrity in government, they acquiesced to sending him to Washington as Assistant Secretary of the Navy. Less than ten months later, the battleship *Maine* exploded in the Havana harbor.

Roosevelt quickly prepared the Navy for the war he knew was inevitable. In addition, he volunteered for service as commander the First U.S. Volunteer Cavalry, a unit known as the Rough Riders -- an elite company comprised of every type of soldier ranging from Ivy League gentlemen to western cowboys. But Roosevelt led his men in an assault of a fortified Spanish position just outside Santiago, losing over a hundred men but eventually overtaking the position.

The war was a lopsided affair that was over in four months. The United States received not only Cuba, but also Puerto Rico, the Philippines and Guam. America not only cemented its leadership in the Caribbean, but also assumed a new presence in the Pacific.

Now a war hero, Roosevelt ran for governor of New York and narrowly defeated a popular Democrat who was the candidate of Tammany Hall. Roosevelt owed his victory to the state's Republican party boss, Thomas C. Platt, but Platt and Roosevelt would clash over a number of issues including patronage, municipal utilities and business regulation.

෴ ෴ ෴ ෴ ෴

Platt knew that so long as Roosevelt remained in power he would lose much of his influence as party leader. Consulting with Mark Hanna, the top Republican political boss in the nation, Platt and Hanna considered several options to remove Roosevelt. When William McKinley's Vice President Garret Hobart died in office, they saw their chance. They convinced Roosevelt to run as McKinley's running mate in 1900.

Taggart was also looking for a strong candidate to field in the gubernatorial election of 1900. He settled on a seasoned politician from his Mayoral administration in Indianapolis, John Worth Kern.

John Worth Kern was born December 20, 1849, not far from Kokomo in Howard County, Indiana. He took an interest in politics at an early age, and while still in his pre-teen years had actively supported Stephen Douglas among his friends and neighbors in the election of 1860.

Kern became an accomplished speaker and this, combined with his strong academic aptitude, led him to a career in law. After earning a law degree at the University of Michigan, he began his law practice in Kokomo in 1869. Early in his career he mounted a vigorous defense of one of his clients and gained the respect of the local prosecuting attorney, Thomas A. Hendricks. Hendricks, who had served in the Senate and was destined to become both the Governor of the State and Vice President under Cleveland, became Kern's mentor and would have a strong influence on Kern's political career.

While Kern's Democratic affiliation meant he had little chance of electoral success in heavily Republican Howard County, he gained respect from political leaders on both sides of the aisle and was appointed as the municipal attorney for the City of Kokomo.

Kern's ability and enthusiasm brought him to the attention of the state party leaders, and he was elected reporter of the Indiana Supreme Court in 1884. In 1888, however, with Republican Benjamin Harrison at the top of the ticket Kern was unsuccessful in his re-election bid.

Kern followed this loss with a successful bid for the Indiana State Senate in 1892. In this position, he developed a reputation as a strong supporter of the labor union movement, which at the time was still in its infancy. After an unsuccessful strike by Indianapolis streetcar workers, Kern played a pivotal role in passing legislation legalizing the right of labor to organize. He also developed the strident political philosophy that would endear him to the Democrats and make him the bane of conservative Republicans. "For years and years organized capital was fostered and fed by favorable legislation, until it grew defiant and insolent," Kern said. "As a result labor organized that it might live."[72]

While in the State Senate, Kern developed a friendship with a young politician who would play an important role in Kern's political career and the national political agenda. Despite his liberal background Kern was opposed to the free silver democrats and actively promoted the maintenance of the gold standard. During his travels he would often cross the path of the nation's leading free silver advocate, William Jennings Bryan. Though opposed to each other ideologically, the two soon developed a warm friendship and during the campaign of 1896 Kern put aside their monetary policy differences and actively campaigned for Bryan. Bryan would not forget Kern's willingness to support him, even at the cost of alienating Democrats who supported the gold standard.

Also at this time, Kern caught the attention of Thomas Taggart, who had recently been elected Mayor of Indianapolis. Knowing of Kern's experience as the city attorney in Kokomo – and also of his unshakable adherence to the Democratic Party – Taggart appointed Kern as the Indianapolis city attorney.

While Kern was hesitant to mount another statewide campaign, he reluctantly agreed to be the party's nominee against Republican candidate Winfield Durbin. Durbin had been an officer in the Spanish-American War, and closely aligned himself with the candidacy of William McKinley.

After the Democrats had again nominated William Jennings Bryan, the election was largely a replay of the contest in 1896. Bryan campaigned rigorously, and McKinley seldom left the White House. While McKinley was easily winning reelection, Durbin defeated Kern for Governor by 35,000 votes. While Democrats tried to make currency and silver the major issue, general economic prosperity over the previous four years ultimately decided the election and McKinley won by a higher margin than he had gained four years earlier.

❧ ❧ ❧ ❧ ❧

On September 6, 1901, President William McKinley traveled to Buffalo, New York to attend the Pan-American Exposition. He was standing outside the Temple of Music, shaking hands with a long line of people, when a young anarchist named Leon Czolgosz stepped out from the crowd and fired two shots into McKinley with a .32-caliber revolver.

McKinley was taken to a nearby home, and initial reports indicated that he would recover. Theodore Roosevelt, having been assured that McKinley was out of danger, continued with a trip he had planned to climb to the top of Mount Marcy, the highest mountain in the State of New York.

At the time McKinley was shot, vice presidents had succeeded to the Presidency just four times.

John Tyler had been elected as the Vice President to William Henry Harrison in 1840. Under the slogan, "Tippecanoe and Tyler Too," Harrison and Tyler defeated Martin Van Buren. But Harrison gave a rambling two-hour inaugural speech outdoors in freezing weather without coat or hat, became ill, and died several weeks later. Because no President had ever died in office before, some felt that Tyler should be considered merely an acting or interim President. Tyler was clear, however, that the Constitution gave him full and unqualified powers of office and had himself sworn in immediately as President.

In 1848, Millard Fillmore was elected as the running mate to Zachary Taylor. Two years later, at a Fourth of July celebration in 1850, President Taylor tried to cool down by licking on ice and eating cherries. He contracted cholera, and suddenly began to experience intestinal cramps. Within five days, Zachary Taylor was dead.

In 1864, Abraham Lincoln was elected to his second term of office. Just six weeks after the inauguration, on April 15, 1865, Lincoln was assassinated. Vice President Andrew Johnson rushed to Lincoln's bedside when he was told of the attack. A few hours after Lincoln's death, Chief Justice Salmon P. Chase swore Johnson in as President of the United States.

In the election of 1880, James Garfield and Chester Arthur were narrowly elected. Soon after taking office, on July 2, 1881, Garfield was traveling to his reunion at Williams College in Massachusetts when he was shot twice by Charles Julius Guiteau, who was upset because he had failed to gain an appointment in Garfield's administration.

Garfield remained fully conscious after he was shot, though he went into shock. He was rushed to the White House, where doctors discovered that one bullet had grazed his arm but the other had come to rest in his abdomen.

Garfield would linger for eighty days, conducting state business from his bed. But the decaying bullet was rapidly poisoning his blood. Within a month Garfield's weight dropped from 220 pounds down to just 130 pounds, with new infections throughout his lungs.

As Garfield's condition grew worse, Chester Arthur faced a difficult decision. Should he assume the presidency? If so, who would approve the action? The Constitution called for vice presidential succession if the President was disabled, but was silent regarding the method of succession. The government was paralyzed, but Arthur could be accused of effectively staging a coup if he assumed presidential power. Adding to the confusion was the fact that Garfield and Arthur had significantly different viewpoints on crucial policy matters such as patronage and civil service.

Arthur did nothing, and eventually the question was resolved. James Garfield dies of blood poisoning and related infections on September 19 and Chester Arthur, using the precedent set by John Tyler, became President.

In Buffalo, William McKinley's condition grew worse, and three days later, as Roosevelt was walking down from the peak of the mountain, he noticed a park ranger rushing towards him, a telegram in his hand. Before he even opened the message, he knew he had become the fifth Vice President to succeed to the Presidency of the United States.

❧ ❧ ❧ ❧ ❧

As America entered the new century, the nation was moving from the ostentatious wealth and political power of big business that characterized the Gilded Age to the reforms that comprised the Progressive movement. Marshall embraced many of these reforms.

Though a precise definition of the Progressive viewpoint remains to this day difficult to completely describe, the Progressive Movement consisted of a series of reforms that spanned the social, economic and political arenas at all levels of government that were designed to address emerging problems in the era of industrialization.

One set of reforms focused on urban life and the problems created by massive migration from farms to cities. Overcrowding, poor sanitary conditions, child labor and sweatshop working conditions were just a few of the issues targeted by Progressive politicians.

Reforms at another level were directed at the power of corporations. These reforms included trust-busting, public health issues such as conditions at meatpacking plants, and reforms intended to prohibit business practices in restraint of trade.

An overarching principal underlying the progressive movement was the belief that scientific reasoning and new discoveries, along with creativity and ingenuity, could defeat any technological, social or political barrier to change. Driving the energies of Progressive reformers were a series of astounding breakthroughs in engineering, technology and science that boosted optimism and fed the public's belief that any problem could be solved if only enough wisdom and hard work was applied to it.

❧ ❧ ❧ ❧ ❧

Henry Ford was born in 1863 on a farm near Dearborn, Michigan, just west of Detroit. As the eldest of six children, he learned responsibility early when his mother died when he was just twelve years old. He remained in school until he was fifteen, working on the farm during his free time.

At an early age, he was interested in working with his hands and tinkering with inventions. Though his father tried to discourage his interest in mechanical devices, when he was thirteen he dismantled a watch and put it back together again, just to learn how it worked. When he turned sixteen, he ran away from home and walked to Detroit to work as an apprentice in a machine shop.

He soon returned to his father's farm, and set about trying to build a new type of tractor that would be smaller and less costly than those that were available to farmers. Each of his attempts utilized one-cylinder steam engines, the most effective technology at the time. But steam engines were large, heavy and difficult to maintain, and Ford realized he would need a more efficient engine to make the type of tractor he was seeking.

An avid reader, Ford remembered an article about the use of internal combustion engines in a device that had been called a "horseless carriage". The internal combustion engine fed gasoline directly into a cylinder, with a spark igniting the fuel and pushing the cylinder which, when attached to a drive shaft, could propel the car forward. He was convinced that it was the technology to make a vehicle light and affordable.

In 1890 he returned to Detroit and set up a workshop in his backyard, experimenting on evenings and weekends. Two years later he created a vehicle that had a two-cylinder engine and could generate about four horsepower. Ford was pleased that he had found technology that was both light and powerful enough to propel a carriage that had previously required four horses to pull. His vehicle was the first car in Detroit, and Henry turned a lot of heads as he steered his new invention through the City's dirt roads. Eager to move on to new technologies, he sold the car in 1896 for $200.

Ford had been promoted to chief engineer for the local electric company, and was offered the position of general superintendent – on the condition that he give up his experiments with gasoline vehicles and devote his efforts to the electric company. The offer must have certainly been tempting. As an executive with a fast-growing utility, Ford could expect a good salary along with a chance to advance as the company grew. But the thirty-six year old Ford was looking for a challenge, not a secure paycheck. He knew he had a chance to become a pioneer in the newly emerging automobile industry. He quit his job in 1899 and persuaded a group of men to organize the Detroit Automobile Company.

In the decade after the turn of the century the automobile industry blossomed. In 1900, twenty car companies manufactured and sold vehicles that ranged in price up to thousands of dollars. Most car companies – the Detroit Automobile Company included – developed a business model that produced a small number of customized cars that were sold with high profit margins.

This mode of operation also fit well with America's newly-created wealth at the turn of the century. Not many families could afford the high prices of motorized vehicles. Men who gained riches in the industrial revolution, though, purchased automobiles not only for the practical purpose of transportation, but also to impress their neighbors.

Large profits in the industry attracted new companies. By 1913, there would be nearly ninety different car makers. Ford, however, envisioned a different way of doing business. Rather than produce a small number of cars with high profit margins, he wanted to lower costs – and prices – and increase the volume of cars sold, making them affordable for many American families.

The other investors in the Detroit Automobile Company disagreed with Ford. The low-volume, high profit-margin strategy worked well, they felt, and opposed Ford's low cost-high volume philosophy. Unable to reach an agreement, Ford struck out on his own to create the Ford Motor Company. In 1903 the Ford Motor Company sold 1,708 two-cylinder, eight horsepower automobiles. He continued to find ways to lower costs and increase production, and on October 1, 1908, he began production of the Model T.

Lightweight, affordable (at just $850) and easy to maintain, the Model T soon dominated the market as a cheap and reliable car. While wealthy car owners paid up to $7,000 for custom-made vehicles, Ford mass-produced the Model T and customers were happy to take the vehicle in whatever design or color it came off the assembly line. When asked about getting the car in different colors, Ford replied "any customer can have a car painted any color he wants, so long as it is black." [73]

Ford's idea revolutionized the industry. No longer a plaything for the rich, cars became an indispensable part of family life for the burgeoning middle class. Automobile registrations boomed. Across the country, 8,000 automobiles were registered in 1900. By 1913, the number of automobile registrations exceeded one million. As more families hungered for the new device, Ford continued to push his costs lower and production higher. By 1913, Ford had cut the time required to make a Model T to just ninety-three minutes, and production was nearly 250,000 per year. The price also continued to fall, reaching $500 by the end of 1913.

Part of the savings came from the way Ford organized production. Under the old factory system, one worker would construct an entire part, using many different tools and performing several different operations. Ford set up a system where each worker performed just one operation. A moving conveyor belt carried the raw material along a line of workers, and each worker performed a single task and moved the part along on the conveyer belt. Ford also realized that he could control output by varying the speed of the conveyer belt, rather than letting each worker do the work at their own pace.

As his company prospered, he passed the benefits along to his employees. In January, 1914, he established a minimum pay rate of $5 a day for an eight-hour day. Observers pointed out that not only would the new higher wages spread quickly throughout the manufacturing sector, but the wage enabled more workers to purchase Ford cars.

❧ ❧ ❧ ❧ ❧

Wilbur and Orville Wright were the sons of a bishop in the United Brethren Church and his wife. In 1884, when Wilbur was fourteen and Orville was twelve, Bishop Wright and his wife Susan moved their family to Dayton, Ohio. Susan became ill with tuberculosis, so Wilbur delayed his plans for going to college to care for his mother. When she died five years later, both Wilbur and Orville had established their own printing business.

While their printing business was moderately successful, they developed a side business of repairing and selling bicycles. The bicycle was soaring in popularity, and soon the Wright Cycle Company was more profitable than their printing business.

But the young brothers were fascinated by stories of flying machines that filled the newspapers in the years prior to the turn of the century. Inventors around the world were developing aircraft that could glide long distances. But while many inventors tried to increase the distance a glider could fly, the Wright brothers devoted their time to trying to solve two technological problems.

First, they wanted to create an aircraft that could be controlled by a pilot. They wanted to give the pilot the ability to move the airplane to the left or right, or up and down, using manageable controls. Second, they dreamed of a craft that would be self-propelled. This would require a strong yet lightweight engine.

They began testing their designs at Kitty Hawk, North Carolina. The strong winds off the ocean helped launch their planes, and the soft sands would cushion the landing if the plane crashed.

After several years of testing, the brothers were prepared to attempt a test flight. On a cold December morning in 1903, they attached their aircraft to a test track and prepared it for flight. The brothers flipped a coin to see who would fly first Wilbur won. Soon after it cleared the rail, however, it banked to the left and landed in the sand. The flight lasted just three-and-one-half seconds.

After several days of repairs, the brothers were ready again on December 17, 1903. This time, it was Orville's turn. At around 10:35 in the morning, the machine began to move down the rail while Wilbur ran along side. Orville kept the device airborne for 12 seconds, and the flight covered a distance of 120 feet. An hour later, Wilbur covered 175 feet, and before the day was over Orville was able to travel for 200 feet.

Aviation history had been made. The young brothers from Dayton, Ohio had created a flying device that had taken off from level ground, traveled through the air, and landed under the control of its pilot.

❧ ❧ ❧ ❧ ❧

In 1904, residents of Bern, Switzerland could often watch a young man pushing a baby carriage through the streets, stopping occasionally to scribble in a notepad that he always carried with him on his walks. It is unlikely that anyone watching the examiner in the Government Patent Office and his son could have understood the importance of the ideas captured in that notebook.

In the following year, the ideas that the man thought of as he walked with his infant son were published in a series of four articles in scientific journals. In one paper, he described light as a series of tiny particles, which he called photons. In another, he proposed that the universe was made out of very small chunks of energy and matter.

Next came the special theory of relativity, and perhaps the most famous equation in physics: $E=mc^2$. (Which says that the energy content of a body is equal to the mass of the body times the speed of light squared.) The equation predicted that an extraordinary amount of energy could be released from a single atom. Forty years later, the concept would lead to the creation of the atomic bomb.

Over the next twenty years, those ideas and others from this young scientist would change the way mankind looked at the world, from the smallest atomic particle to the vastness of the galaxy. A century after the young father from Bern began scribbling ideas in his notebook, the world is trying to understand the secrets of the universe unlocked by Albert Einstein.

∾ ∾ ∾ ∾ ∾

Theodore Roosevelt was the favorite for the Republican Presidential nomination in 1904. Some in the party made efforts to convince Mark Hanna to seek the nomination, but Hanna died of typhoid fever early in 1904, and Roosevelt won the nomination without opposition.

For the first time in a dozen years the Democrats passed over William Jennings Bryan and settled on the nomination of Alton B. Parker, a New York judge. Parker embraced the gold standard, a significant departure from Bryan's embrace of the silver issue. But Bryan campaigned hard for Parker, and Roosevelt lost support among conservatives for inviting Booker T. Washington, a prominent black leader, to the White House.

Kern was, once again, asked to lead the Democrats in the statewide elections. This time, the prodding came not from Tom Taggart – who strongly supported Kern – but from the Democratic nominee Alton Parker. Parker and

Kern had become good friends, and the judge from New York asked Kern to run as a personal favor. Parker knew he needed to win Indiana, and felt that a strong showing by Kern would garner him enough votes to win the Hoosier state.

But the divisions of 1896 again hampered the Democrats. Free silver Democrats were unwilling to work for a candidate other than Bryan. In addition, the Republicans fielded a strong candidate in J. Frank Hanly.

Born in a log cabin, Hanly lived in Warren County and was admitted to the bar in 1889. In 1880 he was elected to the state senate, and in 1894 he won a congressional seat. He moved to Lafayette in 1896 and sought the Republican nomination for United States senator in 1898. He was defeated by the young up-and-coming firebrand of the GOP, Albert Beveridge.

Hanly was a strong campaigner and not only won election by a margin of more than 80,000 votes, he also swept into office a slate of Republicans for the Indiana General Assembly, such that when Hanly took office Republicans outnumbered Democrats by three to one.

Roosevelt won the election of 1904 by a wide margin. Only the southern states supported the Democratic nominee. Kern ran well ahead of the national ticket, but Parker was soundly beaten by Roosevelt.

But the stage was set for a series of events that would combine to propel Thomas Marshall to national office. Soon after the election Roosevelt made the crucial strategic mistake of announcing he would not seek a third term. He would spend much of his second term overcoming the inherent leadership problems faced by a lame duck politician.

Governor Hanly proved to be an able politician who felt more strongly, however, about prohibition than Republican electoral success. Hanly would soon take action that would prove to be of great help to the Democrat Marshall.

Thomas Taggart would also plot a strategy that would benefit Marshall. Indiana had not voted for a Democrat for President or Governor since 1892, and some within the party were questioning whether Taggart had lost his touch. Unless he could field a winning candidate, Taggart was facing not only the loss of candidates from his party, but his own position of leadership, as well.

In the early years of the 20th century, the Democratic Party in Indiana was in disarray. Normally a very competitive state, no Democratic governor had been elected since 1892. Republicans had enjoyed ever-increasing majorities culminating in the landslide year for Republicans of 1904.

The Democrats looked through their ranks to find electable candidates. In 1906, local leaders approached Marshall about running for Congress. The idea held some appeal to him, as his law partner, William McNagny, had served a term in Congress ten years earlier.

> *Things drifted along politically until the year 1906. I considered an active interest in political affairs not only my duty but my diversion from the practice of my profession. In that year there was an effort to nominate me as candidate for Congress. I promptly killed the movement. I had had a partner who had been in Congress and I thought one from the firm was sufficient. In the course of conversation with the leaders of the party it was suggested that I ought to run because every county in the district, save ours, had furnished a candidate and all had been beaten since 1896. The pleasure of running for office and being licked, however, never appealed to me. I had not the slightest desire to be classed among those who also ran.*[74]

Tom and Lois were content with their Columbia City life and had no desire to uproot to Washington. Marshall was then asked if he would ever again be a candidate for public office. "To get rid of the situation, I intimated that I did not think I ever would," Marshall replied, "But if I did I would be a candidate for governor."[75]

CHAPTER THREE:

From His Accidency to His Excellency

(1908)

Despite Tom Taggart's wealth and power, it was clear that unless he could deliver a victory in the Indiana gubernatorial election of 1908 he would not long remain as the leader of the Democratic Party. The Democratic Party in the State was splintered into different groups, and lacked the cohesiveness needed to engineer election victories. Marshall knew that, unless the different groups could be brought together, his party would continue to face electoral defeat.

> *From 1896 to 1908 the Democratic Party in Indiana had been torn into factions. It was a somewhat difficult thing to find a man who was a Democrat – just a plain, unadorned, undiluted, unterrified Democrat. You could find Jacksonian Democrats, Jefferson Democrats, Parker Democrats and Bryan Democrats; the party was a party of hyphenated Democrats. I had long since ceased to attend what were advertised as harmony banquets. The most difficult thing in the world is to produce harmony when nobody cares to harmonize. These harmony banquets were really incipient riots.*[76]

The unification of the Democratic Party achieved by Taggart and Marshall began a partnership that was both unusual in its nature and beneficial for both men involved. Tom Marshall was popular and outgoing, scrupulously honest, a small-town lawyer of impeccable character and a proven vote-getter. Tom Taggart was a feared and distrusted but well-connected political boss who was a master at making deals in smoke-filled rooms.

The leading Democratic candidates for Governor of Indiana in 1908 were Sam Ralston, who had the support of Tom Taggart, and Ert Slack, who was supported by both the temperance advocates and the anti-Taggart forces. Ert Slack, just thirty-three in the summer of 1908, had served four years in the Indiana House of Representatives and three in the State Senate when he ran for governor. He would eventually serve a term as Mayor of Indianapolis. Ralston, an attorney from Lebanon, had experience running for statewide office, as he was the unsuccessful candidate for Indiana Secretary of State in 1898.

Tom Taggart and Tom Marshall knew of each other prior to 1908, but neither viewed the other with respect or admiration. Marshall was well aware of Taggart's power both in Indianapolis and in statewide Democratic circles, but loathed political bossism and refused to try to curry Taggart's favor. Taggart knew that Marshall was a popular Democrat committed to party principles, but he was concerned that Marshall was too independent to take orders from him. Marshall in the governor's chair, Taggart feared, would do little to advance Taggart's political power. Marshall might be electable, but what Taggart really wanted was a Democratic governor who would turn to him for advice and direction.

Marshall, though, was clearly a serious contender. Thanks to a front page that had appeared in the Fort Wayne Journal-Gazette, the delegates to the state convention that year from Northeast Indiana were committed to Marshall for governor.

> *I was lost, or thought I was, in the pine forests of northern Michigan in the summer of 1907 when word reached me that my good friend, Louis Ludlow, had taken his life and reputation in his hands and had dared to assert that he thought I would make a good Democratic candidate for governor. His suggestion was immediately approved in a two-column editorial in the Fort Wayne Journal-Gazette by the most loyal soul who ever lived on earth, Andy Moynihan.[77]*

Marshall claimed, probably with sincerity, that he never sought an elected office, but the office sought him. After the *Journal-Gazette* had effectively started his gubernatorial campaign, Marshall insisted that he was still not convinced he was the right person for the job. His description of how he eventually decided to become a candidate represents his self-deprecating humor, his ability to spin stories his listeners adored, and his connection with the common man.

> *I told the Charlie Munson story. Munson was a young man in the City of Fort Wayne, who was desirous of becoming a candidate for sheriff of Allen County, an office he subsequently attained, and afterward was elected auditor of state. It was in the good old days when the liquor interests still had to be recognized and conciliated, if possible. There was an Irish saloon keeper in Fort Wayne by the name of Mike Somers. This man either had or was presumed to have in his vest pocket an entire ward. So one night at about closing time Munson went into Somers' saloon, stood around until the blinds were drawn, shuffled from one foot to another, and finally said to Mike: "Mike, I have thought some of being a candidate for sheriff. I thought I would better consult you about it before I reached any determination." After a few moments' pause, Somers replied: "Go in, Charlie. Sometimes the weakest man wins."[78]*

Marshall told his supports that the weakest man might win the nomination at the state Democratic convention so, yes, he would go ahead and put his hat in the ring.

Each congressional district sent a slate of delegates to the state convention. Ralston and Slack both brought significant support from the various congressional districts to the meeting at Tomlinson Hall on March 25, 1908. The Twelfth Congressional District, which comprised most of Northeast Indiana, remained firmly, if not unanimously, in the Marshall camp. His supporters tried in vain to make sure that the delegates from their congressional district were unanimous in their support of Marshall.

> *My old time friends in northern Indiana, who had more*
> *confidence in me than I deserved, came gallantly to my colors.*
> *When the delegates were elected to the state convention it*
> *was discovered that the Twelfth Congressional District was*
> *unanimous for me, save one delegate in my own county who*
> *had not spoken to me in ten years.* [79]

Before the convention, several of Marshall's friends urged that he visit the recalcitrant delegate and induce him to change his vote. Marshall declined, and in doing so highlighted one of the qualities that made him such a popular candidate.

> *I refused to permit anybody to see him, told my friends that he*
> *had been selected as a delegate, that I believed in representative*
> *government, that he had a perfect right to vote his choice, and*
> *if he cared to vote against me they would hear no complaint. He*
> *went to the convention, came up to my modest little room in the*
> *Grand Hotel, stuck out his hand and said that he would like to*
> *shake hands with me and return to friendly relations, as he had*
> *made up his mind to vote for me and do everything he could to*
> *procure my nomination. Of course, we were friends again. He*
> *told me that if any attempt had been made to keep him away*
> *from the convention he would have spent a thousand dollars to*
> *get every enemy I had to come down to Indianapolis and try to*
> *defeat me. Because I had played what he thought was a square*
> *game he was for me.* [80]

Marshall was the type of candidate whose personality and style attracted supporters. He was not identified with any particular political movement, be it temperance, soft money, or any one of a variety of factions. He did not, therefore, alienate any voting bloc active in the 1908 race. Part of his appeal was that he was universally well-liked, and thus became an acceptable compromise candidate. One reporter remembered a visit with Marshall in Columbia City:

Because in the early stages of the state convention few thought his nomination possible, there was no feeling against him in any quarter. When, like most delegates, I called at his headquarters, I found a slightly built man with a big mustache (not closely cropped, as in his Washington days) and humorous eyes who amused callers with his whimsicality and gave the impression of being a modest man capable of poking fun at himself while paying compliments to his opponents. His visitors left his room with a kindly feeling for an old-fashioned Democrat. Thus it was that in the end organization forces dumped their votes into Marshall's lap.[81]

Delegates from across the state gathered in Tomlinson Hall in Indianapolis to nominate the Democratic candidate for governor. Tensions were high as the preliminary business of the convention was conducted, and both Ralston and Slack supports were confident as the voting began. After the first ballot, Ralston led, followed by Slack and Marshall. The delegates fought the contest bitterly, and as the hours dragged on tempers began to rise. Taggart could see that the convention was spinning out of his control – or anyone else's. As one historian described the scene:

The convention chairman had to call policemen to the floor to restore order during the gubernatorial voting after the sergeant at arms and his assistants failed to do so. At one point a rabid anti-Taggart delegate was hustled off the floor by police only to be brought back shortly thereafter by Taggart himself.[82]

On the fourth ballot, Taggart's candidate, Ralston, fell into second place and it was clear that the momentum had shifted to Slack. Taggart knew what he had to do. He didn't want Marshall to be governor, because he didn't think he could control him. But he also knew that if Slack were nominated, his days as party leader would be over. On the floor of the convention, he turned to Ralston, and stated "I want you to withdraw, and give your support to Marshall." As Ralston made his way to the podium to give his withdrawal speech, the Marshall forces erupted into cheers

> *Marshall supporters, all of whom had been supplied with small*
> *American flags, were on their feet shouting hoarsely, overturning*
> *chairs, and waving their emblems madly, as one county after*
> *another that previously had been in the Ralston column joined*
> *the Marshall supporters and cast solid votes for the Columbia*
> *City man.*[83]

On the fifth ballot, Thomas Marshall was nominated with 719 ½ votes versus 630 ½ for Slack, who escorted the victorious candidate into the hall for his acceptance speech. "Through the inability of the leading candidates to obtain a majority of votes of the convention," Marshall wrote, "I was transformed from His Accidency to His Excellency."[84]

Marshall knew that he needed to take action to cement the unity among the party leaders at the convention. To ease the sting of defeat for his unsuccessful rivals, he opened his remarks to the delegates by reaching out his hand to Ralston and Slack:

> *Mr. Chairman, Gentlemen of the Convention, Ladies and*
> *Gentlemen – It has always been one of the fortunes of my life*
> *that the bitter and the sweet should be intermingled. I never*
> *overcome a rival that I do not feel mercy for him, and when*
> *I overcome friends there is a feeling of sadness as well as of*
> *gladness. It is so here today.*[85]

In a scenario that would be repeated four years hence, Marshall was aware that his victory was a combination of his own personal qualities along with the benevolence of other powerful men.

> *There have been a good many men who have made me politically.*
> *I owe all these friends an infinite debt of gratitude for their*
> *faith, their zeal, and their charity and frequently for their*
> *mistaken enthusiasm, but as I conceive it, I have never been*
> *anything more than a nickel-plated politician.*[86]

Knowing that the hall was filled with Democrats of all types, many of whom had come to the convention in support of someone other than

Marshall, the newly-nominated candidate sought to bring unity to the hall. Turning once again to his training in classical history, he made reference to the practice among Roman legions which would "pass before the new ruler and swear allegiance to him".[87] He asked for the same from the assembled delegates.

> *You have chosen me to lead you in this fight, and I accept your commission with the most sincere thanks and appreciation of the honor, but in this hour I tender the nomination back to you if there be one man in the convention who will not stand behind me.*

Marshall's move was without question bold and risky. Had a single delegate spoken out, the nomination might have collapsed. Rather than hearing a contrary voice, however, those present heard nothing but the roar of approval.

> *I called attention to the fact that we had these hyphenated Democrats in Indiana. I was determined to know none among them save just plain Democrats; that I appreciated the great honor of the nomination but that unless every man in the convention would rise to his feet, lift his hand to Heaven and pledge me from that time forward to be just a Democrat and nothing else, I should be compelled to decline the nomination. It was a rather theatric moment. The delegates arose to their feet and the nomination was an accomplished fact.*[88]

The Republican nominee in 1908, Congressman James Eli Watson, was a shrewd and experienced politician. He knew that his party had the numerical advantage in the statewide election, and that he would have the advantage of a well-liked Republican presidential candidate – William Howard Taft – at the top of the ticket. Taft was thought to be unbeatable in Indiana, and the Hoosier State had not given its presidential vote to a candidate from one party and gubernatorial nod to a candidate from a different party since Republican Ulysses Grant and Democratic Thomas Hendricks did that in 1872.

ക്ക ക്ക ക്ക ക്ക ക്ക

William Howard Taft was Theodore Roosevelt's hand-picked successor as the Republican presidential nominee in 1908. Taft's experience in government was unmatched. He had formerly been a federal judge, a diplomat who helped America slog through the morass of the Philippines, and a cabinet secretary. His integrity, furthermore, was beyond reproach. In behavior and political philosophy, he seemed, in Roosevelt's eyes, to be the best successor to his legacy.

Taft had little of the ebullient personality of Roosevelt. Though genial and sincere, he was viewed as timid and slow by the leadership of Washington. He lacked Marshall's wit or the charisma of Roosevelt or Wilson. He could be humorous at times, as he loved to retell the story of a group of ladies who presented him with a petition asking him to halt the proposed construction of public urinals in the neighborhood surrounding Washington's DuPont Circle. Taft thanked the ladies for their interest, and then politely asked if they could recommend a better location for the project. Taft had to stifle a laugh when the women suggested, apparently without understanding the irony, that the public urinals might more appropriately be placed on P Street.

Teddy may have regretted announcing publicly that he was forgoing a third term; Taft, while seemingly in step with Roosevelt's philosophy, had proven his mettle in his handling of the insurrection in the Philippines. Once Taft had been given the nod, other GOP candidates – such as Charles Warren Fairbanks – backed away from the race.

For Taft's running mate, the Republicans nominated James S. Sherman. Sherman was born on October 24, 1855, in Utica, New York, where his grandfather ran a profitable glass factory and owned an impressive farm, which happened to be adjacent to the family farm of future Senator Elihu Root. He attended Hamilton College, where he became a popular student known for his public speaking skills. He graduated from Hamilton in 1878, received his law degree there the following year, and was admitted to the New York state bar in 1880.

Drawn to politics at an early age, he won election as mayor of Utica before he turned thirty. In 1886, he was elected to the U.S. House of Representatives. Sherman's political philosophy was firmly entrenched in the conservative wing of the Republican Party. He supported a high protective tariff and the maintenance of the gold standard.

While serving as a congressman, Sherman developed a reputation as a noteworthy parliamentarian. With 435 members, debate in the House of Representatives could easily turn chaotic without the firm hand of a presiding officer. Sherman developed a reputation as a decisive and able parliamentarian. This, combined with his commitment to conservative beliefs, meant that the "Old Guard" Republicans supported his nomination for Vice President. Sherman's strength in New York also brought geographic balance to the ticket.

The Democrats had once again settled on William Jennings Bryan as their running mate. The poor showing by Alton Parker in 1904 had energized the free silver Democrats. By this time, however, adherence to the free silver ideology had faded into the background. By 1904, a new political philosophy, known commonly as progressivism, had emerged.

The progressive movement began to gain strength among America's growing middle class. Not as far left as liberalism but well to the left of conservatism, much of the growth of progressivism can be traced to a backlash against the growth of corporate power. Perhaps the mainstay of progressivism was the call for a reduction of tariffs, which were viewed as an unfair advantage for corporations at the expense of the average family. In its place, progressives advocated for the passage of a constitutional amendment to enact a federal income tax.

But progressivism was much more than just an economic viewpoint. It also embraced such ideas as government regulation, establishment of a federal agency to oversee monetary policy, the direct election of senators, and women's suffrage.

Importantly, the progressive viewpoint had adherents in both the Democratic and Republican Party. Both parties had their conservative and liberal wings, but the progressive movement would eventually bring together the liberal wing of the Republican Party with conservative Democrats.

Because Bryan faced no serious contenders at the Democratic Convention in Denver in 1908, attention quickly focused on his selection of a running mate. To balance the ticket, strategists looked for a candidate from large urban states, preferably one that was not as strident as Bryan on the free silver-gold standard question.

Because of his role as a member of the Democratic National Committee, Tom Taggart was well aware of what Bryan was looking for as his running mate. He knew that Indiana's John Worth Kern would provide balance for the ticket both geographically and philosophically. Furthermore, Kern would be warmly welcomed by the growing labor union movement. Taggart used his campaigning skills to elect John Worth Kern as Bryan's running mate on the first ballot.

Any Democrat would face a tough challenge in a statewide election in Indiana in 1908. The last Democratic governor to be elected was Claude Matthews in 1892. The Republican margin of victory had increased every year since then. It was 18,000 votes in 1896, a margin of 26,000 votes in 1900, and J. Frank Hanly had defeated John Worth Kern in 1904 by a seemingly insurmountable difference of 84,000 votes.[89]

To win as a Democrat in Indiana, Marshall had to take a middle ground and appeal to moderate Republican voters. He began the campaign by focusing on a number of issues, including a new primary election law, the direct election of United States senators, stronger insurance for bank deposits, reform of the trusts, and reductions in government spending.[90]

Watson's strategy was to prevent voters who normally voted Republican from switching parties. To do this, he needed an issue that would both solidify his support with solidly Republican voters and prevent ticket-splitting independents from voting for Marshall. He chose to highlight an issue on which both the Democratic Party and Marshall personally appeared weak – the temperance question.

Hoosiers in 1908 were generally in agreement that the sale of liquor should be controlled at the local level. The Republican state platform called for control of liquor sales to be at the county level. That is, each county could decide whether or not to permit the sale of liquor, and that rule would apply to the entire county.

Democrats also favored the local option, but their platform called for the question to be determined at the city or township level – geographic areas smaller than counties. For example, Indiana has 92 counties and 1,006 townships (as each county made up of six to twenty townships.) Under the Democratic plan, cities or townships could choose to be "dry", but those rules would not apply to the rest of the county. Larger urban areas, in general, tended to support the sale of liquor, while the more rural portions of counties were opposed. Not coincidentally, the Democratic Party garnered much of its support from urban areas, while most rural areas, particularly in northern Indiana, were predominantly Republican.

Raising the liquor issue to such prominence also gave the Republicans the opportunity to publicize Marshall's alcoholism. From all indications Marshall in 1908 had not had a drink in over ten years, but his prior record of public intoxication was something too valuable for the Republicans to ignore.

Republicans helped to spread the rumor that Marshall was not a "sober man". While Watson did not personally mention the issue, talk of Marshall's drinking continued throughout the campaign. The whispers became so vicious that the minister from the Presbyterian church in Columbia City publicly denounced the attacks. "Mr. Marshall is not only not a drunkard," said Reverend Alexander D. Sutherland, "but on the contrary is a total abstainer; a practical, consistent temperance man, yet not a hypocrite nor a fanatic."[91]

Watson also sought to attack Marshall as a puppet of the alcohol manufacturers and distributors, and claimed that the brewers were contributing a million dollars to Marshall's campaign fund. Marshall, however, deftly parried the charge of receiving money from the alcohol interests.

While political campaigns were not as expensive in 1908 as they are today, money could still influence elections. Many voters, both Democratic and Republican, were concerned about the influence of corporate campaign contributions. Marshall, however, was determined to avoid any semblance of contributions buying political influence. To finance his gubernatorial campaign, Marshall borrowed $3,750 from a local bank.

On Monday morning I went to my office, which I had not seen in six weeks. There I found a vast number of letters from loyal Democrats all over the state containing checks ranging from five to twenty-five dollars, and aggregating more than seven thousand. These were sent to me by good Democrats to assist me in the expenses of the campaign. It is needless to say that they were all returned uncashed. I had the rather remarkable record of walking into the governor's office of the state of Indiana at a total expense of three thousand seven hundred fifty dollars. People may wonder how I know the exact amount. It is easily told. I had no money when I started; I borrowed it all at my bank, and I didn't succeed in repaying all of it until after I had escaped from the Senate Chamber for a little while and had filled in an interval on the Chautauqua platform, between the disappearance of the snake charmer and the appearance of the sword swallower.[92]

He made sure his audiences knew that it was his personal funds, not those of the brewers that were paying for his campaign.

I am not the brewer's candidate for Governor of Indiana. Not a dollar has been raised for me by any brewer … I have not a dollar of any man's money in my pocket, except what I borrowed of the First National Bank of Columbia City, Indiana, and unless you fellows are kind to me in November I'll have to work like sin for three years to pay that back. But when I say that I am not the brewers' candidate I mean that neither am I the lawyers' candidate, the blacksmiths' candidate, the preachers' candidate nor the Anti-Saloon League candidate. I am the candidate of the Democratic part and I stand upon its platform.[93]

In 1908, before radio and television, campaign messages were delivered though speeches, not sound bites. As a result, most of Marshall's campaign expenses were for travel. By the end of the campaign, Marshall had spent only $2,000 for travel, and he donated the remaining $1,800 to the state Democratic Party.

For voters who judged candidates by their physical appearance, Marshall would not have ranked high. He was a small man – standing five feet, six inches tall, and weighing about 125 pounds. His ears were out of proportion to his head, and his face was dominated by a bushy mustache. Viewers were distracted from his small frame by his immaculate dress.

You would not guess it from his photographs, but he is urbane, from his well-cut locks to his small, well-shod foot and the tips of his perfectly manicured fingers. The taste that selects his ties transcends all criticism. To silence the slanders of the camera, it remains only to note the Phi Beta Kappa key (of unusual weight

and elegance) on his bog, the ring on his finger, the stick in the
gloved hand, and the large, round, real, tortoise-shell spectacles
which add distinction while they relieve the wearied eye of the
wearer.[94]

Marshall's speaking style was extraordinarily effective. He combined references to Greece and Rome (from his courses at Wabash College) with a Hoosier style of wit. While his stories at times poked fun at his neighbors or other politicians, more often than not he was the brunt of his own humor.

Thomas often used his humor to disarm his opponent. Marshall at one point had commented that he felt it was the duty of the Governor to sign laws passed by the legislature unless there was some doubt about their constitutionality. Watson seized on this by asking in one of his speeches if Marshall would sign bills to legalize murder and gambling if the legislature passed them. Marshall quickly retorted:

> *Mr. Watson asks me if I will sign such bills if a Republican*
> *legislature passes them ... All I have to say is that Mr. Watson*
> *certainly has a very poor opinion of the Republican candidates*
> *for the Legislature if he thinks they will pass such bills.*[95]

As the question of the local option for control of liquor sales heated up, he again used wit to make his point (though by today's standards he would clearly open himself to criticism):

> *I am a believer in local self-government. I believe that no man*
> *has a right to call in his neighbor to help him lick his wife until*
> *he finds he can't lick her himself.... I don't talk to Democrats*
> *this year ... it is not necessary. I have been in fifty counties of*
> *Indiana and every Democrat I have met has had a smile on*
> *his face just such as he had when he kissed his wife for the first*
> *time.*

Humor was only one weapon that Marshall used in his oratorical arsenal. He also had the ability to clarify issues in a way that appealed to listeners.

*Do you believe that any man or combination of men has the
right to obtain legislation that will inure to the few and be to
the detriment of the many? Has any one any such rights, God-
given or man-bestowed? If you believe they have not you are
a Democrat, and though I am not a preacher and have never
taken on holy orders, I will do so now and take you into full
communion ... the Republican party and prosperity are not
trotting in double harness this year. The bottom is out of the
full dinner pail.*[96]

Marshall was probably at his best, however, when he was inspiring his
audiences. He had the rare ability to understand his audience and gain the rapt
attention of his listeners. At one rally, when he spotted elderly men wearing
the buttons of the Grand Army of the Republic, he said

*If you boys who wore the blue had not offered yourselves as a
sacrifice there would have been an aristocracy in this country
that would have ultimately destroyed the republic.*[97]

No orator was better at understanding his audience and making a connection
with their hearts and minds. While at a packed rally in Crawfordsville, the
location of his alma mater, he said

*Different things have stirred men's hearts in ages past. To the
Greek, it was thoughts of Marathon and Thermopylae; to the
Roman, it was the Rubicon and Carthage; to the Frenchman, it
was Hastings and Waterloo; to the American, it is Valley Forge
and Gettysburg, but the thing that makes my heart beat faster
are thoughts of Wabash College in Crawfordsville.*[98]

At times during the campaign, some would approach Marshall with very
personal appeals:

*In a little town in Indiana, where I was spending Sunday,
during my campaign for governor, the landlord of the hotel
told me that his cook would like to see me. I said that we were*

going to church, and that I would see her after dinner. So in the
afternoon a modest little woman, holding with each hand a small
child, came in and said she wanted to ask a favor of me. She said
she wanted me, when I was elected, to look up Jake's record and
see whether he was entitled to any mercy at my hands. I learned
that he had been a constable; was of Democratic faith; that in
a drunken brawl he attempted to serve a subpoena, which he
did not distinguish from a warrant, shot and killed a man who
was a prominent Republican, between whom and himself there
was no friendly feeling. In the excitement of the hour he was
convicted of murder in the first degree and sentenced for life to
the penitentiary. I said to her that I was only a candidate; that
the chances were against me. She replied that she was sure I was
going to be elected, and would I just look into Jake's case and see
whether or not he was entitled to any mercy. I promised her if
elected I would investigate his conviction and his record.[99]

The Democratic platform in 1908 covered a wide variety of issues. Progressive reforms had grown in prominence, and the Democrats sought election reform through a new primary election law and the direct election of United States senators. Business issues also were important to voters, and Marshall's campaign advocated for a guarantee of bank deposits, the strengthening of the Employee's Liability Law, and more regulations against the trusts.[100]

But the Republicans focused their attention on the single issue of prohibition. Prohibition and the local option question ended up as the deciding factor in the election – but not in the way that Watson and the Republicans had planned.

Governor Hanly was a leader who worked with fierce determination for issues towards which he felt strongly – he opposed gambling, was determined to root out corruption during his administration, and strongly supported prohibition. Hanly gained a reputation as a political maverick. In that role, he didn't hesitate to take a position contrary to those of his own party, or even to take action which could hurt Republicans at the polls. Despite the potential political consequences for his Republican Party, Hanly was determined to shut down alcohol sales in the State of Indiana (He was to eventually become the

Prohibition Party's candidate for President in 1916). He knew that the county option for liquor sales would lead to prohibition in most counties.

Hanly made it clear to his Republican colleagues that he intended to forcefully press his campaign against the sale of liquor. At the GOP's statewide convention in 1908, he made an impassioned plea to his party to take up the cause of prohibition.

> *I hate it as Abraham Lincoln hated slavery. And as he sometimes saw in prophetic vision the end of slavery, and the coming of the time when the sun should shine and the rain should fall upon no slave in all the Republic, so I sometimes seem to see the end of this unholy traffic, the coming of the time when, if it does not wholly cease to be, it shall find no safe habitation anywhere beneath Old Glory's stainless stars.*[101]

Hanly called a special session of the Indiana General Assembly in September to enact the county-option liquor sales bill. On September 18, 1908, six weeks before the general election, both the House and Senate passed the legislation, which was quickly signed by Hanly.

The special session, however, assured Marshall's victory. Democrats and others who favored the city or township local option were motivated to elect their supporters, including Marshall. Those who supported the county option had already achieved victory, which sapped their energy as the election neared. "When this was done," Watson later wrote, "it took my platform squarely out from under me and thus relieved any Democrats who believed in county local option from the necessity of voting for me to get what they wanted."[102]

Given Marshall's popularity the issue many not have been the deciding factor in the election. But the issue on which Watson had staked his campaign was now settled, and voters were able to focus on the strengths of each candidate.

In a popularity contest, Marshall was an overwhelming favorite. As Marshall aggressively traveled throughout the state, he gained supporters with each campaign stop. Marshall's oratorical style continued to gain him votes over the more mundane Watson. Marshall claimed to have made 169 speeches between the start of the campaign in Salem on August 22 until election eve

November 1. At that rate, Marshall was average about two speeches a day, seven days a week.

> *Mrs. Marshall and I started on our weary way over Indiana. Now and then I forget what should be the prayer of every public man on arising in the morning: "Oh, God, keep me humble this day." Once in a while I thoughtlessly begin to brag, and so on one occasion in her presence I bragged that I had made the most strenuous campaign that was ever made in the state of Indiana; that I had made one hundred sixty-nine speeches in that campaign. Mrs. Marshall has been my best friend because she has been my severest critic. She at once stopped me, and said: "Oh, Tom, don't tell that story! I was with you all the while. What you mean to say is that you made one speech one hundred sixty-nine times in the state of Indiana. And if you dare to deny it I'll deliver it now, and tell them anything else you said!"* [103]

As farmers, factory workers and others gathered to listen to the Democratic candidate for governor, Marshall was able to connect with his listeners and create a personal bond that would convince listeners to support the diminutive lawyer from Columbia City. His effect on a crowd was captured by the local paper after a stop in Evansville:

> *A man with a bull dog jaw, every line of his countenance showing vigor, determination and earnestness, his step quick and firm, a kindly smile showing over his features, walked onto the stage at the People's theater last night to receive the plaudits of a great audience. What manner of man he was, no one knew because he had never spoken in Evansville. He was on trial before an audience of thinking men in the second city of Indiana. He began like a fighter stripping for action, his eyes afire with the light of a message he was about to deliver, his manner showing he was prepared to say it with solar plexus force. Before he was done he had conquered the doubters, had won applause from strangers and stamped himself as the greatest campaigner that Indiana has known since Blue Jeans Williams.* [104]

Many of the speeches were before large and increasingly enthusiastic crowds. Audiences of one or two thousand were not uncommon, with attendance of 4,000 in Huntingburg and Petersburg, 5,000 in Covington and 12,500 when Marshall gave a series of four speeches in Indianapolis.[105] The heavy travel and nonstop speechmaking continued up to Election Day.

> *The last Saturday of the campaign Mrs. Marshall and I got up at five o'clock, in the city of South Bend, managed to secure a cup of coffee and a sandwich, and took the train for Goshen, where I talked for an hour. At twelve o'clock I was talking again in Middlebury; at two o'clock, in Shipshewana; at four o'clock, in La Grange; ant six o'clock, in Kendallville; at eight o'clock, in the Princess Rink, in Fort Wayne, and as the midnight bells announced the ushering in of Sunday I quit talking, on the steps of the court-house, in the city of Fort Wayne. We took the train at four o'clock for home.* [106]

Across the country, Democrats would generally not fare well in the election of 1908. The Panic of 1907 caused some to believe there would be a Republican backlash, but by the fall of 1908 economic prosperity had returned to most parts of the country. William Howard Taft's campaign appealed to voters who embraced the progressive philosophy as he called for a reduction in tariffs and regulation of trusts.

Taft also gained support by allying himself closely with his predecessor, Roosevelt, who was still viewed as a powerful and successful leader. But while Bryan was an extraordinary speaker and Kern was admired, neither could show the voters much success in their records. As the *New York Times* noted, the Democratic candidates were a "ticket that was consistent, at any rate, for a man twice defeated for the Presidency was at the head of it, and a man twice defeated for the Governor of his State was at the tail of it."[107]

Ultimately, Taft and Sherman garnered fifty-one percent of the vote, winning in twenty-nine of the forty-six states. Despite the fact that Republican Taft was winning Indiana by 10,000 votes, Marshall won the state by 14,000 votes. He outpolled all of the other Democrats on the statewide ticket, besting the candidate for Lieutenant Governor by 8,000 votes, and the Secretary of State by 9,000.

Though Taft was nominally now the President of the United States, in the minds of most Americans Theodore Roosevelt was still their leader. Teddy did his best to pass the mantle of governance on to Taft. Referring to the newly-elected President, Roosevelt in 1908 felt complete congruence with his goals and ideals. "He and I view public questions exactly alike," Teddy wrote, "In fact, I think it is very rare that two public men have ever been so much at one in all the essentials of their public beliefs."[108] When a journalist suggested that the American people might ask him to be their leader in 1912, Roosevelt was adamant. "No," came the reply, "Revolutions don't go backward."[109]

William Howard Taft was now President, but Theodore Roosevelt was such a magnetic personality it was difficult for the country to divert its gaze from the fascinating Colonel and his equally interesting family. Those who knew Colonel Roosevelt were fully aware that it would be difficult for him to remain out of the spotlight. His children had teased him that he wanted to be "the bride at every wedding and the corpse at every funeral."[110]

To avoid the attention of the press, Roosevelt decided to go on a year-long safari in Africa. Deep in the jungle, it was presumed, the ex-President would be far from the public's eye and Taft could be given the uncrowded stage that he needed to govern. J.P. Morgan, who had clashed numerous times with the man from Sagamore Hill, was pleased with Roosevelt's impending departure. Upon hearing the news, he raised a glass and proposed a toast: "America," he declared, "expects every lion to do its duty!"

Marshall's success drew national attention. While Marshall was one of several Democratic governors elected in 1908 – including the states of Minnesota, Montana, North Dakota and Ohio – Marshall's strong margins in a state that gave the nod to Taft made party leaders take notice.

Despite his defeat, William Jennings Bryan reached out to Marshall:

> I have sent you a telegram of congratulations, but I beg to acknowledge your note in addition, and to say to you that I have never for a moment doubted the sincerity of your assertion, frequently made, that you would be willing to be defeated to see me elected, if your defeat would elect me. Let me assure you that my defeat is softened by the fact that a number of good friends like yourself have been more successful. Personally I am relieved rather than disappointed, but I regret the delay in the

carrying out of your reforms. I wish you every success in your administration, a wish in which Mrs. Bryan joins, as she does in my regards to your wife. Say to Mrs. Marshall that I have as much confidence in the "First Lady of Indiana" as I have in the new governor.[111]

Republicans were bitter about having lost their first gubernatorial election in twelve years. Governor Hanly may have been particularly incensed that Marshall, whose background included a weakness for alcohol, was succeeding him in office.

The day before Marshall's inauguration, Hanly delivered his final address to a joint session of the General Assembly. The chamber was embarrassingly silent as the departing Governor was accompanied to the podium by the legislative leadership. More a sermon than a political speech, Hanly warned against any attempts by the Democrats to reverse the new law on county option for the selling of alcohol. The new law, he said, "is the livest wire in the political machinery of the commonwealth, and is charged so heavily that it will electrocute the party that repeals it."

As Hanly droned on regarding the evils of alcohol, his speech was seldom interrupted by applause, and then only from the Republican side of the chamber. Reporters noted that many Democrats read newspapers during the oration.

Hanly's mood soured even further on inauguration day, January 11, 1909. His dislike of Marshall was so complete that he, at first, declined to attend the ceremonies.

So intense was the bitterness of the campaign of 1908, and so sure was my predecessor in office, Governor Hanly, that my election would blight the crops, blot out the churches and destroy the civic sense of justice in the state, that he tendered me no courtesy whatever with reference to my inauguration. Fortunately (a friend) came to the rescue and succeeded in inducing Governor Hanly to call up my house, ride with me to the Capitol and preside over the ceremonies.[112]

Convinced by Republican Secretary of State Fred Simms, who also happened to be a friend of Marshall's, that that the absence of the departing governor would be a serious embarrassment to the State, Hanly grudgingly agreed to accompany Simms in a carriage to pick up Marshall for the ceremony.

> *Simms sat between the old and new governors during the excruciatingly long ride to the State House. Not a word was spoken until the carriage reached the Capital. Wishing to take a mischievous stab at his discourteous host, Marshall stated, "Governor Hanly, I think it is only fair to tell you that when I become governor one of my first official acts will be to sign the Vincennes Bonds." Hanly had refused to sign the bonds which would have settled a long-standing claim held by Vincennes University against the state. Sims thought Hanly, his anger already held in check by only a slim margin, might erupt at the governor-elect. Instead, without even looking at Marshall, Hanly said, "Mr. Marshall, when you are the governor, you may do exactly as you please about signing the Vincennes bonds."* [113]

The atmosphere during the ceremony improved little. After the Lieutenant Governor had been sworn in during a ceremony in the Senate chamber, the legislators, led by Marshall and Hanly, walked in two lines to the first floor rotunda of the state house. There, Marshall was met by Lois, whose dress was topped by "a picture hat with an immense plume". Mrs. Hanly, on the other hand, appeared to be dressed for a funeral, complete with a black veil. Reporters, wishing to convey to careful readers the contrast between sour demeanor of Mrs. Hanly and the youthful enthusiasm of Mrs. Marshall, noted that Lois was "younger" and "unveiled".

The invocation was presented by Reverend George Mackintosh, President of Wabash College and a fellow member, with Thomas, on the Board of Trustees of Wabash. At 12:30, Thomas Riley Marshall as the new Governor of the State of Indiana.

CHAPTER FOUR:

Governing a State

(1909-1911)

The Indiana over which Governor Marshall took the reins in 1909 was in the middle of one of the most significant periods of transition in the State's history. Indiana was changing from part of the rural, agricultural frontier to an urbanized industrial and manufacturing state.

In many ways, the transformation of Indiana around the time of Marshall's term of office reflected changes that were occurring in other mid-western states. Illinois, Michigan, Ohio and Pennsylvania were all experiencing the economic, social and demographic changes that followed the Industrial Revolution. But knowledgeable observers pointed out that Indiana soon after the beginning of the twentieth century was a state that reflected the makeup of the rest of the nation. Indiana had been at the center of national politics for a generation, and to a great extent this reflected the fact that Hoosiers tended to look like the rest of the country. As one historian wrote:

> *Indiana approximates an average of America and closely*
> *resembled the composite that the various corners of our country*
> *might present could they be brought together and intermingled.*
> *It is an average that makes a State with fewer of the very rich,*
> *with fewer of the very poor, with fewer of the foreign born, with*
> *a larger proportion of the home born that most of our other*
> *States; that makes a community born within itself, enlarging*
> *its own traditions and carrying on its own ideals; and because*

of the trend of its history it is singularly American in its point of view.[114]

The centrist nature of the population was mirrored in its geographic location between the urbanized east coast and the newly emerging cities of Chicago and St. Louis. Demographers calculated that the population center of the United States in 1900 was near Columbus, Indiana.

During the period from 1880 to 1920, Indiana added nearly 1 million in population, an increase of almost one-third. When Marshall took office in 1909, there were more than 2.6 million Hoosiers, up from just under two million thirty years earlier. Of those, about 1.6 million lived on farms. Indiana was home to around 220,000 farms that employed around one-third of a million adults. By today's standards the average farm was small – just under a hundred acres. On those hundred acres, though, farmers and their families would provide for themselves, their neighbors, and the rest of the nation.

In 1909, Indiana's farmers produced $341 million in agricultural products. Much of that production was corn, hay and oats and most of that was consumed on the farm on which it was grown to support hogs, cattle and chickens. Nearly $100 million in livestock was slaughtered in 1909 – most of it hogs – and that figure would double over the next ten years. Chickens, and the eggs they produced, would also be important for the farm economy.[115]

Farm life in Indiana in 1909 was characterized by long days of work using few modern conveniences to produce an income which families hoped would allow them to live a decent life. Despite the invention of the internal combustion engine, the heavy work on Hoosier farms was still done by men and animals. Windmills were often used for pumping water, but as late as 1920 less than five percent of Indiana farms used a tractor and fewer than two percent had trucks.

The work was hard, but some modern conveniences helped to reduce the burden on the farmer and his family. The widespread use of the telephone helped to break centuries of isolation for rural farms. By 1920, two out of three Indiana farms had a telephone.

For those farmers fortunate enough to live near cities, the use of electricity helped reduce dependence on kerosene lamps. Electricity was installed in one of ten Hoosier farms by 1920. Another time saving convenience was the washing machine (not electric, but with manual rollers), which had been purchased by one out of four farms by the time of World War I.

To guard against the vagaries of weather and farm prices, Indiana farms diversified their crops and livestock. A detailed study of farming during the time of Marshall's governorship showed the average farm had revenue of around $3,000 from at least a dozen different farm products.

The breeding of hogs was often the most significant revenue source, accounting for about 40% of revenue on the average farm. Corn, wheat, oats and hay were grown, but most of that was used as feed for hogs and cattle. Chickens and eggs also provided a steady stream of income. A typical farm sold over three-hundred dozen eggs a year, and when prices were good they may get twenty-five cents a dozen. Chickens were also sold for their meat. Horses were used for much of the heavy work around the farm, and the occasional sale of a fowl would provide a small amount of income. While milk from the cattle could be sold, city dwellers would pay more for butter, and the typical farm sold over three-hundred pounds of butter a year.

During Marshall's years as governor, farmers benefited from rising prices for their product. A bushel of corn sold for sixty-three cents the year Marshall took office, and wheat was $1.13 a bushel. Prices were fairly stable during the next four years, but the increased demand from World War I pushed the price of a bushel of corn to $1.50, while wheat soared to $2.16 by 1919.

Farm revenue was dependent on the vagaries of the weather, the market price at which crops and livestock were sold, and how hard the farmer and his family worked. Farm expenses were minimal. Food was plentiful; clothes were usually hand made. But the largest expense item each year that was beyond the control of the farmer was property taxes. Both the State of Indiana and local governments in 1909 relied on property taxes for their revenue. By today's standards, though, expenses were miniscule. The entire budget for the State in Marshall's final year in office was $900,000. This provided for state government administration, a state police force, and some social services for mentally ill and handicapped Hoosiers.

Local governments also relied on property taxes. Education was provided through township governments, as were services for the indigent. The cost of road building would rise during this time period as the use of the automobile became widespread. In 1900, only 8,000 cars were registered in the United States; by 1920, 9.2 million automobiles were in use. The gasoline tax to pay for the construction and maintenance of roads would not be enacted in Indiana until 1923.

The State's dependence on property taxes served to limit the growth of government. An increase in property taxes was a sensitive issue in rural areas, as a farmer could not increase the price he received for his crops or livestock to pay for an increased property tax bill. With no other revenue source to finance expanded services, property tax rates were kept low by politicians who understood that Indiana was a rural state, and many farm families would be hard pressed to pay a higher property tax bill.

❧ ❧ ❧ ❧ ❧

Marshall brought with him to the governorship a political philosophy that had been instilled by his father, nurtured by his education at Wabash, and enforced by his life experiences. His belief in the rights of individuals might today earn him a Libertarian label; above all else, he was committed to honoring the constitutional form of government, the balance of power, and the ability of elected officials to vote their conscience:

> *I have always been a believer in the three coordinate departments of government – the legislative, judicial and executive. I believe that each is supreme within its own realm. I was and am satisfied that the attempted usurpation by one department of the clearly defined constitutional rights of another could result in but one thing – turmoil and bad government. I did not believe then, nor do I now believe, that an executive has any right to use his power, his prestige and his right of appointment to overawe or coerce the legislative department of government. I believed then, as I now believe, that it was the duty of the executive as much as the duty of the humblest citizen to obey the judgments of the court although he might believe them to be erroneous and usurpations of power, trusting to argument and education to rectify the wrong. I was not then any more than now, impressed with the rights of bodies of men, large and small, to remedial legislation, unless it was legislation not for their business or trade or calling, but in furtherance of their rights as*

*American citizens. No member of the Indiana Legislature will
dare say that I ever offered him an office, threatened him with
punishment, or even pleaded with him to vote for any measure
pending before that body as against his better judgment.*[116]

Believing in the importance of representative government, Marshall felt
that each branch of government should respect the responsibilities of the other
branches and the limitations of their own. He also believed that government
existed for the "everyday citizen", and not for special interests. He had little
regard for the army of lobbyists who would descend on the state capital while
the legislature was in session.

*The everyday citizen has no time to hang around the lobbies of
the General Assembly urging right things and fighting wrong
things. My observation convinces me that nine out of ten of the
men who buttonhole legislators, insist on dining and wining
them and seek to make appointments for secret conferences are
inspired by motives which may well be scrutinized.*

As with all newly-elected governors, patronage questions arose immediately
after the election. Marshall was the first Democratic governor in sixteen years,
and many Democratic Party faithful were eager to be rewarded with state
jobs. Marshall, though, held back the onslaught of office seekers. He felt an
obligation to his party, but also knew he was committed to appointed qualified
office holders.

*Any man who says he has a promise from me directly or
indirectly, tells me what is not true and if his name is given me,
I will promise now that he will not get the appointment; and
no appointment will be made on a man's ability as a politician,
but on merit. I shall appoint Democrats, real Democrats who
will give the state service for the pay they receive.*[117]

Marshall and Taggart clashed early in his administration over the subject
of patronage appointments. Taggart complained to Marshall that none of the
men that Taggart was recommending for office were being appointed. Marshall

replied that none of them were fit to appoint, but if the State Chairman would submit the names of men of proven character and ability, he would take pleasure in appointing them. Marshall had made his point and Taggart was more thoughtful in the names he put forward. This relationship worked well over the next four years.

One of Marshall's first appointments was one who would remain loyally by his side for the rest of his career. Mark Thistlethwaite was a young reporter with the Indianapolis News who covered Marshall's campaign. After the election, Marshall asked Thistlethwaite to be his confidential secretary, and his first job would be to come to Columbia City and respond to requests from patronage seekers. From that day and throughout Marshall's lifetime, Thistlethwaite remained a loyal and devoted advisor, confidant and friend.

❧ ❧ ❧ ❧ ❧

During Tom Marshall's term as governor the number of Indiana citizens who lived in urbanized areas began to grow, and has been growing ever since.

The reason for that growth was the increase in the industrialization of the economy. In 1904, around 175,000 Hoosiers were employed by manufacturing firms. In the next fifteen years that figure nearly doubled, to 330,000 workers. While nearly half of the workforce of Indiana was in agriculture in 1890, by 1920 that figure had fallen to one in four. The industrial sector growth meant that that by 1919 the value of output in the industrial sector exceeded agricultural products for the first time in the state's history.

Indiana was well-positioned during Marshall's tenure as governor to grow its manufacturing sector. Geographically, the State was in the center of commerce between eastern and western states. Railroads and high quality roads criss-crossed the region and manufacturers who located in Indiana were close to large quantities of forest and agricultural products, as well as limestone and coal in the southern counties and natural gas in the central part of the State.

The benefits of growth in manufacturing, however, were not evenly disbursed around the State. Firms such as iron and steel, glass manufacturing, and the newly-emerging automobile industry were concentrated in Indianapolis and the northern portion of Indiana. These economic differences would have political repercussions, as well, as the northern portion of the State generally supported the Republican Party, while the southern counties were strongholds of Democratic support.

No area of the State changed more dramatically during this time period than the far northwest corner – Lake County, which borders Chicago. In the early years of the twentieth century, a coalition of iron and steel manufacturers were looking for ways to expand their production capacity in the Midwest. They settled on the Lake Michigan shoreline in Lake County for a variety of reasons. Ports could be constructed to receive raw material – such as iron ore – from the mines in northern Minnesota. Railroad connections were excellent in and around the Chicago area, and finished goods could be transported quickly and cheaply to a variety of markets. A number of large manufacturing facilities were built in Lake County, culminating in the construction by United States Steel of the world's largest and most modern steel plant. To house workers, U.S. Steel developed a city next to the factory which they named Gary after the Chairman of the Board, Judge Elbert Gary. Similar company towns grew in Hammond, East Chicago and Whiting, such that by 1920 the four had a combined population in excess of 125,000. In just two decades, the swampy, barren marshland had been transformed into a vibrant center of manufacturing.

While many young men left the drudgery of farm life for the city, factory jobs during the time of Marshall's term as governor provided little of the glamour sought by farm boys. Work weeks in excess of sixty hours were not uncommon, and the jobs were often dirty and fraught with danger.

Worker safety became a key plank in the platform of the progressive movement, and several laws in this area were signed by Governor Marshall. In 1911, a new law reorganized industrial safety regulations by creating a Bureau of Inspection with responsibilities for factories, mines and boilers. Also in 1911, the General Assembly passed legislation strengthening worker compensation laws, which provided support for workers injured in industrial accidents. Marshall supported reform to the worker compensation laws:

> *The intricacies of modern manufacturing demand of the State that it take steps to protect itself from the liability to support those who are disabled and the families of those whose lives are snuffed out. The state has a right for its own protection, if for no other reason, to declare for compulsory compensation. This may deprive*

*a few of large damages but it will result in a more equitable
distribution than can possibly arise under the common law ...*[118]

But perhaps no area of labor reform was more prominent during Marshall's
tenure than that of child labor. When Marshall took office, Indiana's child
labor laws were among the weakest in the nation – and even those laws
were rarely enforced. Indiana law prohibited workers under age fifteen from
working in high-risk industries, and limited children under that age working
legally to no more than an eight-hour day.

But problems remained. A 1906 inspection found that over six hundred
boys between the ages of fourteen and sixteen were working in glass factories.
As late as 1910 over thirty thousand boys and girls between the ages of ten and
fifteen were in the workforce. The U.S. Department of labor reported in that
year that only two states had a higher proportion of child labor than Indiana.

Legislation spearheaded by the Indiana Child Labor Committee was
introduced in the 1909 legislative session, but strong opposition from business
prevented approval of anything other than a study commission. The Indianapolis
Star ran a series of stories after attempts to pass child labor laws failed, and the
articles had a strong impact on public opinion due to their inclusion of photos
taken by Lewis Hine. (Conspicuously missing from the stories were photos
taken by Hine of boys as young as six on street corners selling newspapers.)[119]

Supporters tried again in 1911, and Governor Marshall eventually signed
a new law that fell far short of that sought by reforms. The new law extended
the ban on employment of children under age fourteen except for agriculture
and domestic service – but the canning industry successfully lobbied for
exclusion for boys as young as twelve during the summer months. Children
under sixteen were prohibited from working after 6:00 p.m. or before 7:00
a.m. in any place "where their health may be injured or morals depraved". The
law still permitted, however, children under the age of sixteen to work as many
as forty-five hours in a week with the consent of their parents.[120]

ঙ ঙ ঙ ঙ ঙ

On the morning of September 21, 1910, Benjamin Corkwell was the
motorman for Union Traction Company Car #303, traveling north on the
interurban track between Fort Wayne and Bluffton. His train was filled with

passengers heading for a day at the county fair in Fort Wayne. Charles Van Dine was at the controls of southbound engine #233 of the Fort Wayne and Wabash Valley railroad. He was heading back towards Bluffton with an empty car to pick up more passengers for their day of fun.

Van Dine knew that, just about the same time each morning, he would nod to his counterpart Corkwell who would be waiting at a siding as the southbound train passed. But this morning something went terribly wrong. For reasons that still remain a mystery engine #233 never moved to the siding, and the two trains struck head on at nearly full speed. Built using stronger materials, Van Dine's engine remained intact but traveled through the midsection of Corkwell's train. Remarkably, both Corkwell and Van Dine would survive the wreck, but forty-one of Corkwell's forty-two passengers were dead. Corkwell's grief led him to be committed to a mental institution, where he subsequently died.

The crash was the worst in interurban train history. As a result, Governor Marshall supported the passage of new safety legislation for both railroads and interurbans. New regulations required the construction of highway crossing signs, inspection of locomotive boilers, switching signal lights, and windows in the compartments of the engineers to allow an unobstructed view of the track ahead.

◈ ◈ ◈ ◈ ◈

In the years before Marshall became governor, United States Senators were chosen by state legislators. This system meant that Senators were chosen by a caucus of leaders of the party in power in the statehouse. In 1903, when the Republican Party controlled both houses of the Indiana legislature, Charles W. Fairbanks was easily re-elected to the United States Senate. After the election of 1904, the landslide for Roosevelt for President and Hanly as Governor gave the Republicans a three-to-one margin in the Indiana General Assembly. The Republicans, then, were able to fill both U.S. Senate seats in 1905. Albert Beveridge was easily re-elected, and James Hemenway was elected to fill the position vacated by Vice President Fairbanks.

By 1909, though, control had swung to the Democrats, and for the first time in recent memory the outcome of the Democratic caucus would have real meaning in selecting Indiana's senator. John Worth Kern was viewed by many as the leading candidate, in part because of his strong principles and unblemished record and in part because it was felt that he should be rewarded for his efforts in the unsuccessful gubernatorial campaigns of 1900 and 1904 and the presidential election of 1908.

But Kern also had detractors among his party, and when the Democratic caucus met it took twenty ballots before former congressman Benjamin Shively got the nod. Kern and his supporters were outraged not only by the outcome, but also by the nature of the voting – secret balloting, in a closed caucus.

Marshall was among those upset by the methods used to elect Shively over Kern. Progressives from both parties had advocated for the direct election of senators. While Marshall did not publicly endorse such a reform, he was adamant in calling for the nomination process to be open and visible. He asked for a commitment by Democratic leaders to a plan which would have the delegates to the statewide convention in April, 1910 choose a Senate candidate. When the General Assembly gathered next to choose a Senator, the Democratic members would be bound by the decision of the convention.

During the debate of the method of selecting the Senate candidates, Marshall faced the difficult task of having to rebuff Tom Taggart's opposition to the plan. In a letter of April 10, 1910, Marshall wrote to Taggart:

> Owing to many pressing matters I have delayed writing you for several days. In announcing my opinion with reference to endorsing a candidate for us senator, I had not the slightest intention of doing any candidate an injury or of booming any person's candidacy. Your relations and mine have been uniformly agreeable and satisfactory to me, and I would be the last person in the world to criticize you for taking any position which you may choose to take with reference to this proposal. You have a right to favor it or to oppose it. Whatever you do will not change the friendly relations existing between us.
> If this were a question simply between you and me and I could do you a personal kindness by withdrawing my proposition, there would not be a moment's hesitation. But upon a full study of the question, it seems to me that it is neither your question nor my question; that nobody has given either you or me the right to settle it; that having been announced, it becomes the

right of the Democratic party to settle it as the delegates please.
If, therefore, you are opposed to this proposition, I beg to assure
you that I will have no personal political feeling at anything that
you may say or do looking toward the defeat of the proposition.
I still, however, feel that it is an honest and wise one for our
part to adopt, and we must continue to say so. If the delegates
decide otherwise I will gracefully submit, as I believe them to
be the final arbiters.[121]

The governor's plan was approved by a narrow margin, and at the next convention the delegates voted to support the senatorial candidacy of John Worth Kern. The selection of Kern also had the effect of healing the rift between Taggart and Marshall, as Taggart was pleased to see his good friend and political ally Kern win the nomination, and Marshall won a victory when the selection process took place in the way he had proposed.

᠄ᠻ ᠄ᠻ ᠄ᠻ ᠄ᠻ ᠄ᠻ

During Marshall's term as governor, laws were enacted creating the State Board of Accounts. This unit of state government was charged with creating a uniform public accounting system secured with provision for inspection of budgets, supervision of expenditures, and periodic public statements on finance. Up until the enactment of this law, local units of government were free to devise their own accounting systems, and there was little regulation of the propriety of expenditures. The State Board of Accounts continues to provide valuable oversight of local expenditures to this day.

Not long after the new department was created, two accountants relayed a story to Marshall of a township trustee who had taken twenty dollars for the local road fund. When the auditors inspected the books of the trustee, they found that he had dutifully noted the income of twenty dollars, with the entry labeled as "graft". They asked the trustee to explain.

He said he had to buy a road scraper, and there were three or
four agents seeking to sell him one. He liked the appearance of
one young man better than the others, and as the prices were
substantially the same, he bought the scraper of this particular

agent. When he had concluded the contract he walked down to
the train with him and as the young man got aboard he shook
hands and said goodbye. When this ceremony had taken place
he found in his hands a twenty-dollar bill. He said to the agent.
"Here! You have left twenty dollars of your money with me."
The agent replied: "No! That is yours!" The trustee asked:
"Why, how is that mine?" The agent said: "Why, you blamed
old fool, that's graft!"[122]

ख ख ख ख ख

Labor issues were an important part of Marshall's term as governor. For Thomas
Marshall, labor violence – and concurrent actions by state governments – was
an important part of his political education. Though he had chosen to affiliate
with the party most often identified with the labor movement, he was anxious
to avoid the mistakes made by government policies towards labor actions in
the past.

Governor Marshall was asked to use the state militia in labor disputes on a
number of occasions. Philosophically, Marshall believed in the rights of labor
to organize and strike.

> I have felt that if an executive would take firm hold of a strike
> as soon as it occurs; would get the facts on both sides of the case
> and would lay down the law and his intention fearlessly to
> administer it, that an adjustment of these matters could well be
> arranged without the intervention of the militia.[123]

On a practical level, support by labor was important to electoral victory by
the Democrats, and Marshall was often reluctant to use force during strikes.
Labor leaders, strong supporters of the Democratic Party, were generally
opposed to government interference during strikes and work stoppages.
Management often benefited from a show of force by local police or state
national guard forces. During a street railway strike in Vincennes in May,
1910, Marshall wrote to a railroad official that "it is not my business to help
you break the union a bit more than it is my business to help the union break
you." During the same strike, he wrote to the Mayor of Vincennes:

I could not interfere in the local self-government of the City of Vincennes unless the condition of affairs became such as to show to my satisfaction that life and property were unsafe and that the civil authorities either could not or would not preserve life and property, in which event, as I understand my duty under the constitution, it would be necessary for me to send the troops, suspend the civil authorities and put the city under military government.[124]

Despite Marshall's hesitancy to use the force of state government, in one instance he could not avoid it. During a strike at Indiana's stone quarries strikebreakers from Chicago, known more for their fighting skills than their quarry craftsmanship, incited violence in many communities.

In the stone quarries of Indiana there developed a strike. The operators lived in Chicago. They rushed down with their attorneys to see me, demanding that I order out the militia. Trembling and quivering, they said the strikers were keeping out their workmen, and that unless I ordered the militia their workmen would be murdered by the strikers. Now, I happened to have some little general knowledge, and I knew that quarrymen were skilled laborers; that they had to pass through an apprenticeship, and that in this part of Indiana the profession – for I dignify it with that title – had passed down from father to son. I believed there were no quarrymen west of the New England States who could take the place of these striking men. So I asked the operators where they got their new workmen. They told me in Chicago. From the look on their faces I was satisfied there was something wrong, and I said: "Now be frank with me! You might as well be, for I will get the truth. Aren't these men you have taken down to the quarries strike-breakers whom you have hired from a detective agency in Chicago, not one of whom was ever in a stone quarry before, and not one of whom can do the least bit of work in those quarries?" Reluctantly they admitted this to be the truth.[125]

As a Democrat, Marshall knew the voting strength of organized labor was important to his party. While many labor leaders remained critical of Marshall for the McNamara extradition, Marshall himself came to respect labor union members.

The labor union man is a human being; he is neither slave nor autocrat; he is moved with like passions as the rest of us. Like us, at many times he is prejudiced, but in the long run he has as much respect, if not more, for the man who treats him just as a man than he has for the official who shivers in his presence and consents to doing of all sorts of foolish things in order to cater to what is known as the "union vote". There is no "union vote." Some day these shivering politicians will find out that the laboring man is not a man with a dirty shirt, who takes pleasure in fawning and in cowardice, but that he is a self-respecting American citizen, who ultimately judges the conduct of public officials by their desire to uphold the law and do the right thing; who votes as he pleases; who is willing to transfer to somebody else the making of a contract which as to do with his wages and working conditions, but who is not willing, and never will be, to transfer into the hands of a lot of self-constituted agents the discharge of that high duty and the preservation of that great privilege which is his – voting as an American citizen. [126]

❦ ❦ ❦ ❦ ❦

Kentucky's gubernatorial election of 1899 pitted Republican Attorney General William Taylor against the Democratic candidate, State Senator William Goebel. After a bitter election battle, the returns showed Taylor as the victor by a small margin.

Kentucky law required the State Legislature to approve the election tallies. Supporters of Goebel sought to overturn the results, and started proceedings before a packed Democratic legislative committee to unseat Taylor. Taylor's supporters, fearing that Goebel's challenge would be successful, rallied a force of more than 1,500 armed mountaineers who arrived in Frankfort, the capital, on January 19, 1900 and took possession of the town.

The Legislature ruled in favor of Goebel. When Inauguration day arrived on January 30, 1900, due to numerous threats on his life, Goebel was accompanied by a handful of bodyguards as he made his way to the ceremony.

A little after 11:00 that morning, as Goebel entered the gate leading up to the Capitol, a sniper with a rifle in office of the Secretary of State fired five shots, one of which struck Goebel. The wounds were not immediately fatal, and for several days Goebel signed numerous state documents as Governor of Kentucky. But Goebel succumbed to his wounds several days after the attack.

After Goebel's death two sets of state officials claimed to rule in Kentucky. One group was headed by Taylor; the other was headed by J. C. W. Beckham, running mate of Goebel. Beckham was eventually declared governor, and an investigation of the murder led to the indictments of Taylor, Secretary of State Caleb Powers, and fourteen other men charging them with murder. During the trial, several witnesses testified that Powers and Taylor were behind the plot to kill Goebel. One witness said Taylor offered him $2,500 if he would fire the shots.

After the indictment of Taylor was issued, two detectives were sent to take him into custody. Apparently tipped off about the coming arrest, Taylor snuck out a rear door and drove in his carriage to Indiana. In a trial later that year, Powers was convicted and sentenced to death.

Despite the fact that the assassination had occurred eight years earlier, the flight of indicted murderer and gubernatorial candidate William Taylor from Kentucky to Indiana was one of the first issues addressed by Marshall. Taylor's flight was still a passionate issue in both Kentucky and Indiana. There were even stories about attempts to kidnap Taylor and return him to Kentucky to face trial.

Kentucky had repeatedly asked that Taylor be returned from Indiana. The United States Supreme Court had ruled that a state had the right to decide whether or not to return a fugitive from justice to be tried. Marshall, though, exemplifying his life-long devotion to the United States Constitution, said

I felt that under the terms of the Federal Constitution, which reads as follows: 'A person charged in any state with treason, felony or other crime, who shall flee from justice and be found

*in another state shall, on demand of the executive authority of
the state from which he fled, be delivered up to be removed to
the state having jurisdiction of the crime,' I ... believed that
it was the constitutional duty of an executive ... to issue his
warrant for the arrest of the alleged criminal regardless of any
of the facts in the case.*

*I had always felt, as I now feel, that if I take it into my mind
to become a resident among the Yaqui Indians of Mexico and
get into trouble I ought to be man enough to abide by Yaqui
justice.*[127]

The issue of returning Taylor to Kentucky for trial was of widespread
interest in southern Indiana, and Marshall made it clear that he would send
Taylor back. As it happened, Augustus E. Wilson, a Republican, was elected
Governor of Kentucky in 1907. Before Marshall could act, Wilson had
pardoned Taylor, and the issue became moot. Despite his pardon, Taylor still
feared for his life if he returned to Kentucky, and he remained in Indianapolis
until his death in 1927.

ക‍ ക‍ ക‍ ക‍ ക‍

Harrison Gray Otis, owner and publisher of the Los Angeles Times, was a
political conservative and strongly anti-union. That viewpoint was reflected
both in the editorials of the newspaper and in his company's relationship with
its employees. Otis organized the business community of Los Angeles against
any type of union activity. During the height of business and labor tensions,
Otis would drive around the City in a large car with mounted cannon.

In the late summer of 1910, several unions, including the metal trade's
workers, called a strike against the Los Angeles Times. Union leaders spread the
strike to businesses across the city, and management brought in strikebreakers
from the Midwest. Laws against picketing led to arrests, but juries refused
to convict union leaders who had gained the sympathy of much of the
community.

On the evening of October 1, 1910, a little after one o'clock in the
morning, a series of explosions tore through the printing plant of the Los
Angeles Times. The first explosion was heard ten miles away. The building

collapsed, and the printer's ink exploded in a ball of flame. Twenty employees were killed.

Otis hired a private detective agency to find the bombers, and went on a national speaking tour garnering support from business groups. Union leaders said that the explosion was caused by a gas leak because Otis had taken inadequate safety precautions. Hoosier Eugene Debs argued that Otis and his executives may have planted the bomb themselves to gain public sympathy against the strikers.

Early one Saturday morning, two law enforcement officials sent by Governor Hiram Johnson of California entered Marshall's office. A few minutes later, the Governor asked the Secretary of State to keep his office open after the ordinary Saturday closing hour, which was noon. Papers were filed with the Secretary of State, and later that day police arrested John McNamara, secretary of the Structural Iron Workers Union, for the bombing of the Los Angeles Times building.

Union supporters were outraged at Marshall for extraditing McNamara without the benefit of an attorney or a hearing. But Marshall had addressed the question of extradition long before the McNamara incident:

> *Although the Supreme Court of the United States had decided that it is discretionary with the state whether a fugitive from justice shall be surrendered or not, it had further decided that persons who were charged with being fugitives from justice have no constitutional right to demand a hearing, and a governor of a state who is requested to issue a warrant of extradition must act upon such evidence as is satisfactory to him.*[128]

Despite Marshall's reasoned approach, labor leaders were unmollified. They felt McNamara was unjustly charged and unfairly extradited. The rhetoric intensified and grew vicious.

> *The labor unions of Indiana proceeded to meet and resolve. They resolved in such virulent and vicious language that no partisan press could be found willing to print resolutions.*[129]

Fearing that Marshall would be attacked by union sympathizers, Marshall was followed by Secret Service agents for six months after McNamara was extradited. McNamara's trial drew national attention, and Clarence Darrow was hired as his defense attorney. But Darrow quickly concluded that McNamara and his brother James were responsible for the bombing. They pled guilty, and John received a sentence of fifteen years; his brother James was sent to jail for life.

As the trial of McNamara came to a close, late one afternoon a reporter came to the Governor's office. The reporter berated Marshall, telling him he had sold out to "the predatory interests in American life" for agreeing to extradite McNamara and, in his view, supporting the viewpoint of business against labor.

> *Instead of ordering him out of my office, as in justice to my position I should have done, I simply smiled at him and told him to wait — that the returns were not all in. Just then the custodian of the state house opened the door and asked me if I would like to see the Indianapolis News — McNamara had pleaded guilty. I said, "No, I do not care to see it, but the young man sitting beside me perhaps would like to look at it."* [130]

❧ ❧ ❧ ❧ ❧

Near the midpoint of his term, Governor Marshall was asked to describe the greatest need of his state. Marshall's response was "contentment"

> *A man who expresses an opinion today is much like the discoverer of a patent medicine — he is quite sure that it will cure all ailments. Indiana needs many things. I hope the time will never come when all its needs have been supplied. Just now, from my viewpoint, its greatest need is contentment. By that I mean that it should possess a body of citizens who are content to do a day's work for a day's wage; who are willing to pay a day's wage for a day's work; who are unwilling to shirk work and gain wages by cunning; who are unwilling by enforced employment to increase profits; who believe more in the common*

good than in the larger good; who would rather be buried in a pine box wet with genuine tears than to have a rosewood casket guarded by detectives; who really feel that Indiana is the land of opportunity, individuality and manhood, and not the land of knavery, trickery and cunning; who believe he is not wise who is not just, and that justice is as much the other fellow's right as his own. Maybe a majority of Indiana's citizens are such. I hope so.[131]

❧ ❧ ❧ ❧ ❧

Soon after taking office, Marshall followed up on a request from a young mother asking that her husband Jake be pardoned from the state penitentiary.

Just before Christmas I issued a thirty-day parole for this man to go home and see his family, on the condition that he not enter a saloon or drink a drop of intoxicating liquor. I may, by way of parenthesis, say that this condition was included in every parole I ever put my hand to. I was not for the prohibition amendment but I can cheerfully certify that the saloon ruined more men than all other evil influences in society. I told the warden to have Jake stop to see me on his way home. He did, and I asked him if he had any money to get a little Christmas present for his wife and children. He said the warden had given him some. I cautioned him about the saloon and the trouble he was in; said to him I had made arrangements to get reports as to his conduct; that if he behaved himself for thirty days I would extend his parole to sixty days; that I would let him stay out as long as he behaved himself. Shortly after Christmas I found a good soul in his county who had a farm some twenty miles away from town, where all temptations to drink were removed. I discovered that his wife had fallen heir to a few hundred dollars which would enable them to buy horses and agricultural machinery, and this good man promised, if I would extend the parole, he would rent the farm to Jake and would keep a watchful eye over him to see that he grew strong enough to avoid the further use of intoxicating liquor. I extended the parole from time to time, and shortly before the expiration of my office I found a little boy had come to them whom they had named Thomas Marshall, and I pardoned Jake. He is today a good, clean, upright moral citizen of this state.[132]

❧ ❧ ❧ ❧ ❧

During his administration, Marshall's connection with Tom Taggart proved to be both an asset and a liability. With the rise of the Progressive movement, national newspapers railed against such bosses as Roger Sullivan of Illinois, Charles Murphy and the Tammany Hall gang of New York, and Thomas Taggart of Indiana.

In his memoirs, Marshall remained respectful to his relationship with Tom Taggart and the work Taggart had accomplished on behalf of the Democratic Party.

> *So far as I have any knowledge there has never been the slightest personal difference between us. In matters political we have been as far apart as the poles. In making this statement it is not to be implied that I deemed myself right and him wrong. It is only the difference in viewpoint. He has believed in the power, efficiency and necessity of organization. I was never able to divorce myself from the idea that the appeal for principles should be made to the individual. I was foolish enough to think that an honest presentation of a cause to the people is enough. Perhaps he was right; perhaps I am wrong. He deserves this tribute: That he never wavered in the defense of the Democratic Party regardless of whether his personal choice was the candidate or not. Few men have been more misinterpreted than he.*[133]

Marshall tried to steer clear of Taggart's business dealings, but this was not always possible. In 1908, gambling was illegal in the State of Indiana, but Tom Taggart was the owner of the hotel in French Lick, Indiana, which was adjacent to the nation's most popular casino. The crusading Governor Frank Hanly had made a strong effort to shut down Taggart's gambling operations.

Hanly was supported in his efforts by William Randolph Hearst. Hearst and Taggart had become bitter enemies when the latter had failed to support the publisher's presidential bid in 1904. Taggart's position as the chairman of the Democratic National Committee meant that the accusations against Taggart in the Hearst newspapers would receive wide coverage. A reporter sent to French Lick described the scene:

> *I saw all kinds of gambling – faro, roulette, poker, Klondike, 'the ponies', books on the races, slot machines, etc. I saw men and women gambling … Gambling at the French Lick Springs is undisturbed by law. Any guest of the French Lick Hotel or of the West Baden or other hotels may gamble there if they have the card of admission, which is a mere formality for the hotel guest to obtain.*[134]

Government officials from both parties had tacitly agreed to ignore the violations that were taking place at French Lick. But Frank Hanly was not the type of man to look the other way when gambling and drinking were involved. He was given an opportunity to move against Taggart's casinos when he discovered the state auditor had lost a large amount of the state's money at the gaming tables. In July, 1906, the state raided the casinos and confiscated a large supply of gambling equipment. Taggart attempted to build his defense by pointing out that he had merely rented the property to the French Lick Springs Company, which was accused of operating the casino. Pointing to the anti-gambling clause in the lease, he sued the lessee for breach of contract.

Taggart was defended in the prosecution by John Worth Kern. Taggart knew of Kern's skills when the latter had served as municipal attorney during the time when Taggart was mayor of Indianapolis. The case also provided additional copy for the Hearst newspapers. "The Republican Party has exchanged its principles for Mr. Morgan's bank checks," read one Hearst editorial, "and the Democratic Party has cashed its principles for Tom Taggart's blue chips."[135]

Though he was causing a scandal for the state party, Hanly vigorously prosecuted and removed from office the secretary of state, the attorney general and the state auditor (who was also convicted of embezzling state funds).

Despite the fact that Hanly had vigorously prosecuted the gambling operations at French Lick, at the time Marshall took office the casino was still open. Marshall faced the tricky task of potentially prosecuting the man who had helped elect him as Governor. He asked the local prosecuting attorney from Orange County to investigate, and when it was reported back that the casino was no longer operating, Marshall was skeptical.

> *I note that you say that the gambling places are not open at the Springs. I am glad to know that this is so. I, however, desire you to investigate and if gambling has been going on to prosecute the same.*[136]

Eventually, the local prosecutor brought charges against those involved with the French Lick casinos. The Attorney General's office helped to prepare the case, but Marshall knew that it would be difficult to get a conviction using a local jury. He told a nearby newspaper:

> *I understand there are sixty-eight indictments outstanding and am informed by (the local prosecutor) that they will all be tried in due time. I will instruct the Attorney General to assist (the local prosecutor). But if Orange County juries will not convict, if they choose to judge the law and the evidence in such a way as to enable the game keepers to continue, what are we to do? The law makes me chief executive of the state, but it does not constitute me a jury to judge the law and the evidence.*[137]

When the trial eventually began in March of 1910, the prosecutor and Attorney General took several days to present the evidence. But when it came time for the jury to deliberate, it took only a few minutes to return a verdict for the defendant.[138]

Marshall also faced another gambling-related challenge. Roger Sullivan – the political boss from Illinois -- had taken action to shut down horse racing operations in and around Chicago, not because they were illegal (which they were), but because the were competition for Sullivan's own horse racing businesses. The competing horse races left Chicago but moved across the border into Porter County, Indiana.

And yet I did have the troops out on one occasion, this not arising over any controversy between labor and capital, however. I assume that there is hardly a more crooked game on earth than that of the small bookmakers in the large cities, taking bets on running races from bootblacks, elevator boys, clerks, stenographers – anybody who has the gambling instinct and the hope of making something for nothing. The races are never run for sport, but always to make money. Driven out of Illinois, they started one of these race tracks up in Porter County, and the bookmakers of Chicago were reaping a rich harvest. The officials of Porter County were totally indifferent.[139]

Marshall made several attempts to stop the Porter County horse races, without success. While traveling to the Wyoming, newspapers in the northwest corner of the state published a series of articles about the horse racing operations. Reporters continually hounded the governor about his inability to shut down the operation. He sent a telegram to his secretary, Mark Thistlethwaite, saying, "Stop Porter County gambling at once or I will come back and do it." Thistlethwaite, in consultation with the Adjutant General, ordered the Indiana National Guard to stand shoulder-to-shoulder at the finish line, with fixed bayonets. As the horses rounded the final turn, the crowd waited anxiously to see who would back down first – the race horses, or the national guardsmen. A few hundred feet before the finish, the jockeys orders their horses to stop, and racetrack was shut down.

⚘ ⚘ ⚘ ⚘ ⚘

As Governor, Marshall had to authority to commute death sentences. Like all in this position of authority, he struggled with his own personal viewpoint of capital punishment versus the realities of the penal system.

The question of inflicting the death penalty is a serious one. Personally, I am opposed to capital punishment. I do not believe it rests in human hands to say when a life shall cease; and if there were some way devised to prevent – What I, perhaps, was guilty of – the extension of executive clemency to men who are

*sent up for life, if there were some way to keep them in for life,
then I believe the public would be satisfied with the abolition
of capital punishment.*[140]

As it happened, Marshall never faced the question of commuting a death
sentence during his four years in office. While one man in Lake County was
sentenced to be hung for murder, the case was reversed on appeal.

Marshall was, however, critical of subsequent governors, and their
willingness to overturn a life sentence when he felt the punishment was
warranted. In his memoirs, he was critical of a gubernatorial pardon in a case
with which Marshall was very familiar:

*In 1907 I was appointed to prosecute a man for one of the foulest
cases of wife murder that I ever knew. I accepted it with the
understanding that I did not believe in capital punishment. I
tried the cause. When the jury went out for the first ballot it was
eleven for hanging and one for life imprisonment. The one for
life imprisonment happened to be a staid old Hollander, who
called to the attention of the other eleven the fact that I was
opposed to capital punishment. The second ballot was twelve
for life imprisonment, and in six minutes after the jury left the
box the verdict had been returned. It is not seventeen years since
I tried that case and yet this man is walking the streets today a
free man by the action of some subsequent governor of Indiana,
who pardoned or paroled over my protest.*[141]

∽ ∽ ∽ ∽ ∽

The elections of 1910 gave Governor Marshall greater ability to enact his own
agenda. The legislature that served 1909-1910 was split between Republican
control of the house and Democratic majorities in the Senate. The Democrats
gained enough seats in the election of 1910 to capture control of both
chambers.

In opening the sixty-seventh session of the Indiana General Assembly on
January 5, 1911, Governor Marshall signaled his desire to make changes to
the State's Constitution. He noted that there were "certain provisions of our

constitution which do not meet present conditions", and that, while he did not want to see the document "radically altered", he made it clear that he would soon propose changes.[142]

Thomas Marshall was not known for making rash decisions or taking bold chances. He lived with his parents until in his forties; he agreed to run for Governor only after being recruited by friends and colleagues. But few could have expected the magnitude of his proposal to the legislative session of 1911.

> *After consultation with those in whom I placed confidence, I had introduced into the General Assembly an act submitting to the voters of the State a new constitution.*[143]

Legislators, newspapermen and most of the electorate were stunned by the sweeping magnitude of Marshall's proposal. It was clear from Marshall's opening speech to the legislature that changes would be proposed, but almost no one expected an entirely new constitution. The new constitution, it turns out, was written by a local reformer, "in whom" Marshall had "placed confidence". That reformer was Jacob Piatt Dunn.

Jacob Piatt Dunn was born April 12, 1855, in the southern Indiana town of Lawrenceburg. His family moved to Indianapolis while Jacob was a young boy, and, after earning a degree from Earlham College, studied law at the University of Michigan. He returned to Indianapolis to enter a law practice, but, like many young men of those days – including Theodore Roosevelt -- was smitten by the idea of earning his fortune in the West. When a silver mining venture in Colorado failed to provide him with financial success, he returned to Indianapolis to begin a career as a writer and journalist.

Dunn would write numerous books of historic interest, and would be elected state librarian by the legislature in 1889 and 1891 and serve two terms as Indianapolis city controller. He developed a reputation as one of the early proponents of municipal reform, focusing his attention reforming Indiana's electoral process by adopting the Australian ballot system. These reforms were eventually adopted in 1889. In addition, Dunn played a major role in adopting a new city charter for Indianapolis. Dissatisfied with the changes that he thought the ballot reforms of 1889 would bring, Dunn saw the Indiana Constitution as an impediment to true reform.

The new constitution that Governor Marshall would propose was designed to address a number of issues. The hallmark of the new constitution were two devices to return more power directly to the voters. Language regarding initiative and referendum would allow citizens to propose their own issues and take them directly to a vote of the people. Also included was the ability to recall any elected official other than a judge.

Several items were included to strengthen the power of the governor. The governor would have the power of a line-item veto, meaning that only a portion of approved legislation could be vetoed, rather than the entire bill. This power was designed to override the common legislative practice of including special interest language in a popular or important bill. In addition, the new constitution would require an affirmative vote from three-fifths of the legislature, rather than a simple majority, to override a gubernatorial veto.

The powers of state officials were changed in other ways. The Indiana House of Representatives would be expanded from one hundred to one hundred and thirty members, and the number of Supreme Court justices would rise from five to as many as eleven.

Dunn included suffrage provisions common to Progressive Era reforms. Voting would be limited to male citizens twenty-one years of age or older who met certain residency requirements. Voters would be required to pay a poll tax, which Dunn felt would sharply limit the practice of vote buying. In addition, voters would be required to prove that they could "read in English or some other known tongue any section of the Constitution of the State."[144]

Marshall felt particularly strong about the issue of voting rights for new immigrants. His views were summarized in a letter he wrote to Elbert Gary, chairman of U.S. Steel Corporation. His steel mill adjacent to Lake Michigan in Indiana was such a powerful force that the city of Gary, Indiana was named in his honor. Marshall wrote to Gary in December, 1909:

> *I am convinced ... by the testimony which was taken after the last election, that more than two thousand of the employees of your corporation voted at the election when they had only landed in America in February and March of that year ... Our State Constitution is weak in that it permits the man who as been in America a year upon declaring his intention to become a citizen, at the same time to become a voter.*

> *A large number of us would feel much more kindly toward your corporation if you would see to it that those in charge of the actual work do not become so zealous in politics as to vote in droves, ignorant foreigners who, after they have voted, and are taken to a restaurant to get something to eat, can only say in response to the inquiry of the waiters — what will you have to eat — "Taft."*[145]

Republicans were uniformly opposed to the new constitution. Little of the debate, though, focused on the reform proposals within the document. Opponents focused on Marshall's method of adopting the new constitution. Rather than call a constitutional convention, which was the commonly accepted method of constitutional adoption, Dunn had advised Marshall that the new constitution could be put into effect with a majority vote of the legislature and signature by the governor, followed by approval by the voters at the next general election.

Marshall was opposed to convening a constitutional convention He felt it would provide an opportunity for special interests across the state ranging from prohibitionists to women's suffragists to gain favor through a provision in the new document. Such a convention, he felt, "would be fraught with great danger and would shake the state into a great passion."[146]

Knowing that they lacked the votes to stop the Governor's plans, one Republican senator took a different approach. He introduced a resolution that appointed the Governor as a committee of one with the power of adopting a new constitution. In addition, Marshall would be given the power to

> *revise the Lord's prayer, amend the Declaration of Independence, repeal the Mosaic Law, bring the Thirty-Nine Articles of Faith down to date, abridge the Sermon on the Mount, and do all other things as will appear in his infinite wisdom and supreme interest in the welfare of the people, to be fitting and proper.*[147]

The Marshall Constitution, included in Senate Bill 407, was approved by the Indiana Senate on February 27, 1911, and by the House three days later. Governor Thomas Riley Marshall signed the new constitution into law on March 4, 1911.

Judicial review of the new legislation was certain, and it came quickly. A Democratic judge from Marion County granted an injunction that prohibited the question from appearing on the ballot for the election of 1912. That ruling was appealed to the Indiana Supreme Court.

Indiana adopted its first Constitution in 1816. This document contained a provision that required voters to decide, every twelve years, whether to create a constitutional convention to make changes. The electorate rejected changes when the question was on the ballot in 1828 and 1840.[148]

But in the late 1840s, the situation changed dramatically. Owing to the Mammoth Internal Improvements Bill of 1836, Indiana had borrowed significant amounts to link the state with a system of canals and toll roads with the intent of fostering commerce. Revenue from the tolls would repay the bonds. Owing to poor planning and fraud, when the money was spent little had been accomplished. Despite numerous efforts to repay the bonds, the State was forced to declare bankruptcy.

A constitutional convention met in the years 1850-51, and the Constitution of 1851 contained numerous provisions designed to prevent another financial debacle. Borrowing by the State was forbidden unless in an emergency, and local units of government could not commit to indebtedness in excess of two percent of their assessed valuation.

The Constitution of 1851 also described procedures for amendments. After an amendment had been approved by two consecutive legislative sessions, it was put to the electorate for a vote. If the amendment received a majority of all votes cast, it was approved.

In the late 1890s, a group of attorneys proposed a change to the portion of the Indiana Constitution that described the qualification of applicants for the bar. The Constitution of 1851 required that the only qualification for admission to the bar was good moral character – a provision that Marshall used to become an attorney without attending law school. Stricter qualifications were proposed, and the language was approved by two consecutive sessions of the Indiana legislature (in 1897 and 1899). The question went before the voters in November of 1900, and the amendment received 240,031 votes in favor and 144,072 votes against.[149] A prospective attorney opposed to the new requirements challenged the amendment on the grounds that, while the question received more votes in favor than votes opposed, it did not receive a majority of all of the votes cast in the election. The Indiana Supreme Court ruled that the amendment did not receive sufficient votes for passage.[150]

More importantly for constitutional reformers, however, the Court also blocked further attempts at changing the constitution. The attorney qualification question was neither approved nor defeated; therefore, the question was still before the voters. Nearly 390,000 ballots were cast on the constitutional question put before the electorate. Slightly more than 240,000 voters supported the measure, but records showed that more than a half a million people actually went to the polls that election day. Thus, the question did not receive a majority from all voters. Since the Constitution of 1851 blocked any further amendments while a decision was still pending before the voters, no additional amendments could be considered until the attorney qualification question was resolved.

Marshall's ability to make any constitutional amendments was blocked, therefore, by the unresolved attorney requirement issue.

> When I came into office there was a pretty generally well-established idea in the mind of the legal fraternity that the law of Indiana was, that an amendment to its constitution had to receive a majority of all the votes cast at the election at which it was submitted to the people for ratification or rejection, and that if it failed to be either accepted or rejected it was the duty of the General Assembly to dispose of it in the same way by re-submission or withdrawal of submission from the voters of the state; and that, in accordance with the terms of the constitution, no new amendment could be submitted until a pending one was disposed of.[151]

With three of the high court's five judges Republicans most expected the Marshall Constitution to be voided by the Supreme Court. On July 5, 1912, by a three-to-two vote, the Indiana Supreme Court upheld the injunction. Surprising, though, the vote was bipartisan, as two of the Republicans were joined by a Democrat in the majority. That Democrat, the Chief Justice, wrote for the majority that the General Assembly did not have the power to replace or amend the constitution, other than by the method described in that document.

The minority opinion held that the Indiana Supreme Court had overstepped its authority when it voided the measure before it had been voted on by the electorate. Suppose the General Assembly had enacted a bill, and asked a messenger to take the law to the governor for his signature. "Would anyone imagine," the justice wrote, "the progress of the messenger could be arrested by an injunction?"

Long after the question had been decided, Marshall continued to believe the Indiana high court had erred in their opinion.

> *I think no fair-minded man, now unmoved by the excitement of these times, will dare dispute the logic and the law of the minority opinion. It was never intended by me that in the event of its ratification and adoption at the general election any person, injured in person or property or civic rights thereby, might not raise the question as to whether it had been lawfully or constitutionally enacted, and that when so raised the Supreme Court of the state of Indiana could, if the fact and the law warranted it, declare it unconstitutional and void. But my contention was, is now, and ever shall be, that there was never a more flagrant interference on the part of the judicial with the rights, privileges and duties of the legislative and executive branches of government than is contained in the majority opinion of the Supreme Court of the State of Indiana.*[152]

Marshall was urged to ignore the ruling of the court; he declined.

> *I did not feel that I could afford to show any disrespect to the majority of the Supreme Court of the State of Indiana, or to lessen the respect in which I was teaching the people to hold the court's opinions, by myself openly flaunting one of its opinions. And so I obeyed the judgment of the court. I had no respect for it, and I now have a supreme contempt for it.*[153]

The decision of the Indiana Supreme Court was appealed to the United States Supreme Court. Due to a technical error, the United States court refused to hear the case.

> *I made bold, at a dinner party in Washington, to ask the justice who denied the writ why he did so; why he took advantage of the slight technicality, and his answer was: "If we had gone into the case we should have been compelled to decide that you were right and that the Supreme Court of Indiana was wrong, and that was a thing we did not care to do unless we had to, it being the invariable policy of the Supreme Court not to interfere, if it can avoid doing so, in any political questions arising in any of the states of the Union."*[154]

The battle over the Marshall Constitution would eventually be lost by the Governor. But it was a bold and innovative effort to change the structure of government to reflect the needs of the new century. In the hundred years since Governor Marshall attempted to introduce innovations such as initiative and referendum and supermajorities for veto overrides many states have adopted the new language. Indiana, to this day, has not.

But the Marshall Constitution would also have the effect of bringing Marshall to national prominence. He was known as a popular, well-liked Democrat who could attract votes from Republicans. His fight for the Marshall Constitution showed that he had substance, as well. Informed political observers – including Thomas Marshall – knew that this could be the right combination to help lead his party to victory in the next presidential election.

CHAPTER FIVE:

The Vice Presidential Candidate

(1912)

In order to garner more support in Midwestern states, the Democrats scheduled their annual National Jefferson Day Banquet for Indianapolis in 1910. Some speculated that Marshall supporters planned the dinner in Marshall's hometown in order to move him into the national spotlight and remove some of the focus on Ohio Governor Judson Harmon who was also a leading contender for the Democratic presidential nomination.

Knowing that his views would have a national audience, Marshall took the opportunity just before the dinner to talk about the state of his party. Speaking to a reporter from the *Indianapolis Star*, he described his strategy for a presidential victory:

> *The Democratic party has failed to elect a President because it has spread itself over and exhausted itself with unnecessary and unpopular issues. We have piled plank upon plank and principle upon principle, giving some support here but losing more there and being more soft than when we started ... the one great question before the people is the tariff. I should like to see the Democratic Party go to the country with two issues – protection and economy and not a single line about anything else.*[155]

The National Jefferson Day Banquet was held on April 13, 1910, and was attended by over six hundred Democratic leaders. Senator John Worth Kern, the Vice presidential candidate in 1908, gave a rousing introduction to his governor, which was followed by shouts for Marshall. "I am not a candidate for anything under the sun," said Marshall somewhat coyly, "I am simply the Governor of Indiana, desirous of serving the people of Indiana."

As he had in his gubernatorial campaign, Marshall's style was that the office should seek the man. He was opposed to open personal political ambition. But Marshall's speech that night made it clear that he was speaking to a national, not a statewide, audience. He criticized Theodore Roosevelt and attacked President Taft on an issue over which the Republicans were particularly vulnerable -- the Payne-Aldrich tariff bill.

In most of the years of Thomas Marshall's adult life, the federal government played only a small role in the lives of most Americans. With the exception of times of war – such as the Civil War or Spanish-American War – national government had little influence on the daily operations of commerce, agriculture, or family life.

Common governmental responsibilities were the responsibility of state and local governments. Police and fire protection, education, the criminal justice system, care for the poor and disabled, and the levying of taxes were administered by the state governments or by local counties, townships, cities and towns. The federal government provided for national defense, administered a federal court system, and governed the import and export of goods as well as collecting tariffs on certain imported items.

With a few exceptions, until the time of Woodrow Wilson's presidency federal government operations were financed by a system of tariffs on imported goods. Tariffs were not only a source of revenue, but also served the function of aiding industries that faced competition from foreign firms.

The sugar industry provides an example of the value of tariffs. In the period after the Civil War, southern states such as Louisiana saw sugar crops as a means of diversifying their economy against dependence on cotton. But other countries, such as Cuba, could produce sugar at a cheaper cost – a cost that might even be subsidized by the use of slave labor, which was used to harvest the Cuban sugar crop until 1880.

To provide an incentive for the growth of the sugar industry in southern states, the federal government imposed a tariff on the importation of sugar. Sugar produced overseas may cost less when it reached American ports, but the tariff increased the effective price of a pound of sugar. American sugar producers could sell their sugar for the price of the imported sugar plus the amount of the tariff.

This meant that Washington lawmakers had two powerful incentives to impose tariffs and keep them high. Not only did they provide the revenue to run the government, but they protected industries in their home states, as well. The system also encouraged the growth of an army of lobbyists in the Nation's Capital funded by industries committed to keeping tariff protection on the goods they produced.

But by the turn of the century many had become disenchanted with the tariff system. Tariffs were a form of hidden tax, and in the early 1900s that tax increased the price of household goods by rates of thirty to forty percent or more. Industries that sought tariff protection were often extremely profitable and could no longer argue that they needed protection from foreign competitors.

Theodore Roosevelt angered corporate supporters within his own party by advocating increased regulations of corporations and limiting the powers of monopolies. But he stopped short of making tariff reform part of his administrative agenda. Business titans such as Morgan and Rockefeller were already angered by the President's actions to break up the trusts, and Roosevelt couldn't risk further alienation among his party by making tariffs a political issue.

It was William Howard Taft who, almost unwittingly, began the process that would lead to the tariff and tax reforms that would be completed in the Wilson administration. As the growing middle class became more discontented with the hidden tax imposed by tariffs and less willing to "protect" powerful industrial trusts, the Republic Party platform responded to economic anxieties exacerbated by the Panic of 1907 and called for the immediate "revision of the tariff" by the next president. Most voters interpreted "revision" to mean "reducing", but as time would soon prove not everyone viewed that platform plank the same way.

William Jennings Bryan had gone even further. Knowing that the income tax enacted in the late 1890s had been ruled unconstitutional by the Supreme Court, Bryan called for a constitutional amendment that would enable Congress to enact an income tax. Opponents of the income tax felt they had little to fear from legislation on such an amendment, because enactment would require the approval of three-fourths of the states. Preventing the amendment from adoption would require opposition of only thirteen of the forty-eight states, and while states in the Midwest and west were known to generally support the constitutional amendment, a solid coalition of states on the East Coast and New England could prevent approval.

But the election of 1908 showed that the Republican Party's dominance of national elections was beginning to erode. Taft won less than fifty-two percent of the popular vote, and three states that had voted for Roosevelt in 1904 had switched to Bryan in 1908. In addition, the 1908 elections put Democrats in control of the governor's chair and the state house in several states. Some newly elected Democrats who rose to prominence after the election of 1908 wasted no time in talking about what they viewed as the most important issue facing the electorate.

"The one great question before the people," said Governor Marshall, "is the tariff." Marshall's public pronouncements about the tariff might have seemed out of place, since state governors had absolutely no authority over tariff rates and schedules. But Marshall knew he could help his party – and his own political ambitions – by speaking out on the topic on which the Republicans were most vulnerable.

> *Ask the voter if it is right in morals, laws or justice to put a dollar in one man's pocket that has been taken from the pocket of another man. So long as there are schedules there will be bargains back and forth in Congress – Smith calling for a tariff on one thing and Jones on something else, and each yielding to the other and getting exactly what he wants.*

Marshall recognized that the tariff was not only designed for protection; in 1911, it was also the source of most of the revenue for the federal government. Elimination of the tariff, in the absence of an income tax to make up the lost revenue, would be fiscal suicide for Washington. Instead, Marshall wanted to make the tariff more uniform across all imported goods.

> *I would first ascertain the yearly cost of an honest and economical administration of the national government. Then I would get the approximate value of the goods that are annually imported by the United States. Dividing the one by the other and*

*ascertaining what rate of percentage levied on imports would
equal the cost of government, I would make the quotient one
fixed rate of tariff duty on each class of goods that came from
abroad.*

This method, Marshall proposed, would be fairer than the current system
of different rates for different goods. He used the example of a thousand dollars
worth of silks, which would under his system be taxed at the same percentage
rates as a thousand dollars worth of hides. "Diamonds, pig iron, cotton fabrics,
woolens, pottery, everything would be taxed at a uniform rate based on value,"
Marshall asserted. "Trading in schedules would be at an end, scandals would
cease, and every American would get a square deal."

Vice President John Sherman helped to convince Taft to support the high
protective tariffs in the Payne-Aldrich bill. When the Taft administration began,
Sherman's conservatism at times clashed with Taft's Progressive tendencies.
Taft had asked Sherman to help lobby the conservative congressional leaders.
"You will have to act on your own account," was Sherman's reply. "I am to
be Vice President and acting as a messenger boy is not part of the duties as
Vice President."

One issue on which Taft and Sherman differed was the tariff. Taft's
personal preference was for modest reductions; Sherman, on the other
hand, supported the higher levies proposed by Senator Nelson Aldrich. The
Republican platform of 1908 declared "unequivocally for a revision of the
tariff by a special session of Congress, immediately following the inauguration
of the next President". For much of the electorate, tariff issues had a direct
effect on their standard of living. A high tariff meant higher prices for the
goods most Americans purchased. When Taft and the Republicans called
for a "revision" in the tariff, most assumed the levies would be revised in one
direction – downward.

Many businesses, however, supported tariffs that made their goods more
competitive against foreign competition. While much of the country applauded
when Taft called a special session of congress to pass a tariff measure, business
lobbyists sought protective tariffs for their own industries.

After months of legislative maneuvering, a new tariff bill was framed
under Sereno E. Payne, Chairman of the Committee on Ways and Means,
and Nelson W. Aldrich, Senator from Rhode Island. It was Aldrich who

loaded up the bill with protective tariffs for his business friends. In the end, the Payne-Aldrich Tariff, while lowering 650 tariff schedules, raised the rates on 220 more and left 1,150 unchanged. Once it became clear that the new tariff would hurt as much as it helped, many hoped that Taft would veto the measure. But it would be difficult for Taft to veto a measure drafted by his own party, particularly since the Republicans had campaigned aggressively on the issue in 1908.

Aldrich was a powerful Senator, but public sentiment was clearly in favor of tariff reduction. To replace the lost revenue, Democrats and moderate Republicans advocated for a tax on corporations and a constitutional amendment to enable the enactment of an income tax. A compromise soon emerged.

Aldrich was adamant in his opposition to significant tariff reductions. The Payne-Aldrich bill that would eventually be approved would lower some tariffs but raise others, with the overall effect minimal. In addition, a one- percent tax on corporations "for the privilege of doing business" would make up for lost tariff revenue. Proponents hoped that language would pass a constitutionality test before the Supreme Court, which eventually gave its blessing.

Many of the voters who supported Taft thought that the platform plank which called for a "revision" of the tariff would mean, for them, a square deal. But skepticism rose when, not long after the election, Senator Aldrich responded to a reporter's question about the lack of tariff reduction by stating, "Where did we ever make the statement that we would revise the tariff downward?" Sherman echoed those sentiments by telling people that the Republican Party "had fulfilled every campaign pledge in passing the Aldrich bill." In the end, President Taft sided with Sherman and the protectionists and signed the bill. Progressives in the Republican Party began to reevaluate their assessment of Taft, and the Governor of Indiana saw an opportunity to gain national prominence.

As had happened so often when the tariff question was raised, a commission was assembled to examine tariff schedules and proposed changes. Marshall was skeptical of this approach.

A tariff commission is just about as valuable as a letter written by an inmate of an insane hospital. To pretend to organize a commission that will tell the difference in the cost of production

at home and abroad, is no more possible than it is for a one-
legged man to dance the hornpipe.[156]

In addition, on July 12, 1909, Congress approved legislation to begin
the process of amending the constitution to allow for an income tax. By
overwhelming majorities, both the House and Senate approved new
constitutional language, which would read:

> *The Congress shall have power to lay and collect taxes on*
> *incomes, from whatever source derived, without apportionment*
> *among the several States, and without regard to any census or*
> *enumeration.*

Soon after the compromise was reached, public dissatisfaction with the
new tariff began to increase. Working class families noticed almost no changes
from the new Payne-Aldrich tariff schedule, and increased tariffs on such
widely used articles such as wool led to increased public anger. Taft himself
added fuel to the discontent when he declared that "I think the Payne bill is
the best bill the Republican Party ever passed." Woodrow Wilson and Thomas
Marshall would make sure voters remembered those words in the presidential
election of 1912.

Taft not only signed the Payne-Aldrich Tariff Bill; he actively promoted
it in speeches across the country. Republican opponents of high tariffs and
protectionism began to look for new leadership for the elections of 1912.

Taft's stance on the tariff put Thomas Marshall in an enviable political
position. It was well known among political leaders across the country that
Marshall had long been opposed philosophically to protectionism, and he
echoed that theme in the National Jefferson Day Dinner and elsewhere. He
positioned his party as defender of the public against special interest groups
and legislation harmful to the working man.

> *Let me tell you that the best thing that the old chariot of state*
> *ever had put on it was a brake – a brake to keep the blamed old*
> *thing from going too fast down hill; and the Democratic party*
> *has been the brake that has kept this country from being plunged*
> *into an aristocracy or a monarchy before its time.*[157]

❧ ❧ ❧ ❧ ❧

In his capacity as presiding officer of the Senate, Vice President Sherman tried to show fairness, an even temperment, and good humor. Marshall would use Sherman as a role model when his turn came to serve as the leader of Senate debate.

Like Marshall would in later years, Sherman also came under criticism for some of his rulings as presiding officer. One day, Vice President Sherman ruled against Texas Democrat Joseph W. Bailey, who

> *instantly declared that the independence of the Senate had been invaded by the Vice President who was not a member of the Senate but only its Constitutional presiding officer; that he had no right to use a position which was largely one of courtesy to violate the traditions of the most august body in the world and deny, or attempt to deny, to a Senator the rights to which every Senator was entitled.*[158]

One observer noted that Sherman listened to Bailey without anger or other emotion.

> *He was the presiding officer personified. With perfect calmness, good humor, and dignity, he stated the case to a breathless Senate. He did it so clearly and convincingly that the Senate sat down upon the tumultuous senator, and Sherman's decisions were never after questioned.*[159]

Like Marshall after him, Sherman was able to bridge political differences and make friends on both sides of the aisle.

Indiana Democratic Senator John Worth Kern, who squared off against Sherman for the vice-presidency in 1908, recalled his arrival in the Senate in 1911. To patch their differences, Sherman reached out to Kern within minutes after the Indiana politician had taken the oath of office, inviting him to take the gavel and preside over the Senate. "I protested that I was a stranger, not only to this body but its procedure," said Kern, *but he insisted, saying, "It will be only for a few minutes and it is for my own pleasure and gratification that I ask you to do me this personal favor." And from that time on until the last he never lost an opportunity to make me feel that however wide our political differences—and they were irreconcilable—I had in him a friend on whose fidelity I might always rely.*[160]

In January 1910, Taft fired Gifford Pinchot as head of the U.S. Forest Service. Sherman supported Taft's decision. But Theodore Roosevelt was livid over the firing of Pinchot. Not only did Roosevelt feel that Pinchot was supporting conservation efforts which were opposed by big business (a stance that Roosevelt wholeheartedly endorsed), but Pinchot was also Roosevelt's close friend.

The Taft-Roosevelt split first played out in the fight to control the New York State Republican convention in 1910. Governor Charles Evans Hughes had resigned to become a Supreme Court justice, triggering a battle for the seat between conservative and progressive Republicans. Conservatives selected Vice President Sherman as chairman of the state convention to nominate the next governor. Roosevelt ran against Sherman for chairman. Nominally a contest between Sherman and Roosevelt, it was clear that the fight would pit the progressive Republicans against Taft and the Old Guard. When Roosevelt defeated Sherman, it marked a split in the Republican Party that reverberated to the ballot box. In the 1910 congressional midterm elections, Republicans lost eight seats in the Senate and their majority in the House to the Democrats. The schism would carry on to the presidential election of 1912.

✖ ✖ ✖ ✖ ✖

Woodrow Thomas Wilson was born December 28, 1856, in Staunton, Virginia. His father, Dr. Joseph Ruggles Wilson, was a pastor at the First Presbyterian Church in that town; his mother, Janet, would also have three other children: Woodrow's brother Joseph, Jr., and his sisters Marion and Anne Josephine.

As part of his church responsibilities, Reverend Dr. Wilson would move his family throughout the south to churches in Augusta, Georgia, Columbia, South Carolina and Wilmington, North Carolina. He would eventually serve thirty-four years as the clerk of the General Assembly of the Presbyterian Church of the United States.

Woodrow, who was called Tommie by his family and friends, was described as a quiet and studious child. Athletics played little role in his upbringing. He was extremely close to his mother, and later in life indicated that he was considered something of a "mama's boy". But his attachment to his mother was deep, and when she died in 1888 it left an emotional scar that would stay with him for the rest of his life.

Woodrow Wilson began his higher education at Davidson College in North Carolina, but was dissatisfied and left after one year. When he entered Princeton University (then called the College of New Jersey), it was the logical choice for the son of a prominent Presbyterian minister. The University had close ties with the Presbyterian Church, as every president had been an ordained minister from that denomination. Princeton Theological Seminar, a leading institution for training Presbyterian ministers, was located next to the campus. Wilson's affiliation with Princeton would last far beyond his student days.

While a student at Princeton, Woodrow developed a strong interest in government and politics. He was a member of the debating society, and as part of his studies had written a paper entitled "Cabinet Government in the United States". He submitted it for publication to a journal entitled International Review, whose editor was a young Harvard-educated Bostonian named Henry Cabot Lodge.

Upon graduation, Wilson entered the University of Virginia Law School, but began to be plagued by ill health. Owing to a "digestive" problem, he left law school six months before graduation. Despite his lack of a law degree, he was admitted to the Georgia bar in October of 1882.

Wilson was unhappy with his law career, but while in Georgia he met Ellen Louise Axson, herself the daughter of a Presbyterian minister. Ellen studied at the Female Seminary in Rome, Georgia and had plans for a career as an artist. Woodrow and Ellen announced their engagement in September, 1883.

Soon afterward, Ellen's father suffered a nervous breakdown and was placed in a mental institution in Georgia. He died there in May of 1884, probably the result of suicide. Ellen, shaken by her father's death, used her inheritance to move to New York City and continue her study of art. Woodrow also continued his studies, at Johns Hopkins University pursuing a doctorate's degree.

Despite their separation, the couple continued their correspondence and their relationship deepened. In June, 1885, they were married in Savannah, Georgia, with Woodrow's father and Ellen's grandfather presiding over the ceremony. Later that year, in October, Woodrow was awarded his Ph.D. from Johns Hopkins and accepted a teaching position at Bryn Mawr College, ten miles northwest of Philadelphia.

Woodrow and Ellen Wilson settled into their new lifestyle at Bryn Mawr College in 1885. Woodrow was an associate professor of history, and due to his annual salary of $1,500 Woodrow told Ellen she did not need to find a career as his salary would be sufficient for their family. Within four years they would have three daughters—Margaret, born in 1886, Jessie, in 1887 and in 1889 their third and final daughter, Eleanor, was born.

By the time of Eleanor's birth Woodrow had accept a position at Wesleyan University in Middletown, Connecticut. His reputation as a lecturer, researcher and instructor had spread through the academic community and Woodrow was recruited throughout the country. Soon, an offer would come from his alma mater, Princeton University, and in 1890 he returned to Princeton as professor of jurisprudence and political economy. Within the next few years the nature of his offers would escalate, and no fewer than six universities asked Woodrow to become their president. Each time he declined, as by this time he knew that he had the reputation and ability to choose the job he coveted most. As a young man in his mid-thirties, he had the patience and foresight to wait until the day came when he would be offered the position he most wanted – the presidency of Princeton University.

In early 1902 the presidency of Princeton University became vacant. While the search to fill such a position can sometimes be a long and drawn-out process, close observers knew that the trustees of Princeton would have little difficulty finding a successor. By a unanimous vote of the twenty-six trustees, Woodrow Wilson was chosen on the first ballot, becoming the first Princeton president who was not an ordained Presbyterian minister.

On October 25, 1902, Woodrow Wilson, just shy of his forty-sixth birthday, was inaugurated as the President of Princeton University. On a bright, sunny day just steps away from Nassau Hall, Wilson looked not only across the campus but also across the years, peering into the future of both the students and their new University president. "In planning for Princeton, we are planning for the country," Wilson said.

The service of institutions of learning is not private, but public. It is plain what the nation needs as its affairs grow more and more complex and its interests begin to touch the ends of the earth. It needs efficient and enlightened men. The universities of the country must take part in supplying them.[161]

As the stress of the Presidency of Princeton weighed more heavily on Wilson, his health suffered. Wanting desperately to provide the relaxation her husband would need, Edith insisted that Woodrow take time away from his work and go to Bermuda, where he could relax and restore his health.

While there, however, Woodrow met Mary Allen Hulbert Peck, the wife of a woolen mill owner from Pittsfield, Massachusetts. Her first husband died when Mary was just twenty-six; her second marriage was hardly a close one. Mary often traveled without her husband, and local gossip linked Mary to several men, including the widowed governor of Bermuda.

Woodrow and Mary first met in January of 1907. When Woodrow returned to Bermuda the following winter, he traveled without Ellen – despite writing her that she would accompany him. When Wilson returned he immediately began his relationship again with Mary.

The true nature of the relationship between Woodrow Wilson and Mary Peck remains shrouded in ambiguity to this day. They met at least ninety times – including ten times at the White House – and at least 227 letters between the two remain to this day. Mary herself claimed that the relationship was, "Tender, yeas; but hardly erotic, nor by any means measures of passion." Nevertheless, as Wilson rose to national prominence he maintained his ties to Mary – much to the chagrin of his political advisors.

Several years into his administration, Woodrow Wilson turned his attention towards significant reforms of both graduate education and social life on campus. At a dinner on campus, he called for numerous changes but two would lead to the most significant controversies of his career up to that point.

His first target was the "eating clubs" on campus. Much like fraternities, the eating clubs were the center of social activity for their members. Students could join one of a variety of clubs – Triangle, Tiger, and others. Members took their meals at the club, and club leaders organized dances, receptions, and other social gatherings.

But the social clubs were highly stratified institutions that sorted students by their social standing and excluded some (including Jews and minorities) entirely. Students from the best prep schools would tend to stay together in the same club – those from Andover when to one club, Exeter to another. Students without wealth or connections were excluded from the best clubs. Furthermore, nearly half of each class was unable or unwilling to join any eating club. The result was a fragmented student body, and little cohesion among each class.

Wilson also took the initiative to build a facility for graduate students, and wanted to construct it within the current campus, in the center of undergraduate activity. By exposing undergraduates to the more serious scholars in graduate school, Wilson believed he could create an atmosphere that would raise the academic standards of everyone at the University.

Few doubted the wisdom of constructing a new graduate school, but feelings ran high regarding the location. The school had received a bequest of $250,000 to build the graduate college if it were located on vacant land a mile west of the main campus. Wilson opposed the location as too far from the other students, and was successful in soliciting a gift twice as large from another alumnus to locate the site within the current campus.

But Wilson underestimated the power of influential alumni and other administrators and faculty. Many alumni had fond memories of their affiliation with their eating clubs, and threatened to reduce their annual donations if the clubs were abolished. The eating clubs were skillful at organizing their past and current members to oppose Wilson's plan.

The plans to build the on-campus graduate college were opposed by the dean of the graduate school, who gained significant support when ex-president Grover Cleveland, who had retired to Princeton, backed the off-campus site. Despite the strong opposition, Wilson thought he had won the battle of the graduate college until a $2 million bequest was received for the graduate college – if it was located away from the main campus.

Wilson lost both battles. The eating clubs remained, as they do to this day. The graduate college was built a mile west of the main campus and each day graduate students walk or bike to their classes – which are often on the eastern edge of campus.

Showing behavior that would reemerge nearly ten years later in the fight over the League of Nations, Wilson felt his opponents had personally betrayed him. He sought the removal of staff members who did not support his proposals, and turned his back on some who had been close friends to he and Ellen. When the trustees refused to dismiss the dean of the graduate school, Wilson had made up his mind to leave.

But as with most of his career, Wilson was still aggressively courted by those who knew of his leadership abilities. This time, though, he would not be asked to become the chief executive of a college or university. State Democratic leaders would ask Woodrow Wilson to become the Governor of New Jersey.

Joseph Patrick Tumulty was born May 5, 1879, the son of grocer and Civil War veteran active in local politics in Hudson County, New Jersey. As was expected for a son in an Irish Catholic family, Joseph attended a Catholic elementary and high school, and earned a degree from a Jesuit college in Jersey City. An aspiring politician, Tumulty soon learned that he was gifted as an orator, winning the gold medal for elocution at his graduation. He studied law after graduation and opened a practice in his hometown, using the fees from wealthy clients to support charity work for his neighbors.

Popular and well spoken, Tumulty soon sought elective office. Though his heart lay with the growing strength of the progressive movement, the realities of politics in New Jersey required that he first gain the favor of the local political bosses. Gaining the support of the Hudson County Democratic machine, Tumulty was elected to the New Jersey State Assembly in 1906.

New Jersey at that time had not adopted the progressive reform which called for the direct election of Senate candidates, so the first issue Joseph dealt with was the selection of a United States Senator in 1907. Eager at this time to advance political reform, Tumulty supported a candidate who fought against the New Jersey Democratic machine. The political bosses, though, advanced the candidacy of a new name in statewide elections, the president of Princeton University, Woodrow Wilson.

Tumulty fought hard against Wilson's senatorial nomination, putting the name of his candidate forward with a strong anti-Wilson speech. But eventually a third candidate emerged, and Wilson withdrew from the race.

Tumulty emerged as a champion for the progressive agenda in New Jersey. He introduced legislation providing for initiative and referendum, a civil service commission, and direct election of senators. But without the support of the political bosses, his efforts were unsuccessful.

New Jersey in 1910 was a state whose political structure was not unlike Indiana. The electorate was split among liberals, moderates and conservatives, with a strong and growing progressive movement seeking changes in areas such as direct election of senators and utility regulatory reform.

The business of elections, though, was dominated by political bosses who generally represented a segment of the political spectrum but more frequently would embrace any stance that would keep them and their supporters in power. While some political bosses were of separate parties and battled over voters in the general elections, in New Jersey, as in Indiana, at times the bosses were in the same party and the battles took place before primary election day.

But most bosses were savvy enough to understand that money and energy used in a primary election battle were not available for the effort to win the general election. Fighting among Democratic leaders had helped lead to the election of Republican John Franklin Fort as governor in 1906, and strategists knew that the party would need to coalesce behind a single candidate if they hoped to retake the governor's mansion in 1910.

The leaders of the political machines in Hudson and Essex County, including boss James Smith, joined forces to promote Woodrow Wilson as the Democratic nominee for Governor. They sent Wilson a letter, asking discretely if Wilson would try to overturn their power once in office. "I would be perfectly willing to assure Mr. Smith," wrote Wilson, "that I would not, if elected governor, set about fighting and breaking down the existing Democratic organization and replacing it with one of my own."[162]

Viewing Wilson as a tool of his corrupt sponsors, Tumulty and other progressives proposed a different candidate. They knew, however, that they had little chance of success and it was a despondent Tumulty who attended the Democratic convention that would formally nominate the candidate for governor.

The liberals and progressives had arranged to walk out of the convention after the balloting was complete. Joseph was part of the crowd heading for the exits when he heard among the pandemonium that Wilson was in the convention hall and would formally accept the nomination. Curious, Tumulty returned to the hall to listen to the speech.

What Tumulty heard would not only change his viewpoint about Wilson, but would alter the political careers of both men forever. Rather than deliver a bland and perfunctory acceptance speech, Wilson embraced the progressive platform and announced that he would serve not the political bosses but the people of the State of New Jersey.

America is not distinguished so much by its wealth and material power, as by the fact that it was born with an ideal, a purpose, to serve mankind, and all mankind has sought her as a haven of equal justice. When I look upon the American flag before me, I think sometimes that it is made of parchment and blood. The white in it stands for parchment; the red in it signifies blood. Parchment on which was written the rights of men, and blood that was spilled to make these rights real. Let us devote the Democratic Party to the recovery of these rights.[163]

The crowd loved what they heard, and though Wilson wanted to end his speech those present called for more. Tumulty turned to one of his progressive allies and told him that this was one of the happiest days of his life.

Wilson and Tumulty met soon after the convention and quickly developed a mutually beneficial friendship. Wilson had the charisma and pedigree to be a successful candidate. Tumulty understood local politics throughout the State, and was able to advise the gubernatorial candidate on the best strategy to approach the fall election.

The two campaigned as a team. Tumulty would often speak first at a campaign rally, energizing the crowd with his fiery oratory and instilling in them the same enthusiasm for candidate Wilson that he felt. Often, Wilson's speech was shorter and more pedantic than Joseph's, but the combined effort proved effective for most crowds.

Both national and statewide issues helped Wilson. National dissatisfaction was growing over the newly enacted Payne-Aldrich tariff, and the Republican party was already split into factions supporting either Taft or Roosevelt. In New Jersey, a Republican railroad and utility law recently enacted resulted in a twenty-percent increase in commutation fares in the late summer of 1910. Suburban voters, traditionally Republican stalwarts, gave their support to Wilson.

Woodrow Wilson won the gubernatorial election in New Jersey with the second largest plurality in the history of the State, beating his Republican rival by nearly two to one. As Marshall had accomplished in Indiana two years earlier, Wilson's victory led immediately to talk of the former President of Princeton University as the Democratic Presidential Nominee in 1912.

Wilson was ambitious, and knew that Tumulty had the political savvy that would be required for a successful bid for the White House. Soon after the election, he asked Tumulty to become his personal secretary. Seeing that his political future lay not in his own electoral success but with Wilson's, Tumulty readily agreed.

Wilson became Governor of New Jersey in 1911, with Tumulty by his side as personal secretary. He soon embarked on a cross-country speaking tour, and found that he could energize crowds with his stirring speeches. In places like Richmond, Charlotte and Atlanta, Wilson was embraced as a son of the south. In the Northeastern states, his Princeton background gave him a close tie to his audiences. While ostensibly the chief executive of the State, both Tumulty and Wilson knew that their goal over the next two years was to make Woodrow Wilson the President of the United States.

∽ ∽ ∽ ∽ ∽

Well before Marshall's term as Governor was over, state and national attention began to turn to the Presidential Election of 1912. Experienced political observers could see that while Republicans enjoyed a numerical advantage among the electorate – they had, after all, won every presidential election when Grover Cleveland was not on the ballot since the Civil War. But with Taft's anemic popularity the Grand Old Party faced the difficult choice of backing a weak candidate or declining to nominate a sitting president.

The emergence of Roosevelt as a strong third party candidate gave the Democrats their most realistic chance for victory in a generation. As party leaders developed what they hoped would be a winning ticket in 1912, the importance of key states – such as Indiana – came to the forefront.

Because of the lack of attention paid to Indiana by presidential candidates of today, it is hard to imagine the importance of the Hoosier State to national politics one hundred years ago. But Indiana was seen as a crucial state for election strategists. It was the sixth largest state in the late 19th century, and was equally divided among the Democratic and Republican parties. Between 1880 and 1912, no candidate won the presidential election without winning Indiana.

During the stretch between 1868 and 1916, of the twelve presidential elections, nine included a major party candidate from Indiana. Four of those vice presidential candidates – Schuyler Colfax, Thomas Hendricks, Charles Fairbanks and Thomas Riley Marshall, and one presidential candidate, William Henry Harrison, were successfully elected to office.

The Democrats knew that, with the Republican vote split, they had a good chance of success in the November elections. Even as late as 1912, the Democrats were still in search of a candidate who could garner national support. By this time, the states south of the Mason-Dixon line were solidly Democratic, so the ideal candidate would have southern ties but not be so closely tied to that part of the country to allow the Republicans to once again wave the "bloody shirt".

Three strong Democratic contenders emerged – William Jennings Bryan, who had been the unsuccessful Democratic nominee in three previous presidential elections, James Beauchamp ("Champ") Clark, the speaker of the House of Representatives from Missouri, and New Jersey Governor Woodrow Wilson.

Bryan was still the favorite of the radical wing of the party. He had solid support in the fast-growing western states, as well as the declining but still important agricultural vote. But as a three-time loser in the general election, even his strongest supporters had to question his electibility.

Champ Clark was a formidable candidate, if only because of his congressional power base. Shrewd and highly respected, Clark would prove to be the strongest challenge to Wilson. In April, Clark had outpolled Wilson in the primary by nearly a three-to-one margin, and some felt that this proved that Clark would be the stronger candidate. But more importantly, Clark represented the status quo, and his supporters were generally opposed to the Progressive reforms.

The Governor of New Jersey had only minimal electoral experience, but in the progressive atmosphere of 1912 his intellectualism and academic background proved just as important as political experience. And while Clark could use his political power to gain supporters, the exercise of power is a double-edged sword and those on the losing side of a decision by the Speaker were more than pleased to support his opponent.

Tom Taggart came to the Baltimore convention with control of Indiana's twenty-nine votes. He knew the delegates would be divided, and thought there was a chance that Marshall could emerge as compromise candidate for President. Champ Clark led the voting early in the race, and in each of those ballots Taggart was shrewd enough to keep Indiana's votes united for Marshall as their "favorite son," until he could determine how to use them to the best advantage.

Champ Clark led the voting during the first nine ballots. When the Tammany Hall Democratic machine from New York shifted its support to Clark, the Speaker of the House garnered a majority of the votes. At this point, history was not on Wilson's side. No Democrat who had received a majority of the ballots during the convention had ever been denied the nomination. Wilson, sensing that his campaign was doomed, instructed his managers to release his delegates. Only after numerous phone calls from those closer to the situation did Wilson relent and continued his candidacy.

On the fourteenth ballot, Bryan could see that he was unlikely to garner enough support to be the party's standard bearer once again. He threw his support to Wilson, but this was still not enough to give Wilson the votes he needed for the nomination.

William F. McCombs, Wilson's campaign manager, tells this story of the evening of Sunday night, June 30:

> The night before the nomination was made I had gone to my room entirely worn out. Sleep had been the last thing to think about. I was afraid if I went to sleep something might happen to my candidate's chances. It was about ten o'clock that night when a boy came to my room and asked if I would please go to the room of William Jennings Bryan. Of course I went, wearing only my bathrobe. When I went in I shall not forget the sight. Bryan standing with his profile facing me ....
> Without turning his face toward me he drew his lips in a tight straight line and proceeded: 'McCombs, Wilson can never be nominated. Clark can never be nominated. We must put forward a progressive Democrat for the presidency.'
> 'Bryan', I answered him, 'I could reach out my hand a touch the progressive Democrat you mention. You have sent for the last man in the convention you ought to have called. If this is all you have to say it is not even interesting. Good night.' He made no response and I left him standing looking at the wall.
> I went straight to the room of Tom Taggart. I told him what had passed between Bryan and me. Then I simply said: "How does Wilson look to you at this time as our man for president?' His answer was: 'McCombs, how does Tom Marshall look to

you for vice president?' 'Fine,' I assured him, 'as the running mate of Woodrow Wilson.' We agreed.[164]

Taggart saw his chance. He struck a deal with Wilson's campaign manager to move Indiana's delegates to Wilson, in return for a vice presidential nomination for Marshall. Roger Sullivan of Illinois, remembering what Marshall had done to the horse racing operation in Porter County, also agreed to the deal. On the twenty-eighth ballot, Taggart gave all of Marshall's delegates to Wilson. Illinois switched its support to Wilson, who went on to win the nomination on the forty-sixth ballot.

Taggart contacted Roger Sullivan and leaders from other states. Staying up until early in the morning, the leaders agreed to back the Wilson-Marshall ticket. The next call he made was to Judge Andrew Adams, who was representing Marshall at the convention. Adams knew that it was the best that Marshall could hope for, and quickly agreed to the arrangement.

In the confusion of the convention Wilson was unaware of the deal McCombs had struck with Taggart. After the balloting for President was completed, Wilson contacted Albert Burleson in Baltimore to see if he could contact Oscar Underwood about serving as Wilson's running mate. Burleson, more attuned to the back room maneuvering that had taken place, told Wilson that it was his understanding that the delegates were in favor of Marshall. "But, Burleson", Wilson replied, "He is a small caliber man."

◆ ◆ ◆ ◆ ◆

As the Baltimore convention delegates turned their attention to the selection of a vice presidential candidate, Champ Clark, the runner-up in the presidential balloting, was the natural front runner. A delegate from Georgia nominated Clark. After a brief period of consultation with the Missouri delegation, however, Clark indicated his unwillingness to be nominated for the second position, and his name was withdrawn.

Other nominations soon followed. North Dakota offered up the name of its Governor, John Burke. Next came Elmore Hurst of Illinois.

Marshall was the next to be nominated, along with the argument that an Indiana leader deserved a place on the ticket. Knowing the importance of votes from the other states, it was noted that Indiana was the first state in which

Democrats achieved political power following the Civil War. Indiana "turned the tide of radicalism and helped you to resume the white man's civilization of the South". The speaker also noted Marshall's Virginia ancestry.[165]

Other nominations continued, until Senator John Worth Kern of Indiana interrupted the process to give the report of the Committee of Resolutions.

To give the report at this time may have seemed odd to many of the delegates, who were weary from the fierce fight over the presidential balloting. A problem had arisen, though, which could have stopped Marshall's nomination.

Labor leaders were not pleased with Marshall's pending nomination due to his action in extraditing John McNamara to stand trial in California for the dynamiting of the Los Angeles Times building in 1910. They sent telegrams to the delegates opposing Marshall's nomination. Thomas Taggart, along with Charles Murphy of New York and Roger Sullivan of Illinois, needed time to meet with the delegates to offset the effect of the telegrams.

The strategy worked. After the report of the Committee had been read and adopted, the balloting resumed. Oregon nominated its senator, George Chamberlain, and other states voiced their support for one of the nominated men. But then, yet another roadblock appeared in Marshall's road to the Vice Presidency.

At one point in the process, William Jennings Bryan was nominated for Vice President. Most expected Bryan to immediately refuse the nomination; instead, he asked to address the convention.

As expected, Bryan declined the nomination. He then announced he was supporting the nomination of John Burke and George Chamberlain. He declined to support Marshall.

Bryan's snub of Marshall was a surprise, given what had appeared to have been a close relationship between the two in the past. But Bryan and Marshall had disagreed the previous week over the selection of Judge Alton Parker, the Party's presidential nominee in 1904, as the convention's Temporary Chairman. Bryan had sent Marshall a telegram opposing the selection of Parker. Marshall, though, had a different viewpoint.

> *My unvarying idea has been that principles, and not men, should control the destinies of the democratic party. I cared no more for Judge Parker than I cared for Mr. Bryan. But I did*

not forget that in 1908, when Mr. Bryan was a candidate for President and I was a candidate for governor, Judge Parker had canvassed the state of Indiana for both of us. Mr. Bryan's telegram gave me an opportunity to make a payment on this debt. I was advised that the wise thing to do was to hedge; that Mr. Bryan's influence with the convention was great, that any real or seeming antagonism to him would blight all prospect of my own nomination. But I realized that some time in the future I would meet Judge Parker, and then when I did he would be thinking what an ingrate I was, so I wired Mr. Bryan, in substance, that the man who canvassed Indiana for him and for me was good enough to preside over a Democratic convention.[166]

Nine candidates were eventually nominated. After the first round of balloting, Marshall led with 389 votes, followed by Burke with 304 and Chamberlain with 157. Marshall had just over half of the 726 votes needed for the nomination.

A motion was made to make the nomination unanimous for Marshall, but Bryan rose in opposition and the motion was withdrawn. After a brief discussion, a second ballot was started.

Several states, beginning with Maryland, switched to Marshall. Mississippi followed. After the second ballot, it was clear that it was a two-man race, as Marshall had received 644 votes to 386 for Burke. The North Dakota delegation, seeing that the nomination battle was lost, withdrew Burke's name as a candidate, and made a motion for a unanimous vote for Marshall. The motion was approved.

Tom Taggart strode to the podium in victory to close the proceedings. He thanked the delegates for their work, and also thanked the City of Baltimore for its hospitality. Having accomplished his goal of putting Marshall on the ticket, at 2 o'clock in the morning on July third he banged the gavel for the final time and the convention was over.

Tom and Lois were in Indianapolis while the Baltimore convention was taking place. A few minutes after Marshall was nominated, a local reporter came to the Marshall home asking for comment. Marshall, awoken from his sleep, told the reporter to go away, and that whatever news he had could wait until morning.

Lois, however, persuaded Tom that it could be news from Baltimore, and they let the reporter in. Marshall said little that night, but the next day he informed Lois that he would *decline* the nomination. He was perfectly happy to go back to his life in Columbia City, and felt he could never live in Washington on the paltry $12,000 a year salary of a Vice President. Lois felt differently, however, and her tears eventually persuaded Marshall to accept.

Wilson's telegram to Marshall was prompt but unaffectionate:

SINCERE CONGRATULATIONS. I SHALL LOOK FORWARD WITH PLEASURE TO MY ASSOCIATION WITH YOU.

Wilson's press statement was more cordial. "He is, I am happy to say, a valued personal friend of mine."

Official notification ceremonies were scheduled. Wilson would be notified of his nomination at his summer home in Sea Girt, New Jersey. Marshall's notification would take place in Indianapolis.

The Governor and Mrs. Marshall traveled to Sea Girt in August. Despite sharing the job of chief executive of large and growing states, this would be the first opportunity for Wilson and Marshall to meet. Marshall impressed the presidential candidate with his knowledge of the issues, particularly the tariff question. Wilson was able to show that, despite his reputation as a scholar and academic, he was not devoid of humor. The story is told of one afternoon in 1911, while serving as New Jersey's governor, Wilson received news of the unexpected death of a New Jersey senator and close personal friend. While still recovering from the shock, he received a call from another prominent state politician.

"Governor," the man declared, "I would like to take the senator's place." "It's perfectly agreeable to me," Wilson replied, "if it's agreeable to the undertaker."

While in Sea Girt, Democratic clubs from across New Jersey paraded in front of the nominees prior to the ceremony. "A number of them are my old campaign friends", remarked the New Jersey governor.

"They march," said Marshall, "as well as if they were Jersey militiamen."

"No doubt some of them are," replied Wilson.[167]

Wilson's comments during the ceremony at Sea Girt emphasized the Democrat's themes in 1912. The recent tariff legislation reflected favoritism towards certain elements of big business and against the working man. He noted that the Democratic Party supported the workers, the common man, and struggling families.

At the close of the ceremonies, Marshall presented Wilson with a book by Frank "Kin" Hubbard of the Indianapolis News, who wrote using the character of Abe Martin, a folksy Midwesterner. Marshall inscribed the book: "From your only vice, Thomas R. Marshall."

Marshall invited Wilson to attend his notification ceremonies in Indianapolis the following week. Wilson declined.

On August 20, Alton Parker formally notified Marshall of his nomination before a large crowd in downtown Indianapolis. Parker's address also focused on tariffs and special interests, and also attacked Congress as beholding to special business interests.

Marshall chose a larger theme for his remarks. As was his special gift when addressing large crowds, he talked about justice, humility and the common man.

> *The individualism of Thomas Jefferson is not dead. It has not moldered back to dust in the grave at Monticello. It walks the earth this day knocking at the door of rich and poor, of wise and ignorant, alike, calling upon all men to make this age the millennium of statecraft wherein no one shall claim to be the master and all shall be glad to be the servants of the Republic. It cannot be that it is the system of government that is wrong. It is the unjust use of the system. From Jefferson to Lincoln, the Republic grew in might, in majesty, in pomp and splendor, and the humblest of its citizens could obtain justice, not as a beggar crawling in the sun, but as a man. It has not been the use but the misuse of the powers of government that has produced this discontent in the minds of men.[168]*

Marshall's rhetoric at this point became more partisan. Those who want oligarchy, he said, should vote Republican. Socialists had their candidate. Voters wishing for no separation of church and state should vote the Prohibition Party. But those who longed for equal opportunity should vote Democratic.

> *The hour has come when patriotism must consist in something more than eulogies upon the flag. Whether voting the ticket or not, men everywhere looking upon the awful injustice of this economic system are becoming socialistic in theory if not in conduct ... I do not hesitate to say that if it be impossible to restore this Republic to its ancient ideals, which I do not believe, and I must make the ultimate choice between the paternalism of the few and the socialism of the many, count me and my house with the throbbing heart of humanity.*[169]

❧ ❧ ❧ ❧ ❧

In the summer of 1912 as the candidates prepared for the fall presidential campaign, Marshall was approached by a leader of the Prohibition Party in Indianapolis with an intriguing proposal. Would Woodrow Wilson consider accepting the endorsement of the Prohibition Party, in addition to his role at the head of the Democratic ticket?

The endorsement would probably mean little in the eventual outcome of the election, as the Prohibition Party generally received less than two percent of the vote. While in a close election those votes would look attractive, such an endorsement would also risk alienating Democratic voters opposed to the goals of the Prohibition Party.

But the endorsement of the Prohibition Party could also help Marshall counter the whispers about his history of alcohol abuse. In addition, Republicans had attacked gubernatorial candidate Marshall in 1908 regarding his alleged ties to the liquor industry, and a Prohibition Party endorsement would negate the effectiveness of that criticism.

When Marshall had been approached by C.E. Newlin about the potential endorsement, he knew that it was Wilson, and not himself, who would make the decision. He asked Mark Thistlethwaite to write Wilson, explaining the offer and arranging an appointment with Wilson to discuss it further. Thistlethwaite's letter suggests that Marshall feared that even Wilson was inclined to believe that Tom had gotten too close to the liquor industry.

Mr. C.E. Newlin of this city, a representative of the Prohibition Party, is very anxious to consult with you as to the feasibility of the prohibition party, in national convention, endorsing the democratic ticket.

Governor Marshall declined to express any opinion upon the question to Mr. Newlin, explaining that he felt that you were the person to be consulted.

Mr. Newlin is to be in Atlantic City at the Richmond Hotel and with your consent he will call and talk the matter over with you giving the assurance that the conversation will be private and that his real desire is to benefit the ticket. He wish also to convince you that Governor Marshall is in no wise bound up to the liquor interest in Indiana.

Despite the letter to Wilson, Marshall must have known that a Prohibition Party endorsement was unlikely. The relationship between Marshall and the previous governor, Frank Hanly, was poor as Hanly knew that the rumors of Marshall's drinking contained some elements of the truth. Hanly was also a leader in the national Prohibition Party organization, and would serve as that party's presidential candidate in 1916. Eventually, no endorsement of Wilson was forthcoming, and the Prohibition Party candidate in 1912 eventually garnered less than 300,000 votes.

❧ ❧ ❧ ❧ ❧

The party nomination process in 1912, in a rare result for American presidential politics, produced three viable candidates. Wilson would represent the Democratic Party, Taft the Republican. (When the Taft-Sherman ticket was set, Vice President John Sherman became the first sitting vice president to be renominated since John C. Calhoun, eighty years earlier.) Theodore Roosevelt's nomination by the Progressive Party meant that this would be a legitimate three-way race.

Democrats knew that had their first realistic shot at victory since Grover Cleveland. Roosevelt's candidacy meant the Republican vote would be split. In addition, the solid south could be counted on to support Wilson; that meant that the election would be decided in a small number of northern and Midwestern states.

Wilson advisors defined the issues at the "Two T's" – Tariff and Trusts. "The center of all our difficulties," Wilson said, "is that there is not freedom of enterprise in the United States." The captains of big business, he said, were strangling any potential competition. "The inventive genius and initiative of the American people is being held back by the fact that our industrial field is so controlled that new entries, new comers, new adventurers, and independent men are feared."

Taft was vulnerable for his support of the Payne-Aldrich tariff, now widely viewed as unfairly providing an advantage for special business interests. Roosevelt was painted as the president who did nothing to stop the spread of powerful business trusts that harmed the working man. In a speech in Portland, Maine, Marshall said

> *Does anyone doubt that for seven and one-half years the leader of the Progressive Party was in power in this country? Can any one put his finger upon a single effort made by him to curb the monopolistic tendency that was then rampant? Does any one believe that his new platform, which stands both for socialism and for a system of licensing and curbing, is anything more than a bid for votes?*[170]

By this point in the election it was clear that Taft would run a distant third, and that Wilson's challenger was Roosevelt. Later that week, during his same campaign trip through Maine, Marshall again criticized Roosevelt's record on the regulation of trusts:

> *When he began his career as a trust buster there were only 149 trusts, with four billions in capital. At the end of his career there were more than ten thousand with more than thirty-one billions of capital.*[171]

While Maine had voted for Taft in 1908, Democrats believed they could win back support to their side, and after his trip Marshall reported to Wilson:

> *I thank you very much for your letter of August 22nd that I find*
> *upon my return from Maine. I am told by those who heard me*
> *that I talked like Wilson and this is the greatest compliment that*
> *can be paid me ... Things are in great shape in Maine and if*
> *our vote is gotten out we are sure to win.*[172]

Marshall also helped outline the campaign issues in an article that appeared in Harper's Weekly. The "protective tariff is the source of much of the evil of our present state", he said. He supported the regulation of big business, but felt the term "regulation" was a "condemning" adjective and chose to use other language for governmental oversight of the trusts. He returned to his vision for a new America, saying that "the new spirit" of "fairness" and "brotherliness" should guide the country.[173]

As the campaign progressed, the country was given a clearer picture of the Governor of Indiana. It was a rare reporter who did not quickly warm to Marshall's wit, sincerity and genuine affection for all he met. For newspaper readers who craved the energy and enthusiasm of Theodore Roosevelt, or the learned scholarship of Wilson, Marshall offered little. But compared to the bland personality of figures such as Taft or the excesses of some of the Eastern families such as the Vanderbilts or Rockefellers, the Vice Presidential candidate offered a breath of fresh air.

> *If governor Marshall should become Vice President, the*
> *newspaper and magazine men would have difficulty in finding*
> *anything very spectacular about him. The Governor is not*
> *athletic in build. He is about 5 feet 8 inches tall, and weighs*
> *about 140 pounds. He is well groomed. He does not ride; he*
> *does not shoot; he does not play golf or any other athletic games;*
> *he does not know how to row a boat. But he does like 'a good*
> *game of baseball' and he can tell you a good deal about 'the*
> *team'. He gets his main enjoyment out of reading and the field*
> *of his reading is wide. After he has had a long grind of duties*
> *in the Governor's office, he reads light books – detecting stories*
> *and thrilling adventures – books which Dr. Woodrow Wilson*
> *would undoubtedly condemn as very trashy.*[174]

Marshall's politics were viewed as progressive, since during his term as Governor the State of Indiana had adopted a resolution favoring the direct election of United States Senators, reformed the corrupt practices laws including the creation of the State Board of Accounts, strengthened employer liability laws, and required more public disclosure of campaign contributions.

But Marshall's progressive positions had their limits. He was opposed to the initiative and referendum and to the recall of elected officials. Marshall's views on immigration, as well, could hardly be considered progressive. The Marshall Constitution limited voting rights for new immigrants.

In San Francisco, Marshall addressed immigration in one of his campaign speeches. Clearly an issue of importance in this part of the country, he stated "I am unalterably opposed to the granting of citizenship to any race of aliens which by habit and by nature is absolutely unfitted to amalgamate with the American people."[175]

While Marshall was asked to respond to a wide variety of questions during the campaign, none was more prescient than a letter he wrote to a man from Baltimore. Noting that the most important role of the Vice President was to assume the Presidency if necessary, Marshall responded with a letter that would presage the situation he would face in a little more than seven years:

> *The thought suggested in your letter that Governor Wilson may die during his incumbency in office is too frightful for me to contemplate. This thought involves a calamity to the nation. I believe that Governor Wilson will be elected and that he will live to carry out the democratic platform and to advise the Congress of the United States from time to time as the constitution authorizes him to do. If, unfortunately, I should succeed him, my conduct in the office of president would be the same as in the Governor's office, where I have always held that the legislative branch is the supreme law-making brand of our government; that the executive branch has no right to interfere with, intimidate, or coerce the legislative branch; that the duty of the executive is to enforce the law and that it is also his duty to sign all bills which are clearly not unconstitutional and not vicious in their character. I have protested for four years against*

> *the usurpation of authority by executives and I shall continue*
> *to protest.*[176]

During the presidential campaign, the issue of Wilson's relationship to Mary Peck again surfaced. Her divorce had become final the previous December – an event that the *New York Times* considered important enough to put on their front page. During the divorce proceedings, some of Woodrow's more intimate letters to Mary were presented in court.

A political advisor to Theodore Roosevelt obtained the contents of the letters, and urged Roosevelt to go public with the information.

Despite their obvious veracity and the significant impact the disclosure would have on the election, Teddy declined to use the information. He opposed their use on more than just moral grounds. "It won't work," Roosevelt is said to have retorted, "You can't cast a man as a Romeo who looks and acts so much like an apothecary's clerk."

Marshall was genuinely concerned about the influence of campaign contributions on political discourse. During his gubernatorial campaign he used only his own – or borrowed – funds, and he refused train rides provided by business interests. He brought the same philosophy to his vice presidential campaign.

Late in the campaign, Marshall was asked to visit the western states during the campaign, and the train transportation would be provided by party supporters. He asked his personal secretary, Mark Thistlethwaite, to make his position clear to Wilson's campaign manager, Albert Burleson:

> *It seems to me that there is an undue effort being made to force the Governor to consent to do things contrary to his conscience and his judgment. He positively will not accept money for his political activities. He will not travel on special trains not knowing who is financing the trains and unwilling to accept favors even though he knows the granters of them. The Governor has driven his stake on this proposition and I regret the influence that arises now and then to dissuade him from this purpose. It will be well for your committee to know that during his Western trip to be started tomorrow, that he will not travel on special trains or ride in private cars. He is perfectly willing to pay all of*

his own expenses and those of Mrs. Marshall ... The Governor is
absolutely in earnest in insisting that the use of money in politics
is the bane of our system of government and is determined that
no one shall pay his expenses thereby absolutely eliminating any
possibility of an investigation such as now being conducted in
the City of Washington.[177]

Theodore Roosevelt and his advisors felt that the Progressive Party could carry the state of Wisconsin. Teddy had won Wisconsin with more than two-thirds of the vote in 1904, and the State had voted Democratic only once in the previous nine presidential elections.

But Wisconsin politics was dominated by Robert Lafollette. Lafollette was elected to the House of Representatives in 1884 and served three terms; later, he served as governor from 1900 to 1906. Lafollette was a Republican but fiercely maintained his political independence. Known for his support for progressive reforms and his fiery oratory, he was proud of the nickname "Fighting Bob".

Lafollette created the National Progressive Republican League, hoping to use it as a vehicle to gain the nomination of the Republican Party in 1912. He also had hoped that Roosevelt would support his candidacy.

But Roosevelt wavered in his support for Lafollette. He reasoned – probably correctly – that Lafollette didn't have the support to unseat an incumbent president. As Roosevelt delayed in providing a public statement of support, Lafollette went on a lengthy and physically demanding speaking tour. Near exhaustion – and worried by the news that his daughter would require a serious operation – Lafollette shrugged aside the advice of doctors and appeared before an audience of magazine publishers in Philadelphia.

The decision was a mistake. Lafollette made a rambling two-and-a-half hour speech, repeating whole passages and stumbling over words. Worse, he accused the publishers of abandoning working families in support of business interests. Publishers began walking out of the room, and were harangued by Lafollette as they left.

Within two weeks, a group of Republican governors wrote Roosevelt, asking him to run, in part, to derail Lafollette's ambitions. After Taft was nominated, Lafollette had hoped for the Progressive Party nomination. When

Roosevelt got the nod instead, Lafollette actively campaigned against the former president.

Roosevelt traveled to Milwaukee on October 14 to give a speech before several thousand supporters. That evening, Colonel Roosevelt met some his advisors at a local hotel for dinner. He left the hotel and walked to a waiting car along with Henry Cochems, an official with the Progressive Party, and Albert Martin, Roosevelt's stenographer. A crowd had gathered, and as he entered the car a cheer was raised. Roosevelt turned and waved his hat.

John Schrank, a New York saloonkeeper, stepped from the crowd and aimed his .38 caliber pistol at Roosevelt's head. A bystander saw the gun and deflected Schrank's arm just as he pulled the trigger. There was a brief moment of disbelief and relative quiet before Cochems, a former athlete, and Martin, six feet tall and a football player, grabbed Schrank, wrestled him to the ground and disarmed him. "Don't hurt him," Roosevelt said, "Bring him to me."

Cochems and Martin brought Schrank to the car. "Why did you do it?" Roosevelt asked. "What was your reason?" By this time, the crowd was calling for Schrank to be lynched. Roosevelt quieted the crowd, and turned Schrank over to the police.

Attention then turned to Roosevelt. Not knowing if he was hit, Roosevelt put his hand beneath his coat, and when he pulled it out it was covered in blood. "It looks like I have been hit, but I don't think it is anything serious". A doctor insisted that he be driven to a hospital, but Roosevelt refused. "You get me to the speech. It may be the last one I deliver, but I am going to deliver this one."

When Roosevelt arrived at the auditorium, several doctors examined the wound. Roosevelt had prepared a fifty-page speech, which had been folded in half in his breast pocket. The bullet was slowed as it traveled through his speech. The wound was bandaged, and doctors again urged Roosevelt to go to a hospital. "I will deliver this speech or die, one or the other," was his reply.

Cochems stepped to the stage to introduce the speaker. "In presenting Colonel Roosevelt ... you should know that ... as we were leaving the hotel a few minutes ago a dastardly hand raised a revolver and fired a shot at him, and the Colonel speaks as a soldier with a bullet in his breast – where we don't know." The crowd hushed as the news filtered among the supporters. The man who had led his troops up through enemy fire shuffled slowly to the podium.

"Friends," Roosevelt began, "I shall have to ask you to be as quiet as possible. I do not know whether you fully understand that I have just been shot. But it takes more than that to kill a Bull Moose." Roosevelt spoke for nearly an hour.

After the speech, Roosevelt was taken to a Milwaukee hospital, where he was examined by six surgeons who had been waiting for him. X-rays showed that the bullet had Lodged next to his fifth rib, less than an inch from his heart. Roosevelt was then taken to a hospital in Chicago, where doctors gave him a tetanus shot. The decision was made to leave the bullet where it was.

Taft was genuinely shaken by the news of the assassination attempt. He wrote Roosevelt "I earnestly hope and pray that your recovery may be speedy and without suffering." Taft also announced that he would cease campaigning until Roosevelt recovered.

Wilson also sent expressions of sympathy, and Colonel House urged him to halt his campaign until Roosevelt had recuperated. Somewhat reluctantly, Wilson kept only a few previously arranged speaking engagements, but otherwise stopped his campaign.

As could be expected, though, Roosevelt was not sidelined for long, and announced that he would resume his speaking engagements on October 30. While that meant that only a few days would remain until election day, Roosevelt and his advisors felt the assassination attempt would garner enough sympathy votes to bring him a victory.

As the campaign of 1912 progress, Vice President Sherman suffered a serious illness that limited his campaigning. He had been diagnosed with Bright's disease, a serious kidney ailment. Sherman was able to give his acceptance speech at the Republican convention, but soon thereafter he became bedridden and was unable to campaign for his ticket. On October 30, 1912, Sherman died at the age of fifty-seven.

No candidate on the national ticket had died so close to the election. Taft considered naming a progressive to the ticket to stem the shift of voters to Roosevelt, but was persuaded otherwise. With only a few days before voters went to the polls, the move might be considered an act of desperation from a candidate on the verge of being badly beaten. "You have the worst luck," Mrs. Taft is said to have commented to her husband.[178]

Throughout the campaign, Wilson focused his efforts on Roosevelt, sensing correctly that Taft would run a distant third. Roosevelt had called for a "New Nationalism"; Wilson, focused more on the rights of individuals, labeled his vision the "New Freedom".

When the results were tabulated, Wilson and Marshall won a plurality of the votes and a majority in the electoral college. The Democrats garnered 6.3 million votes, with Roosevelt collecting 4.1 million and just 3.5 million for Taft. In the electoral college, Wilson received 435 votes against 88 for Roosevelt and just 8 for the incumbent president.

Following the 1912 presidential election, William Howard Taft was asked to comment on his third place finish. "Well, I have one consolation," Taft declared. "No candidate was ever elected ex-president by such a large majority."

The nation had spoken, and they wanted change. That five out of every seven voters cast their ballots against the status quo sent a strong message to Wilson, Marshall and others that the electorate was ready for a change. In addition, for the first time since the Civil War Democrats had control of both the Senate and the House of Representatives. Democrats held fifty-one seats in the Senate versus forty-four for the Republicans (with the Progressives holding one seat). In the House, Democrats controlled 191 seats to 127 Republicans and fourteen Progressives.

Marshall and Wilson exchanged telegrams after the victory. "I SALUTE YOU MY CHIEFTAIN IN ALL LOVE AND LOYALTY", cabled Marshall.

Wilson's staff drafted a telegram to send to Marshall. The first draft of the telegram had stated "your part in the campaign was exceedingly effective". Wilson deleted the phrase "exceedingly effective", and the telegram he eventually sent read

WARMEST THANKS FOR YOUR GENEROUS TELEGRAM. YOUR PART IN THE CAMPAIGN WAS A SOURCE OF GREAT STRENGTH AND STIMULATION. NOW FOR THE DEEP PLEASURE OF CLOSE ASSOCIATION IN A GREAT WORK OF NATIONAL SERVICE.[179]

Lois Marshall was extremely pleased. She clearly longed more than her husband did for the Washington social life. Their age difference probably played a factor; Marshall was 58 when elected vice president, while Lois was nearly twenty years his junior. She was disappointed when Thomas had passed up the chance to serve in Congress; now she would finally see Washington.

> *I've always wanted to go to Washington. I used to wish Mr. Marshall would accept the nomination for congress – you know he could have had it. And then I thought he might someday be a senator. I thought I should love the life in Washington. But when he was elected governor and we came to Indianapolis, I knew that was out of the question. And I gave up all thought of Washington. I never dreamed of this ...*[180]

In late December, 1912, Marshall was a guest at the annual dinner of the Phi Gamma Delta fraternity in Indianapolis, termed an ecclesia. Marshall had belonged to the fraternity while at Wabash. Among the fraternity brothers present were Charles Fairbanks, the former Vice President, and the mayor of Cleveland, Newton Baker. While Fairbanks and Marshall had represented opposing parties, their relationship was cordial.

Charles Warren Fairbanks was born on May 11, 1852 on a farm in Ohio. His father's farm and other business interests were successful, and they sent Charles to college at Ohio Wesleyan, and then on to law school at Cleveland Law College. Soon after graduation, he and his wife moved to Indianapolis, where Charles took a position as attorney with the Chesapeake and Ohio railroad system.

The new position proved lucrative and, as his wealth grew, Charles took an active interest in Republican politics. He failed to support Benjamin Harrison in his 1884 Presidential bid, but when discontent grew over Harrison's performance in office Fairbanks was viewed more favorably by other party members. Charles used his wealth to support Republican candidates across the State, and his power and influence grew. In addition, Fairbanks secretly owned the state's largest newspaper, The Indianapolis News, and in 1901, he had also purchased the major opposition newspaper, The Indianapolis Journal. He used both publications to promote his own political career, as well at that of other favored Republican candidates.

Fairbanks had tried unsuccessfully to win a U.S. Senate seat in 1893, but when an opening became available in 1896 he was the clear choice. Six years later, in 1902, he was elected to a second term.

Though his speaking style was lackluster, the tall (at six feet, four inches) and handsome Fairbanks looked like presidential material and his eyes soon turned to the highest office in the land. He performed admirably in his role as Senator, and gained prominence in a number of highly visible positions. When he helped mediate the discussions that determined the U.S.-Canadian boundary in Alaska, leaders of that State were so impressed that they named the city of Fairbanks in his honor.

Fairbanks had become close friends with William McKinley, and had positioned himself to succeed him in the presidency. But McKinley's assassination in 1901 derailed his plans, and the new President, Theodore Roosevelt, was not close to Fairbanks. While Fairbanks represented the conservative wing of the Republican party, Roosevelt carried the banner for the liberals and progressives. Despite Fairbanks' seniority, Roosevelt relied more on the advice of Indiana's junior Senator, Albert Beveridge, whose political viewpoint was closer to Roosevelt's.

Albert Jeremiah Beveridge graduated from Indiana Asbury University (now known as DePauw University) in 1885. Perhaps one of the most intelligent and best-educated politicians in Indiana history, Beveridge was an accomplished historian but was better know as a dynamic orator, delivering speeches which advocated for territorial expansion by the United States and an increase in the power of the federal government. He was elected to the U.S. Senate in 1899, and quickly gained a reputation as a strong advocate for American imperialism. But as the Progressive movement began to gain in strength Beveridge broke with the conservative faction of the Republican party and championed national child labor legislation and stronger regulations over meat packers. He would eventually join Theodore Roosevelt in the Progressive Party, which advocated political views closer to his own but meant that, after he left the Senate in 1910, he would no longer find electoral success. He lost in his attempts as the Progressive nominee for governor in 1912 and United States senator in 1914. Beveridge would turn his energies towards his writing, and *The Life of John Marshall*, published from 1916 to 1919, won him a Pulitzer Prize.

But Republican leaders were looking for an opportunity to balance the ticket in 1904, and they turned to Fairbanks as the Vice Presidential candidate. Not only did Roosevelt and Fairbanks represent both the liberal and conservative wings of the party, they also provided a crucial Indiana connection to the President's New York roots.

Fairbanks proved to be a good campaigner, but after the election he played only a minor role in the second Roosevelt administration. In this, Roosevelt was ignoring his own advice, as he had once written an article which argued that the Vice President should be an active policy participant, attending cabinet meetings and even giving the Vice President a regular vote in the Senate.[181] Like Marshall in a later administration, President Roosevelt seldom included Fairbanks in policy discussions.

Instead, Fairbanks played only a minor role in the passing of legislation. While he was viewed as a fair and attentive presiding officer of the Senate, he never had the chance to break a tie vote.

Fairbanks made a brief attempt to seek the Republican nomination for the election of 1908, but Roosevelt's support of William Howard Taft forced him to drop his bid. He returned to Indianapolis and would have been content to maintain his quiet life there until one more opportunity would present itself.

"The first ecclesia I attended was in 1872," Fairbanks said during the dinner, "here in Indianapolis, and it was here that I first met Tom Marshall, now at my left, then an undergraduate at Wabash. I've always thought a lot of him. If Tom would only change his politics he would be perfection ...".

Marshall returned the cordial greeting, and addressed the limited responsibility of the vice presidency. Speaking to both the young college students and the older alumni, he told the story of a man who had two sons. One son chose the path of seamanship, the other politics. The first son was tragically drowned; the other was elected Vice President. "The poor father died of a broken heart – he never heard of either one thereafter."

In his remarks, Marshall lauded his State and Phi Gamma Delta. He reiterated his bonds with his fraternity brothers, and then turned to the former vice president. "I thank God, Fairbanks, for one thing, and that is that you weren't running against me!"[182]

Marshall may have been thankful that he did not face his fraternity brother in the election of 1912, but he would not be able to say the same in the next presidential race.

CHAPTER SIX:

All the Wise Men in the Land

(1913-1914)

Washington, DC, in ways more pronounced than any other part of the country, views the inaugural of a new president with eagerness, with a sense of excitement and, in some respects, with nervous trepidation. Though the nation's capital is filled with many more ambitious and aggressive office-seekers and office-holders today than in 1913, no observer could doubt the enormous potential for change that Woodrow Wilson brought to office.

Politically, Democrats were in the position of inaugurating one of their own for only the third time in a generation, as the other two Democratic presidential inaugurations had seated the same man – Grover Cleveland, in 1884 and 1892. They knew that part of the power of the presidential office is in the patronage that rewards party leaders and poll workers, and energizes them to continue their partisan support.

But informed scholars also knew that Wilson had gained power without receiving the support of a majority of the electorate. His popular vote gave Wilson the lowest percentage of support since Lincoln had won in the divisive vote in 1860.

If Wilson's first term were to be a success, he knew he would need to inspire not only his supporters but also to persuade moderates from both the Republican and Progressive parties. Progressives – who were mainly former Republicans - felt so strongly about the need for reform that they were willing to tear their party apart in their quest for the passage of their agenda: direct election of U.S. Senators, the creation of an initiative, referendum, and recall process, woman suffrage, a national tariff reduction, child labor laws, old-age pensions, and other social reforms. Wilson had the chance to bind disenchanted Republicans with his base of Democratic support. At least during his first term, Wilson's academic training and background gave him the tools he needed to enact some of the most sweeping policy changes in American history.

Wilson wanted to send the message that his administration would be different from the many Republican presidents who preceded him, and he started with the inauguration ceremony. To the dismay of Washington socialites, Wilson cancelled the inaugural ball, wishing to focus public attention instead on substantive policy questions. "This is not a day of triumph; it is a day of dedication," Wilson told the assembled crowd on March 4, 1913. Members of Congress, Justices of the Supreme Court, and visiting dignitaries from numerous foreign countries listened as Wilson set the stage for what would be an extraordinary period of political change for the country.

> *Men's hopes call upon us to weigh what we will do. Who shall live up to the great trust? Who dares fail to try? I summon all honest men, all patriotic, all forward-looking men, to my side. God helping me, I will not fail them, if they will but counsel and sustain me!*[183]

Upon being sworn into office, the new President and departing President Taft settled into the Senate chamber for the presentation of the new Vice President. After being announced by the Sergeant-at-Arms, Thomas Riley Marshall, accompanied by two Senators, walked to the front of the chamber and took his seat.

Normally, the outgoing Vice President, as presiding officer of the Senate, performs the oath of office to the incoming Vice President. But Taft's Vice President, James Sherman, had died six days before the election, on October 30, 1912, so the oath was administered by Senator Jacob Gallinger of New Hampshire, who was president pro tempore of the Senate. In his first duty as Vice President, Marshall opened the session.

> *The Senate will be in order. Let us reverently attend while the chaplain invokes the blessing of our God and Father upon us.*[184]

After the inauguration, Marshall's speech was a mixture of vision and humor. He said he wanted to take the opportunity to give his views before he "enters upon a four years' silence." He also asked for "peace with all peoples, justice for all Governments, and righteousness the world around." The *New York Times* was pleased by what it heard.

> *There was something very refreshing in the spectacle of the Vice President on the eve of "four years of silence" addressing the Senate as Mr. Marshall did on Tuesday. The form of address was novel and naïve; there were metaphors verging on the grotesque, and there were touches of sentiment on the one hand and whimsical, almost boyish, humor on the other that must have tickled the jaded ears of the older Senators and suggested ventures of their own to new ones...*[185]

The day after the inaugural ceremonies, Marshall greeted well wishers in his new offices. By today's standards, security surrounding key public officials was remarkably light in 1913. Aside from limited access to the White House, most Washington offices were open to visitors of nearly every ilk. This ambivalence seems misplaced even today, as in the two decades prior to the time Marshall became Vice President six heads of state had been assassinated. They were President Carnot of France in 1894, Premier Canovas of Spain in 1897, Empress Elizabeth of Austria in 1898, King Humbert of Italy in 1900, President McKinley of the United States in 1901, and Premier Canalejas of Spain in 1912.[186] The attack on Roosevelt in 1912 was a reminder to Marshall that an armed lunatic could change the course of history. That lesson would soon be relearned.

Tom and Lois showed the same courtesy and friendliness in Washington that made them so popular in Indiana. A classmate at Wabash College tells the following story of a Hoosier who came to Washington for the inauguration.

> *While he was governor of Indiana he was accustomed to ride to and from his home on the street cars. It happened that I lived in the same neighborhood and frequently used the same line and became pretty well acquainted with one of the conductors who was a great admirer of Marshall. When Marshall became*

vice president, this conductor, who had been his loyal support, went to Washington to the inauguration. Shortly afterward, in riding on his car he gave me a very enthusiastic report of his trip to the capital city. He regarded it as the great event of his life. He said that while in Washington he met Marshall who saluted him with "hello, Charlie, are you here too?" Using the street conductors own words, he said, "he seemed just as glad to see me as if I were somebody and treated me just as he used to when he rode in my car. And what do you think, he insisted on my coming around to the hotel where he and Mrs. Marshall were staying. I was very badly scared but I went because he seemed to want me to. And then I went to the big hotel where they were they treated me just the same as they did back in Indianapolis. Just think of it! He is a great man and vice president of the United States and I just Charlie, the street car conductor, and he treated me as though I were his equal".[187]

The Vice President's office is in the Capitol Building, adjacent to the Senate chamber. The close proximity is necessary due to the Vice President's responsibility as the presiding officer of the Senate. Marshall, like his predecessors before him, would need to remain close to the floor of the Senate whenever they were in session. Marshall was surprised by the small size of his office, and by how open it was to visitors. "I don't see that this room differs much from a monkey cage, except that the visitors do not offer me peanuts."[188]

In a town used to the banality of William Howard Taft and the stuffiness of many of the political elite, Marshall quickly earned a reputation for his unassuming manner, pleasant personality and dry humor. Reporters were delighted when he told them that he came to Washington "with the feeling that the American people might have made a mistake in setting me down in the company of all the wise men in the land." The new Vice President, they soon learned, would make great copy for newspaper stories.

Tom and Lois also found that they were invited everywhere to social functions in Washington. They jumped enthusiastically into the social scene of the nation's capital, and Washingtonians were quickly enamored by the self-effacing Vice President and his charming wife. Commenting on their reception in Washington, Marshall wrote

> *I have an idea that what success I had in getting along in the social life of Washington was due to the fact that heaven had given me a nimble tongue; that I could phrase a compliment and tell a story out of the book of my life, which had not then been read by the people of the city.*
>
> *Whether it was real regard – and that I am pleased to believe it to have been – or whether it was mere courtesy, at no time was I ever the recipient of a frowning face, never did I have a cold shoulder turned to me, nor the slightest suggestion that Hoosier manners did not appeal to that which was best and cultured in the social life of the city.*[189]

Marshall reveled in cutting through pomposity and the trappings of social status. Though he shared a surname with the former Chief Justice John Marshall, he was not related, though this did not prevent him from using the connection as an opportunity for a humorous quip. A Senator from Texas and his wife asked if the Vice President was related to former Chief Justice John Marshall. "Yes," Thomas replied, "but my family moved west in 1819, and I guess it's about rubbed off."[190]

Reporters at the time described Marshall as a slight, bespectacled man, with his hat pushed back on his head, a pipe or cigar always ready in his hand. "He is calm and serene and small; mild, quiet, simple and old-fashioned," as one writer described him. "His hair is gray and so is his mustache. His clothes are gray and so is his tie. He has a cigar tucked beneath the mustache and his gray fedora hat shades his gray eyes."[191]

As President Wilson prepared to assume leadership of the nation's government, he frequently looked to Marshall for levity. Marshall did not disappoint. Soon after they took office, Marshall was given a Korean language newspaper that, he was told, provided a verbatim account of the inaugural speeches given by Wilson and Marshall. He sent it to Wilson with a note attached.

I enclose you a Koran paper containing your inaugural and my talk. I find mine correct. If you are not satisfied address the Editor.

Keeping up the jest, Wilson wrote back:

Thank you very much for giving me an opportunity to see how my inaugural looks in Korean: I note one or two typographical errors, but as long as the paper has been circulated, I do not believe I shall go to the trouble of asking the editor to make the corrections.[192]

But while Wilson turned to Marshall for humor, he relied on his Vice President for little else. From the time when Wilson agreed to allow Marshall to balance his presidential ticket in 1912 until the last days of his second term, Wilson kept Marshall at arms length, far from the inner policy circles of the White House. Marshall would occasionally be called upon to deliver a message, break a tie vote or campaign for a key Democrat, but over the next eight years he was kept informed of important matters only when he asked. He seldom asked.

Why was Marshall so far removed from the policy planning and discussions? Part of it was Marshall's own preference. Though he had been chief executive of a state larger than New Jersey (Indiana's population was 2.7 million versus 2.5 million for New Jersey), Thomas knew his own limitations. His training and experience gave him minimal background in banking regulation, tax laws, and foreign policy – topics that would dominate the nation's attention.

Marshall regretted that he did not take advantage of opportunities to gain a better understanding of foreign policy. He wrote in his *Recollections* of passing up, in 1873, the opportunity to work with a respected Wabash College professor at the Centennial Exposition in Philadelphia in 1876. He chose, instead, to begin his law career.

Looking back upon it, I made a great mistake. As his private secretary I could have obtained such a knowledge of world conditions as never came to me until I passed through the experiences of the World War.[193]

Yet while few would look to Marshall for advice on international relations, Wilson himself had only a limited knowledge of foreign policy. Until the Spanish-American war and the annexation of the Philippines, the federal government had little involvement with foreign countries. Wilson's academic background was in U.S. history and government. Wilson spoke no foreign language, and rarely traveled to foreign countries. "It would be the irony of fate", Wilson told a friend soon after he was elected President, "If my administration had to deal chiefly with foreign affairs."[194]

His self-deprecating humor didn't help his stature in policy-making circles. While popular at dinner parties and often quoted in casual conversation, Marshall played a role much more akin to a court jester than a trusted policy advisor. In the climate of enthusiasm and optimism of 1913 Marshall's humor helped to fuel a spirit of cooperation and cordial bipartisanship. Four years later, the carnage in Europe would make his humor seem grotesquely out of place. Colonel Edward House believed that Marshall's wit diminished his standing as a serious statesman and made him appear to be a buffoon. "An unfriendly fairy godmother presented him with a keen sense of humor," House commented. "Nothing is more fatal in politics."

Part of Marshall's exclusion from serious policy discussions must certainly be traced to his non-Eastern academic background. Wilson's experience with serious scholarly research and as head of an Ivy-League institution contrasted sharply with Marshall's career at Wabash.

Wabash College in the late 19th century was without question one of the finest institutions of higher education in the Midwest and Marshall received an education that placed him among the nation's intellectual elite. Furthermore, he knew his history and the classics well enough to intersperse his speeches with historical references and quotations that combined his strong intellect with a folksy speaking style that was very effective with most audiences.

But in 1912, as somewhat today, Eastern schools, particularly those in the Ivy League, considered Midwestern colleges as second-rate, or worse. Marshall's Wabash connection meant a great deal in Indianapolis; it meant much less in Washington.

Marshall seemed unconcerned with his reputation as a simple Midwesterner. While he made no apologies for his Hoosier roots, he respected and admired the many leaders he met in Washington. He also understood the limits of the Vice Presidency.

*Since the days of John Adams there has been a dread and fear
that some Vice President of the United States would break loose
and raise hell and Maria with the administration. Everything
that can be done, therefore, is done to furnish him with some
innocuous occupation. They seek to put him were he can do no
harm. Among the other nameless, unremembered things given
him to do is the making of him a regent of the Smithsonian
Institution. There, if anywhere, he has an opportunity to compare
his fossilized life with the fossils of all ages. The other regents are
usually men of affairs. I found, among others, when I attended
the first meeting, Chief Justice White, Alexander Graham Bell,
Justice George Gray, Senator Henry Cabot Lodge, and others
of like caliber.*

Marshall's humor, at times, was viewed as a bit too lowbrow by some of
the more stuffy American aristocracy. This led to one of the rare times when
Marshall's humor fell flat:

*The agenda was taken up and I maintained a modest silence until
an appropriation of money for an expedition to Guatemala was
up for consideration. Now, the mere mention of money arouses
my interest, particularly when it runs into thousands of dollars.
I am not used to computing it in such large denominations. So I
ventured to inquire for what it was proposed that the expedition
should spend these thousands of dollars. I was informed that it
was to excavate among the ruins of that country in the hope of
finding some trace of prehistoric man. With the breezy manner
of a breezy state I ventured to inquire whether they had dug
into Washington yet. A look of amazement came over the
countenances of all these distinguished gentlemen, and somebody
asked me what I meant. The reply was that from some of the
specimens walking the streets I thought they would not need to
go more than six feet down to discover the prehistoric man. And
then the utter uselessness and frivolity of the vice-presidency was
disclosed, for not a man smiled. It was a year before I had the
courage to open my mouth again.*[195]

Marshall's triumph over alcoholism cannot be ignored as a factor in his policymaking exile. Wilson and his advisors had to know that Marshall was a recovering alcoholic. This alone did not cause the leaders in the Wilson administration to fail to take Marshall seriously. But with Wilson's background as the son of a Presbyterian minister and a southern gentleman, Marshall was accepted but not embraced. The Vice President could be good company at social functions, but when the talk became serious Marshall was viewed not as a source for good ideas but as a former drunk.

Marshall's recovery from alcoholism led to his estrangement in another way. Having faced the depths of despair on those cold, lonely mornings in Columbia City, living with his mother, and with only the memories of Kate and a freshly-poured whiskey to keep him company, Marshall faced his own inner demons and could not have liked what he saw. But he had the courage and fortitude to hang on until a savior named Lois gave him the love he craved and the resolution to change the course of his life. The conquest of his alcoholism gave Marshall a different perspective on his world. He filtered the meaningful from the meaningless. His God reigned supreme; his wife, close thereafter. He valued good friends, honest leaders and hard-working families.

Marshall developed little patience for the social snobbery and caste-consciousness of Washington. He loved to tweak the noses of the upper class. He had a genuine admiration for wealth borne from hard work, but contempt for riches protected by political favoritism. He respected royalty, but felt no need to stifle his penchant for sarcastic remarks or homespun humor even in the company of kings. Observant and insightful leaders like Eleanor Roosevelt would come to respect Marshall's genuineness and lack of airs; the superficial and intellectually insecure, like Edith Wilson, would react to Marshall with disdain. Had Wilson's second wife been more like Eleanor than Edith, Wilson's second term may have had more elements of triumph than tragedy, and Marshall might have changed the course of history.

Whatever the reason, the newly elected Vice President was rarely briefed about Wilson's policy agenda. When Marshall did speak out on current issues, his lack of communication with the President's advisors sometimes resulted in awkward moments. Soon after the election, while being interviewed in Indianapolis prior to moving to Washington, Marshall stated that he felt there was no need for anti-trust legislation in the near future, in view of the fact that tariff and currency legislation had recently been passed. Almost simultaneously, however, Wilson was briefing reporters on anti-trust legislation he was planning on submitting to Congress. The blunder was an awkward way to start his vice presidential career, but would mark the start of a series of miscues that would strain the relationship between Marshall and Wilson's closest advisors.

✄ ✄ ✄ ✄ ✄

Almost immediately upon taking office, Wilson faced a crisis south of the border. Francisco Madero was born into one of the wealthiest families in Mexico. Their far-flung family business included holdings in banks, mines and the production of alcohol. His family's riches meant that Francisco would be educated at only the best of schools – in Baltimore, then Paris, and finally at the University of California at Berkeley.

Despite his wealth, Madero developed both a disciplined lifestyle and an intense hatred of injustice. Though his family's business manufactured wine and hard liquor, he didn't drink. Small in stature (he was only five-foot-two), his compassion and intelligence, combined with his love for his country, soon led him to positions of leadership.

Madero was appalled by the brutal and high-handed behavior of Mexico's President, Porfinio Diaz. Ruthless and authoritarian and wanting to extend his control of the political structure, Diaz had enacted laws that increased the length of the Presidential term. In response, Madero had published a book that criticized the new presidential succession law and called for honest elections.

The book touched a nerve throughout the country, as Mexicans formed clubs and political parties devoted to opposition to Diaz's reelection. It was natural that the movement would promote Madero as a presidential candidate. Hoping to silence his rival, Diaz had Madero arrested in June of 1910, and that October the Chamber of Deputies officially declared that Diaz had been reelected as Mexico's president.

Madero managed to be bailed out of jail by his family's wealth and connections, and on November 20 he fled Mexico for the United States – a date that is still commemorated across the country as the Day of the Revolution. Madero did not lead the final battles of the revolution that led to the downfall of Diaz – others like Pancho Villa and Emiliano Zapata can take credit for that – but in October of 1911 Francisco Madero was elected President of Mexico by a wide margin.

Madero's triumphant rise to power was soon clouded by further intrigues. One of the leaders of the revolution resented the new Mexican President and mounted a counterrevolution. With the help of General Victoriano Huerta, Madero successfully defeated the counterrevolutionaries.

But Huerta secretly wanted to take Madero's place as the leader of Mexico, and he found an ally in the American ambassador, Henry Lane Wilson. Ambassador Wilson preferred a Mexican dictatorship to keep the peasants in line and protect corporate interests in mining and oil drilling. He conspired with Huerta to undermine the Madero regime, and sent inaccurate reports back to Washington which he hoped would lead to Madero's demise. Madero learned of Ambassador Wilson's complicity, and expressed the hope that the newly elected President of the United States, Woodrow Wilson (no relation to Henry Lane Wilson) would recall the Mexican ambassador.

But Madero would not survive until President Wilson was inaugurated in March 1913. Mexican rebels, who were secretly allied with Huerta, began a series of violent confrontations in Mexico City. When the leader of the loyalist military was wounded, Madero, unaware of Huerta's ambitions, appointed Huerta to take his place. Once in power, Huerta placed Madero under arrest.

Ambassador Wilson not only knew of Huerta's duplicity, he helped to ensure that Madero could not return to power. After seizing Madero, Huerta asked Ambassador Wilson what he should do with the former Mexican president. Huerta had considered sending Madero into exile, but Wilson's response made it clear that the country might be better off if Madero was no longer able to resume power.

On February 22, while being transferred to prison, Madero was shot by his guards. Huerta released a fabricated story that Madero was accidentally killed when a group of his supporters tried to rescue him. Ambassador Wilson, to lend credence to the ruse, issued a statement that supported Huerta's story. That evening, Wilson invited Huerta to a reception at the American embassy, where the two conspirators celebrated their good fortune.

After President Wilson assumed the presidency in March, he and his new Secretary of State, William Jennings Bryan, made it clear that they would soon be replacing the Mexican Ambassador. But news stories appeared which

He Almost Changed the World | 165

indicated that Woodrow Wilson was being pressured to retain Ambassador Wilson from an unlikely source – the new Vice President, Thomas Marshall.

The Washington *Times* reported that Marshall had interceded on Henry Lane Wilson's behalf with the new President. Marshall and Ambassador Wilson were known to be friends – both had graduated from Wabash College, and Henry Wilson's brother, John L. Wilson, was in Marshall's graduating class.

Marshall denied that he had made any attempt to influence the newly elected President's decision regarding Ambassador Wilson. In response to a *New York Times* reporter, Marshall released a statement refuting the story:

> *There is no earthly basis for the statement published beyond the bare suspicion that because Ambassador Wilson and I were graduated from Wabash College, and his brother, John L. Wilson, was a classmate of mine, I would attempt to interfere on his behalf. Personally the relations between Ambassador Wilson and myself are cordial, but the handling of the Mexican situation is the business of the Administration, and not my private and social business.*[196]

There is no evidence that Marshall tried to convince President Wilson to retain the Mexican ambassador. Later that March, Marshall had written a letter to the President in which he stated that "certain suggestions have come to me which, if you care to hear, I will be glad to convey at your convenience." The President apparently did not take the opportunity to hear his Vice President's advice on the Mexican situation. Wilson preferred to leave foreign policy to his new Secretary of State, William Jennings Bryan.

The story soon faded from the newspapers, but enough doubt persisted in the minds of State Department officials and others to reinforce their belief that the new Vice President should not be included in foreign policy discussions.

෧ ෧ ෧ ෧ ෧

Andrew Carnegie was born in Scotland in November of 1843, and his family moved to Pennsylvania five years later. Young Carnegie started work at an early age as a bobbin boy in a cotton mill, and a few years later was engaged as a telegraph clerk and operator with the Atlantic and Ohio Company.

Carnegie's outgoing personality caught the attention of a high official of the Pennsylvania Railroad. At twenty-four, Andrew became superintendent of the western division of the railroad. Though his family had little money, Carnegie worked hard and invested wisely. He had early success with an investment in a railroad sleeping car company, which enabled him to pay $850 for a replacement and avoid active duty in the Civil War.

While in this position he met George Pullman, inventor of the sleeping car. Carnegie immediately recognized the potential of this venture and readily joined in the effort for its adoption. His investment paid off, and he used his profits to purchase interests in oil production. That, too, was successful.

After the Civil War Carnegie turned his attention to the newly emerging iron and steel business. After the Panic of 1873, with properties cheap and the Bessemer process coming into its own, Carnegie concentrated all his resources and energies into the making of steel.

By the late 1880s Carnegie Steel was the largest manufacturer of pig-iron, steel-rails and coke in the world, with a capacity to produce approximately 2,000 tons of pig-metal a day. In 1888 he bought the rival Homestead Steel Works, which included an extensive plant served by tributary coal and iron fields, a railway 425 miles long, and a line of lake steamships.

He and his partner, Henry Clay Frick, gained control of the Homestead Steel Works and eventually consolidated those operations into the Carnegie Steel Company. By applying the coordinating and cost accounting techniques he had learned from the Pennsylvania Railroad, holding down wages and salaries, keeping up with the latest technology, and "hard-driving" both his men and his furnaces, he held costs to a minimum and prices below his competitors', thereby capturing an ever-growing share of the market and maximizing the return on his investment. In 1901 Carnegie Steel merged with the U.S. Steel Corporation and Carnegie sold out to J.P. Morgan for $480 million, making Carnegie the richest man in the world.

After his retirement he became a philanthropist and donated more than $350 million to further public education, build libraries and lobby for international peace. Carnegie established over 1600 libraries in the U.S. alone. Among all of his many philanthropic efforts, the establishment of public libraries in the United States, the United Kingdom, and in other English-speaking countries, was especially prominent. Carnegie libraries, as they were commonly called, sprang up throughout the world. The first library was opened in 1883 in Dunfermline, Scotland.

Carnegie's policy was to build and equip the libraries, but only on condition that the local authority provided the land and maintenance costs. In total Carnegie funded some 3,000 libraries, located in every U.S. state except Alaska, Delaware and Rhode Island, as well as Britain, Ireland, Canada, Australia, New Zealand, the West Indies and Fiji. Eventually Carnegie libraries were built throughout northeast Indiana, including Columbia City, Pierceton and North Manchester. When Carnegie's philanthropic project was complete, more libraries would be built in Indiana than in any other state.

∽ ∽ ∽ ∽ ∽

In March of 1913, on the Monday after Easter, Marshall was asked to speak at a YMCA-sponsored event at the Municipal Auditorium in Springfield, Massachusetts.

Marshall used the gathering to criticize the wealthy who earned their fortune from working families and then assuaged their conscious with widespread philanthropy. Marshall noted his "local contacts" had told him that people across the country "seemed apologetic" about their Carnegie library. "The public does not appreciate charity," he said, "that emanates from predatory wealth."

> *I don't wish to detract from Mr. Carnegie in the slightest, but I do believe that he derives more pleasure from giving libraries than the public does from availing itself of them. If you want institutions of which the public will be proud, dig down into your pockets and pay for them yourselves.*[197]

The *New York Times* was quick to rebuke Marshall. They pointed out that Marshall's local contacts were most likely politicians "who are not noted for their literary tastes."

Though Marshall was criticized for his remarks on Carnegie, few felt much sympathy for the industrialist turn philanthropist. But Marshall's verbal blunders were only starting, and a few weeks later, the Vice President's remarks would result in a deluge of criticism from a wide variety of sources.

Marshall was asked to deliver comments at the Jefferson Day Dinner in New York on April 12, 1913. He knew his speech would create controversy. Speaking to the National Democratic Club at the Waldorf-Astoria Hotel, he started by saying he had "come to beard the lion in his den" because "the welfare of the country depends not a little upon the conduct of certain men in this City of New York."[198]

Marshall warned that the accumulation of large amounts of wealth by a few families could lead to socialism, or worse. Though communism had not yet toppled the Russian nobility, socialism was a credible political force in America. Eugene Debs had provided a glimpse of the power that could be garnered with the melding of organized labor and socialist doctrine. It was widely felt that many of the rich had achieved their gains through inappropriate means, such as high protective tariffs.

> *The belief that there is an unequal distribution of wealth in this country has been supplemented by the belief that much of it has been obtained through special privilege, that it did not come by labor, skill, industry, barter or trade, but through watered stocks and bonds, through corners on commodities, through corruption of legislatures, through the sale of impure foodstuffs, through wrecking railroads, through all the devices known to man whereby the law is not abrogated but chloroformed.*[199]

Marshall went on to discuss the imposition of an inheritance tax on estates of the wealthy. He felt passing assets on to offspring was a privilege, not a right, and that this was justified by the manner in which the rich obtained their wealth.

> *Nothing but a desire to arouse thoughtless rich men to a sense of their danger would induce me to suggest this – what might happen to them here in the great State of New York if those who have not should take it into their heads to make common cause against those who have? They talk about vested rights, and in their talks assume they have both an inherent and constitutional right to pass their property down from generation to generation until some reckless descendant shall have dissipated it.*[200]

If Marshall had intended to shock the crowd, he was successful. "The applause he received when he finished," wrote the *New York Times*, "was not nearly so enthusiastic at that which greeted him when he arose to speak."

Thinking that he may have been misquoted, reporters the next day asked Marshall to clarify his views. "Men of judgment have told me," he said, "that they believe if a proposition could be submitted to the people by which all estates over and above the exemption limit of $100,000 should revert to the state it would be carried two to one."[201]

Marshall was raising an idea anathema to most businessmen – an inheritance tax. But he was hardly alone in proposing the idea. Just fifteen years earlier – in the War Revenue Act of 1898 – Republican William McKinley had enacted an inheritance tax to help finance the Spanish-American War. That tax was imposed on "legacies" (personal property) and "successions" (real property) and exempted estates under $10,000. After the War, the federal treasury began to generate large annual surpluses, and the tax was repealed in 1902.

While United States policymakers had considered an inheritance tax as long ago as the War of 1812, the first inheritance tax was approved during the Civil War. Northern politicians approved the measure to ensure that wealthy Americans were helping to pay for the large increase in military expenditures. The rate ranged from 1% to 6%, and varied both on the size of the estate and the relationship of the person receiving the inheritance to the deceased. Congress repealed that tax in 1870.[202]

The reactions to Marshall's proposal were strong and immediate. The Literary Digest, borrowing a phrase that had been used to describe Wilson's program, devoted a portion of its next issue to "The Vice President's New Freedom." Newspapers across the country ran articles for and against Marshall's ideas. The *New York Times* pointed out that "The Vice President may not be far wrong."

But the Times made it clear they felt the Vice President had, indeed, gone too far.

> *Our Vice Presidents have usually been content to refrain from the public discussion of burning questions, and the people of the country have suffered under no sense of loss from this wise habit of reticence. Certainly, if our Vice Presidents are to talk at all, they ought not to talk foolishly.*[203]

Much of the criticism of Marshall was due to political posturing. Republican critics must certainly have remembered Theodore Roosevelt's call for an inheritance tax in the middle of his second term during his annual message to Congress. In addition, by 1913 thirty-five states had enacted an inheritance tax, including New York.

But in the politically charged environment of Wilson's first term, reaction to Marshall's speech continued. The most searing denunciation of Marshall, however, came from George Harvey, the editor of the *North American Review*. In a speech before bankers at the Waldorf-Astoria, Harvey was expected to retort Marshall's comments, and he did not disappoint the audience.

Marshall had "come almost directly from the place of his nativity", which Harvey had incorrectly called "Columbus City, Indiana". Had Marshall forgotten that the "thoughtless rich" had gotten him elected? "I take care to refer to our recent guest as Mr. Marshall, and not as the Vice President. I doubt if he quite realizes yet that he as been elected."

Harvey called Marshall's idea of a confiscatory inheritance tax on estates above $100,000 arbitrary. Why not a $10,000 ceiling, he asked? Furthermore, the country was threatened not by the predatory rich, but by "the incitement of the predatory poor".

Harvey concluded by noting:

> *I may go so far as to admit that, if somebody had proposed the health of Mr. Wilson at the conclusion of Mr. Marshall's speech, the toast would have been drunk with rare enthusiasm.*[204]

The New York Sun, however, probably reflected the feelings of many of Wilson's advisors when they wrote:

> *Friends of the Wilson Administration are beginning to scratch their heads and ask one another, "What are we going to do with the Vice President?" Mr. Marshall's speeches against "the thoughtless rich" are giving them a lot of worry.*[205]

Marshall's comments may have led to consternation for Wilson's advisors, but the Vice President had raised an issue, caused by the confluence of several factors, that was about to lead to a fundamental change in government finance in the United States.

The vast accumulations of wealth that had occurred during the Gilded Age caused many to become critical of the manner in which the federal government was financed. For more than a century after the birth of the United States, the primary source of federal revenue was tariffs on imported goods. Not only were the tariffs lucrative for the government's treasury, but they also served the dual purpose of protecting domestic industry from cheaper imports.

But much of the electorate had grown disenchanted with the political chicanery that had dominated the setting of tariffs. While families had grown rich owning corporations that benefited from protective tariffs, farmers and working men had to pay higher prices on food, clothing, and other essentials. Lowering the tariffs meant the federal government had less money to finance an increasing demand for services, particularly in building and maintaining a strong army and navy.

Marshall may have become a magnet for criticism because of his comments, but his ideas were shared by many. The nation was on the edge of the most significant change in government finance in history.

ക ക ക ക ക

Though not a published scholar of the structure of the government like Wilson, Marshall had a thorough understanding of the federal system of checks and balances. Unlike many casual observers, he viewed the office of the Vice President as part of the legislative, and not the executive, branch of government.

As such, Vice President Marshall devoted his primary efforts to his responsibility as the presiding officer of the Senate. Few outside of government understand the importance of the role played by the Vice President in overseeing activity in the Senate (or, for that matter, a Lieutenant Governor presiding over a State Senate). The presiding officer, using established rules of order, decides which topics are brought to the floor for debate and vote, and who speaks. He (or she) decides when to close the debate – often as important as a decision as the debate itself. Emotions often run high, and the Vice President was responsible for maintaining the decorum of the debate.

The presiding officer's power is not absolute. A Senator can ask for a ruling on a question, and anyone can appeal that ruling. But in the daily operation of business, the presiding officer is like the traffic cop – moving the flow of business along in the manner, speed and direction that they choose.

Marshall often had to use his authority to maintain order in the Senate chamber. During a discussion of the Mexican crisis, spectators in the galleries cheered as a senator made some particularly forceful points during a speech. The Vice President was forced to have the spectators removed. Marshall, in taking action to clear the galleries, also explained his viewpoint of his role as the presiding officer.

> *The Sergeant at Arms will be compelled to clear the galleries. The Chair is not responsible for the rules of the Senate. They were made contrary to the judgment of the Chair. They place upon the Chair the duty of seeing that there are no demonstrations of approval or disapproval in the galleries of the Senate. Three times now this morning attention has been called to that fact, and the Chair has been compelled to clear one gallery, much to the regret of the Chair.*
>
> *The Chair wants to say something further now: The Senate passed this role, but the Senate, if the Chair is an observer of things going on, is largely responsible for the outburst in the galleries. If the Senate expects the Chair to enforce the rule as against the galleries, a decent respect for the feeling of mankind would suggest that Senators should also obey the rule.*[206]

Another critically important role of the presiding officer is that of tiebreaker. According to Article I, Section 3 of the Constitution of the United States, "The Vice President of the United States shall be President of the Senate, but shall have no Vote, unless they be equally divided". Since 1789, the Vice President has cast 242 tie-breaking votes. The first vice president, John Adams, had the distinction of having broken a tie in the Senate 29 times during his two terms in office – a record that remains to this day. Perhaps the most famous instance of tie-breaking occurred in 1881, with the Senate divided between 37 Republicans and 37 Democrats (along with two independents), Vice President

Chester Arthur was forced to break numerous tie votes until President James Garfield's assassination moved him to the presidency.

As presiding officer, Marshall also had several opportunities to use his tie-breaking ability – he would, in fact, vote to break a tie eight times in his career as presiding officer of the Senate.

ᔕ ᔕ ᔕ ᔕ ᔕ

When Marshall became Vice President, the United States relied on revenue from tariffs to support the operations of the federal government. A major goal of the Progressive movement, however, what the enactment of an income tax. Such a tax would be based on a wage earner's ability to pay, rather than the nature of the goods they purchased. Because tariffs generally increased the price of household goods from thirty to fifty percent, it was clear that adoption of an income tax would ease the burden on a working family and raise the tax liability of the wealthy considerably.

In an effort to find revenue during the Civil War, Abraham Lincoln had asked Congress for an income tax. First enacted in 1864, the new tax was five percent on income above six hundred dollars a year, and ten percent on incomes more than five thousand a year. Though most families had incomes low enough to avoid the tax, it was understandably unpopular and was repealed in 1872.

The United States remained without an income tax until the second administration of Grover Cleveland. Elected with a promise to reduce tariffs, Cleveland was successful in asking Congress to approve a two percent income tax on all income in excess of four thousand dollars. This was hardly a widespread tax, as only two percent of Americans had income at that level in 1893.

But opponents argued that the tax was unconstitutional. Article I, Section 2 of the Constitution said that any "direct tax" must be "apportioned among the several States ... according to their respective numbers." The evidence showed that only a handful of urbanized states such as New York, New Jersey, Pennsylvania and Connecticut were paying the vast majority of the new income tax. As a result, the new tax, it was argued, violated the Constitutional provisions for a "direct" tax.[207]

The Supreme Court agreed. In the case of *Pollock v. Farmers' Loan and Trust Company*, Chief Justice Melville Fuller asserted that a tax on rents or other incomes that derived from real estate was equivalent to a tax on that property, which would be a direct tax. Their 1895 decision effectively prevented the enactment of a federal income tax until such time as the Constitution was amended to permit it.

It was William Howard Taft who would start the process of enacting the necessary changes to permit an income tax. In the tariff compromise hammered out in July of 1909, Congress began the process that allowed the states to adopt an amendment to the Constitution permitting an income tax. The amendment would give Congress the power "to lay and collect taxes on incomes, from whatever source derived, without apportionment among the several States and without regard to any census or enumeration."

Opponents of the tax felt they could successfully block the adoption of the amendment. Approval would required an affirmative votes from thirty-six of the forty-eight states, and many felt that a sufficient number of states would withhold their approval to derail the effort. But tax opponents did not foresee the leftward shift among voters that occurred during the Taft administration. Democrats won governorships and statehouse contests across the country, and the Republican Party had a strong progressive faction, led by Theodore Roosevelt.

Alabama was the first state to adopt the constitutional amendment, and the only one to do so in 1909. Eight more states adopted in 1910, including populous Illinois and the eastern state of Maryland.

Democratic victories in the elections of 1910 brought many more adopting states in 1911. Twenty states adopted the amendment that year, including Marshall's Indiana, which became the sixteenth state to approve the amendment. In an important symbol of the political changes that were occurring, New York adopted the amendment after Democrats had gained control of the state house and senate, as well as the governorship.

After New York's approval, the eventual enactment of the amendment was clear. On February 3, 1913, Wyoming became the thirty-sixth state to adopt, reaching the constitutional requirement.

Woodrow Wilson signed the legislation approving the amendment in New Jersey two days later. Barely a month after that, and on the day after his inauguration as President, Wilson called a special session of Congress to reform the tariff system.

After his missteps early in Wilson's first term, when Marshall did speak out after that he was careful to make certain that it was part of a coordinated effort by the Wilson administration either to influence an election or to gain public support for a particular issue. To promote tariff reform, Wilson asked Marshall to help garner support through a speech in Kansas City:

> *We've got to get back to the time when the people of the country had equal opportunities; back to the time when there were old-fashioned competition, old-fashioned rewards of comfortable living and tranquil old age for labor.*
> *If I know Mr. Wilson and old-fashioned Democracy they propose to go back to first principles. We propose first to go back to constitutional tariff. The tariff has corrupted this country more than anything else. It has corrupted good men and made bad men worse. I don't care how good a man is. If you give him a tariff favor at the expense of his neighbor, you weaken his moral fiber.*[208]

The tariff reform legislation was incorporated into the Underwood-Simmons Tariff Bill. This legislation was designed to reduce tariffs across all imported goods, and eliminate them entirely on one hundred items. Business interests that had been protected by the tariffs lobbied hard to keep protection over their own industries.

While support for tariff reduction was building, it was clear that an income tax would be required to make up for the lost revenue, estimated at nearly one hundred million dollars. From today's perspective when the federal budget is measured in trillions of dollars this amount may seem miniscule, but in 1912 the entire federal budget was less than seven hundred million dollars.

Wilson knew that the income tax he would propose had to contain several elements. It had to be simple enough that the return itself could be calculated by the taxpayer. In addition, he wanted to exempt enough income from taxation that most families would not pay any tax. Finally, he felt strongly that the tax rates should be progressive, meaning that higher incomes would be taxed at a rate larger than the tax on smaller incomes.

The compromise that was eventually reached imposed a one percent tax on all incomes above four thousand dollars – eliminating more than ninety-five percent of families from any income tax liability. Additional taxes were imposed on incomes above twenty thousand dollars, with a top rate of seven percent for incomes above a half a million dollars. In addition, the law created a one percent tax on corporate income.

During the debate over the Underwood-Simmons legislation, Marshall became acquainted with Senator Boies Penrose of Pennsylvania. Penrose had served as a Republican in the Senate since 1897, and his political viewpoints were far removed from those of Marshall.

> *I had nothing whatever in common with Senator Boise Penrose of Pennsylvania. I did not believe in a single principle of government for which he stood. I thought that everything advocated by him was distinctly inimical to the best interest of the American people, but I had a profound admiration for him.*[209]

Despite their ideological differences, the Senator from Pennsylvania and the Vice President from Indiana developed a warm friendship – in part because of an ancestral tie Penrose had with Northern Indiana.

> *He came of an illustrious line in his home state and traced his genealogy back to General Anthony Wayne, for whom Fort Wayne, Indiana was named. Maybe it was by reason of the fact that I lived so close to Fort Wayne that somehow, regardless of his opinions, I admired his conduct. There was no shifting for him; no half-hearted advocacy of anything. What he stood for, he stood for. He did not wield the scimitar of Saladin; he had the battle ax of Richard the Lion Hearted and struck down, when he could, all opposition that stood in his way.*[210]

Marshall was amused by some of the debate on the Senate floor during the discussion of the tariff legislation.

Perhaps the wittiest thing I listened to was a speech by Penrose at the conclusion of the discussion on the Underwood-Simmons Tariff Bill; the bill which put wool on the free list but gave a tariff on goats and goat hair. Penrose came into the Chamber with certain works on natural history. He read from them showing the relationship that existed between the goat and the sheep; showed from these works that they were of the same family, and wound up by wanting to know why the sheep of the North should be left to the wintry blasts of free trade while the goats of the South were safely housed in a fifteen percent tariff! [211]

President Wilson signed the Underwood-Simmons Bill, with the attached amendments for the income tax, on October 3, 1913. The law is easily ranked as one of the most important in the history of the United States. By the end of that year, the new Bureau of Internal Revenue, with just thirty employees, would create all the forms that would be required to collect data on income and taxes. For simplicity, they used a sequential numbering system to keep track of each form. Wanting to use four digits, the first form created was assigned the number 1001. Nina Wilcox Putnam was a young accountant who would eventually find a career as a screenwriter for Hollywood movies, including the screenplay for the 1932 hit "The Mummy", staring Boris Karlof. She was assigned the task of developing the form that taxpayers would use to calculate their income tax liability each year. Thirty-nine documents were prepared before Mrs. Putnam had completed her work, so when she was finished the tax return she created was given the moniker Form 1040.

In the first year after enactment, only 368,000 Form 1040 returns were filed, and the total tax paid was a disappointing $28 million. But by the time policymakers had discovered their underestimate of the revenue from the new income tax, hostilities had begun in Europe and increased revenue would be needed for the war effort. The low rates and high exemption levels would not remain for long.

Tariff reduction would provide relief to some areas of the country, while hurting states that had benefited from such protectionism. Wilson was particularly worried about the sugar planters in Louisiana, a heavily Democratic state. After the Underwood-Simmons Tariff Bill became law,

Marshall cut a limerick out of a magazine and sent it to Wilson. The reference to Louisiana, the Pelican State, was not lost on Wilson:

> *Oh, a wonderful bird is the pelican!*
> *His beak will hold more than his belican.*
> > *He can hold in his beak*
> > *Enough for a week –*
> *I don't understand how the helican.*[212]

❦ ❦ ❦ ❦ ❦

Economists say that the financial health of a country is fundamentally controlled by monetary policy. Monetary policy influences interest rates, inflation, exchange rates for foreign currency, and a wide variety of indicators crucial to successful business and commerce.

In the early years of the United States, attempts to develop sound monetary policy were generally unsuccessful. Part of the reason why monetary policy is a sensitive issue is that different political factions may hold radically different viewpoints. The Panic of 1893 highlighted the political differences between the agrarian west, which favored faster growth of the money supply and higher inflation, and businessmen from the east, who preferred a more stable monetary policy.

Attempts by the United States government to develop a central bank to control monetary policy had failed. Alexander Hamilton, then the Secretary of the Treasury, asked Congress established the First Bank of the United States, headquartered in Philadelphia, in 1791. Supported by large banks based in New York and Philadelphia, the bank was opposed by farmers in the western states and, in 1811, when the bank's 20-year charter expired, Congress refused, by one vote, to renew it.

Five years later, in 1816, Congress agreed to charter the Second Bank of the United States. But President Andrew Jackson was elected in 1928 on a platform that included opposition to the Second Bank of the United States, and when the Bank's charter expired in 1836, it was not renewed.

Further attempts at monetary reform over the rest of the nineteenth century were unsuccessful. The Panic of 1893 highlighted the need for central bank reform, but it was the Panic of 1907 that set the stage for the series of events that would eventually lead to meaningful legislation creating a central bank.

∾ ∾ ∾ ∾ ∾

The Industrial Revolution, strong growth in agricultural output, and the soaring prominence of the United States in world commerce led to unprecedented growth in the American economy in the years around the turn of the century. But the critical weaknesses in the banking and financial system that were spotlighted in the Panic of 1893 remained unresolved.

Large corporations that began in the post-Civil War era grew more powerful in the early years of the new century. Railroads, steel manufacturers and mining companies enjoyed growing profits and rising stock prices.

The New York Stock Exchange was the vehicle of choice for the buying and selling of the shares of these corporations. The Stock Exchange traced its roots back to traders who conducted business under a tree at the south end of Manhattan Island in 1791. Over the next century the stock market witnessed rises and declines, panics and periods of relative calm. By the early years of the twentieth century the stock market had become the preferred method of investment for the nation's wealthy families.

But in 1907 the idea of government regulation was anathema to stock market traders. Banks and trust companies were free to hold much of their assets in stocks, and even borrow to purchase more shares. In periods of rising prices, borrowing money to purchase stocks can increase investment returns significantly. But if shares decline, this borrowing – known as "leverage" – can quickly wipe out the net worth of an individual investor or even an entire corporation.

Stock market observers were already nervous as events developed in 1907. A wave of selling had swept the markets in March. A team of financiers had put together a $25 million pool to prop up prices, but this proved unnecessary when prices recovered.

The recovery proved temporary. Speculation continued in shares of copper, mining and railroad stocks. President Roosevelt did little to calm fears when he referred to the wealthy as "malefactors of great wealth" during a speech in August.

Much of the speculative buying during the summer of 1907 came from trust companies based in New York. Regulations prohibited banks from creating trust accounts to hold stock market investments for wealthy customers, so trust companies were created to manage investments for clients who wanted services that went beyond savings and checking accounts.

Because there were few regulations on trust companies, some, such as the Knickerbocker Trust, began to venture into riskier investments, and to use leverage to increase their returns. When stock prices rose their profits soared, and they began offering high rates to attract depositors so they could have additional funds to buy even more shares of stock.

On Monday, October 21, a story appeared reporting on the development of a major new copper mine in Alaska. Fearing a glut in copper and a subsequent decline in copper prices, shares in United Copper fell thirty-five points in just two hours. A large block of the shares of United Copper were owned by the Knickerbocker Trust, and on Tuesday morning many of the Trust's eighteen thousand depositors lined up outside their doors to withdraw their money. In addition, depositors at other trust companies, seeing the panic at Knickerbocker, tried to withdraw their money, as well.

As with the Panic of 1893, again financial leaders turned to J. Pierpont Morgan. Now seventy years old and retired from most of his business ventures, Morgan was still the most respected name in financial circles and nervous bankers, investors and government officials turned to him once again to stop the panic. But Morgan knew that Charles Barney, the President of Knickerbocker, had foolishly overextended his corporation, and even Morgan's intervention might not save the company. "I've got to stop somewhere", Morgan said. Knickerbocker Trust went bankrupt; Barney later committed suicide.

As depositors withdrew funds from other trust companies, they were forced to sell stocks to meet the demands for cash. Banks and trusts needed cash to pay depositors, and their only source was to liquidate their investments, further depressing prices. Seeing that the financial institutions needed a source of cash, the Secretary of the Treasury pledged $25 million in government funds.

It was not enough. On Thursday, October 24, the President of the New York Stock Exchange, Ransom Thomas, told Morgan that if another $25 million was not raised immediately, at least two dozen brokerage firms would fail. Thomas would be forced to close the stock exchange early to avoid the financial collapse.

"At what time do you usually close it?", Morgan asked.

"Why, at three o'clock", Thomas replied.

Morgan pointed his finger at Thomas. "It must not close one minute before that hour today," he said.

At two o'clock, Morgan called together other bank presidents and raised the needed $25 million. Fifteen minutes later the Morgan bailout was announced, and the panic was over.[213]

∾ ∾ ∾ ∾ ∾

The Banking Panic of 1907 led to the creation of the National Monetary Commission, which was designed to study the country's banking problems. That Commission pointed to a critical flaw in the nation's banking system. No central institution existed that could make loans to banks that were suffering from a run on their deposits or other issues that may lead to widespread withdrawals. In 1893 and 1907, J. Pierpont Morgan had used his private resources to bail out failing banks. It had been only fourteen years between the last two financial panics. When the next one occurred, would the government rely again on the good graces of a benevolent banker, or should a government-sponsored central bank be given the role of "bank of last resort"?

Based on the recommendations of the National Monetary Commission, Senator Nelson W. Aldrich of Rhode Island introduced legislation to create the National Reserve Association, which would be given the authority to lend funds to banks and control the growth of the money supply. But Aldrich was a poor choice for the sponsor of the bill. A wealthy Republican with close ties to eastern bankers, many were skeptical that the National Reserve Association was a thinly disguised effort by rich northeasterners to take control of the nation's banking system. Even though many Democrats supported the reforms, they were unwilling to allow the Republicans to claim credit for the landmark legislation.

Concerns were also raised due to the secrecy with which the proposal for a central bank was formulated. Critical elements of the plan were created during a November 1910 meeting at the Jekyll Island Club off the coast of Georgia. Meeting in the mansions created by the selective club – membership was limited to one hundred millionaires – the Wall Street tycoons and bank presidents wanted to create a central bank which they could control.

But with the split in the Republican Party in 1912 and the subsequent election of a Democrat in the White House as well as Democratic majorities in both the House and the Senate, the political landscape shifted in favor of reform. Woodrow Wilson actively supported legislation, as did Carter Glass, Democratic Representative of Virginia and chairman of the House Banking Committee.

Carter Glass came from a family that owned the newspaper in Lynchburg, Virginia. Inspired by the speech that William Jennings Bryan made to the 1896 Democratic National Convention, Glass served in the Virginia State Legislature before being elected to the House of Representatives in 1902. He became an expert in finance and banking, and observed first hand the government's inability to implement policies to minimize the tragic consequences of the Banking Panic of 1907.

The election of 1912 put Glass, as the Chair of the House Banking Committee, in a prime position to enact reforms. Glass was opposed to the centralization of power that had been proposed in the National Reserve Association legislation. Using a suggestion made by Woodrow Wilson, Glass changed the governing body of the central bank from private bankers to a board of governors appointed by the President.

On December 23, 1913, President Woodrow Wilson signed the Federal Reserve Act into law. The bill created the Federal Reserve System of regional banks overseen by a Board of Governors, with Presidential appointments and congressional approval.

Less than four months later, J. Pierpont Morgan, the rescuer of the financial system in the crises of 1893 and 1907, died in the Grand Hotel in Rome. The new law and the death of Morgan marked the end of an era in the American financial system. Gone were the days when a single individual, with their private wealth and power, would control the nation's financial destiny. In its place, for better or worse, was the central banking power of the federal government.

The passage of the Federal Reserve Act brought to a close the remarkable legislative year of 1913. Marshall, however, could see that the world was on the verge of far more dramatic events, and shared his thoughts with his Senate colleagues:

> *When the Federal Reserve Bank measure finally passed the Congress of the United States, in December, 1913, and I had signed it, I went into one of the cloak rooms and said that was the best piece of work Congress had accomplished in many years; that there would be a war in Europe within five years, and that we might be drawn into it; and if we were, that this system would enable us to finance a war. I was laughed at by the senators who were present, some of them even venturing to inquire what sort of liquor I had been drinking, assuring me that the peace of Europe was permanent. I then recited these facts, not all of which were known to any single one of them, and made the statement that the German emperor would either be taken from his throne by the growth of socialism or he would have to justify the standing army, rouse German patriotism and make France pay the bill.*
>
> *It was not five years – it was only nine months – until the awful cataclysm came; that world-destroying war, from the effects of which neither the minds, the consciences nor the business of mankind, on either side of the Atlantic, have as yet measurably been restored to either normality or common sense.*[214]

෧ ෧ ෧ ෧ ෧

A common theme in Marshall's political philosophy was his opposition to large trusts and corporations, and his support for federal regulations. Government regulations against trusts dated back to the Sherman Antitrust Act of 1890, which was the first measure passed by the U.S. Congress to prohibit trusts. The law declared illegal every contract, combination (in the form of trust or otherwise), or conspiracy in restraint of interstate and foreign trade.

Implementation of the Sherman Act, however, was complicated by Supreme Court rulings that limited the ability of federal regulators to successfully bring action against offending corporations. President Theodore Roosevelt had some success with his "trust-busting" campaigns, and in 1904 the Supreme Court upheld the government in its suit for dissolution of the Northern Securities Company. President Taft successfully used the Sherman Act in 1911 against the Standard Oil trust and the American Tobacco Company.

The Sherman Act was strengthened by the passage of the Clayton Antitrust Act, in October 1914. The Clayton Antitrust Act prohibited exclusive sales contracts, local price cutting to freeze out competitors, rebates, and interlocking directorates in corporations. The Act also provided significant advances for organized labor. The new legislation restricted the use of the injunction against labor, and it legalized peaceful strikes, picketing, and boycotts.

The Sherman Act was the first attempt by Congress to regulate trusts and corporations. Yet more than twenty years of pro-business presidents and an uncooperative Supreme Court had removed most of the teeth from that legislation. Wilson, with Marshall's help, restored the federal government's role in business regulation and thus enacted one of the key goals of the Progressive agenda.

స్ స్ స్ స్ స్

As the presiding officer of the Senate, Marshall helped gain legislative approval for Wilson's proposals. Marshall was presiding over the Senate one afternoon when he uttered what has become one of the most often-quoted phrases in American politics. Joseph Bristow, a Senator from Kansas, was droning on and on with a long-winded speech in which each sentence started with the phrase "What this Country needs....". Most of the senators had long ago left, but Marshall, along with the clerks and reporters nearby, were forced by their duties to remain in the chamber. Finally, Bristow concluded his remarks and Marshall, sensing the relief in the room now that the speech was over, turned to the clerks and reporters and said, "Bristow hasn't hit it yet. What this country really needs is a good five-cent cigar."

CHAPTER SEVEN:

I Trust My Chieftain

(1915-1916)

From his post in the front of the Senate chamber, Marshall had the opportunity to observe the workings of the United States Senate, and was not hesitant to offer criticism of the way the chamber did business.

> *As I watched the appropriations during eight years in the Senate I concluded that that cause was utterly foolish which came down to the Capitol asking for less than a half-million dollars. Small items were scrutinized with a microscope and large ones were taken as a matter of course.*
>
> *I well remember one day that the Senate spent three long hours discussing an item in an appropriation bill, of seventeen dollars and fifty cents, an appropriation made to an employee in some one of the government offices in the city of New York. It is the custom to pay certain compensation to a government employee injured in the line of duty. This man was a roustabout, with a set of false teeth. A fellow employee, in some way, swung a crane, struck him in the mouth and broke his false teeth. It cost him seventeen dollars and fifty cents to have them repaired, and he presented the bill to Congress for damages sustained in the course of his employment and in the discharge of his duty. After wrangling for three hours the Senate finally allowed the seventeen dollars and fifty cents. The next item in the bill, as I now remember it, was for two hundred fifty thousand dollars*

to investigate and eradicate something that had already been investigated and has not, up to this time, been eradicated. Nobody raised a protest.[215]

Not all of Marshall's criticisms of the Senate's procedures were whimsical. A common tactic of opponents of legislation was the filibuster.

The word "filibuster" comes from the Dutch word meaning "pirate." The term refers to "a politically delaying tactic such as a long irrelevant speech or several such speeches used by politicians to delay or prevent the passage of some undesired legislation".

Filibusters have been a part of the legislative process since Congress opened its doors. The first attempt to limit the filibuster, however, may have occurred in 1841. At that time, when the Democratic minority hoped to block a bank bill promoted by Kentucky Senator Henry Clay, he threatened to change Senate rules to allow the majority to close debate. Other senators opposed Clay's efforts to restrict unlimited debate, and the new rules were not enacted.

In the early years of Congress, representatives as well as senators could filibuster. As the House of Representatives grew in numbers, however, revisions to the House rules limited debate. In the smaller Senate, unlimited debate continued on the grounds that any senator should have the right to speak as long as necessary on any issue.

By 1915, however, with Europe plunging into conflict, Woodrow Wilson grew impatient with attempts by some Senators to block legislation intended to aid allied nations.

In the final weeks of the Congress that ended in 1915, legislation related to the war in Europe was stalled in the Senate for thirty-three days – a roadblock that also prevented the passage of major appropriations bills. Later, in 1917, as Americans debated the possibility of sending troops to Europe, a twenty-three-day filibuster against the president's proposal to arm merchant ships also failed, dooming other legislation as well. Secretary of State Bryan was attempting to pass a bill that would permit the purchase of the existing ships. Bryan asked Marshall to impose a gag order to limit floor debate but the Vice President, feeling the move would be unethical, refused to do so. The bill was defeated.

Later, the measured was revived in the Ship Purchase Bill, which would enable the government to spend $30 million towards the purchase of new ships. Opponents feared the money could be used to purchase German vessels, providing that government with much-need cash to finance their war efforts.

The vote would be close. The President's supporters needed the support of two senators who were out of town on business, as their votes would result in a tie that could be broken by Marshall's vote. To stall for time and allow the return of the two senators, the President planned a filibuster strategy to stall for time and set up the tie vote. The strategy backfired, however, when several Senators, led by Henry Cabot Lodge of Massachusetts, were angered by the filibuster and withdrew their support.

Despite the fact that he himself had, at times, taken advantage of the filibuster strategy, on March 4, 1917, Wilson fumed that the "Senate of the United States is the only legislative body in the world which cannot act when its majority is ready for action. A little group of willful men, representing no opinion but their own, have rendered the great government of the United States helpless and contemptible." He demanded the adoption of a cloture rule, designed to allow Senators to invoke a process that would set time limits on debate of a particular issue.

Wilson had a willing ally in the issue in Thomas Marshall.

> *One of the remarkable things about the Senate of the United States is its never-ending discussion of the question of cloture. As far as I know it is the only legislative body in the world that has no power to bring debate to a close save by unanimous agreement. Like Tennyson's brook, the words flow on forever, and yet this question of cloture is perennial.*[216]

Within a few days of Wilson's comments, on March 8, 1917, the Senate agreed to a rule that essentially preserved its tradition of unlimited debate while still permitting the Senate to move business forward. The rule required a two-thirds majority to end debate and permitted each member to speak for an additional hour after that before voting on final passage. For the first time in its history, the Senate had agreed to rules that could, in some instances, prevent a filibuster from stopping legislative activity. Wilson did not know it at the time, but the rule would be invoked for the first time within two years to enable a vote on his beloved League of Nations.

❧ ❧ ❧ ❧ ❧

The United States Senate in the early years of the twentieth century was a relatively accessible building, as legislators and constituents alike mingled in the offices and corridors. Physical violence was very rare -- and sometimes it was between the Senators themselves. In 1902, South Carolina Senator Ben Tillman questioned the integrity of his state's other senator, John McLaurin. McLaurin returned to the chamber and called Tillman a liar. A fight ensued, drawing in other senators, and it was several minutes before order was restored.

Capitol Hill security was designed to protect legislators from angry constituents, but in 1917 it was the visitors who needed protection from a Senator. On April 2, 1917, on the day that Woodrow Wilson had asked Congress to declare war on Germany, three antiwar demonstrators visited Massachusetts Senator Henry Cabot Lodge in his Capitol office. One was a minor-league baseball player, who had brought with him a baseball bat, presumably as a souvenir for Lodge.

The men asked Lodge to vote against war, and the conversation became heated. After an exchange of angry words Lodge grabbed the bat and struck his visitors several times, and a fistfight ensued. Security guards quickly intervened. But the altercation would indicate the depth of feelings among Americans regarding the war in Europe. Marshall later wrote:

> *Washington was seething, torn between pacifism and war. A delegation of some ten thousand pacifists came to town. I was compelled to exercise my authority to prevent public speaking from the steps of the Capitol. I was certain as I was of my own existence that, if permitted, it would lead to riot and tumult. Indeed, the only thing the pacifists ever did was when one of them hit Henry Cabot Lodge.*[217]

❧ ❧ ❧ ❧ ❧

Henry Cabot Lodge was born into wealth and privilege in Massachusetts in 1850. His family combined two of the most aristocratic of the Boston Brahmin families. His mother's family – the Cabots – came to America in the 1600s and his maternal great-grandfather – George Cabot – was a United States Senator during the presidency of George Washington. The Lodge family became wealthy in trading and other commercial interests.

Lodge was educated at Harvard and, while there, met Nannie Davis, the daughter of an admiral in the United States Navy. Though Nannie was described by many as both charming and pretty, theirs was never a close marriage. Nannie is barely mentioned in Lodge's memoirs, and though Lodge would write over two dozen books, none were dedicated to her. Nannie would eventually have an affair with Theodore Roosevelt's Secretary of State, John Hay.

Lodge was consumed with his research and his politics. He earned both a Ph.D. in History and a law degree from Harvard. After becoming the editor of the *North American Review*, he began to write over two dozen books beginning with a biography of his great-grandfather, George Cabot.

But his ancestry and his viewpoint of the world drew him into politics. In 1879 he was elected to the Massachusetts legislature, but defeated two years later. In 1882 he lost the Republican nomination for the U.S. Congress. He won the nomination in 1884, but was narrowly defeated in the general election.

Lodge blamed his defeat in 1884 on the schism in the Republican Party caused by the nomination of James G. Blaine, who had been opposed by reformers in the party. At the Chicago convention, Lodge had actively opposed Blaine's nomination. He was joined in his anti-Blaine efforts by a young New York politician named Theodore Roosevelt. The two were bitterly disappointed by Blaine's victory, but they cemented a friendship that would last the remainder of their lives.

Lodge was successful in his election to Congress in 1886, and was reelected for two more terms. In 1892, the Massachusetts legislature elected Lodge to the Senate, and he would remain in that position for over thirty years.

Perhaps due to his patrician background or to his family's political history, Lodge was a fierce advocate of a strong United States military and expansion of American power overseas. Lodge believed firmly in an idea first described by journalist John O'Sullivan in 1839, but which could still describe elements of American foreign policy today:

The far-reaching, the boundless future will be the era of American greatness. In its magnificent domain of space and time, the nation of many nations is destined to manifest to mankind the excellence of divine principles: to establish on earth the noblest temple ever dedicated to the worship of the Most High – the Sacred and the True.

From this blessed mission to the nations of the world, which are shut out from the life-giving light of truth, has America been chosen; and her high example shall smite unto death the tyranny of kings, hierarchies, and oligarchs, and carry the glad tidings of peace and good will where myriads now endure an existence scarcely more enviable than that of the beasts of the field.[218]

Over time, the phrase "destined to manifest" became embraced by some as America's "manifest destiny". Lodge believed passionately that the United States had a mission in the world and, through technology and wealth, possessed the means to fulfill its manifest destiny. Woodrow Wilson would also come to share at least a portion of this vision, as when he would one day call upon the American people to "make the world safe for democracy".

To this end, Lodge advocated for a strong military and the willingness to use it. An early supporter of the Spanish-American war, he actively encouraged the seizure of islands such as Hawaii, the Philippines and Cuba, and even spoke in favor of annexing Canada. At the time of Wilson's first administration, Lodge was both the ranking Minority member of the Senate Foreign Relations committee and Minority Leader of the Senate.

While Lodge was one of the strongest proponents of America's leading role in world affairs, he bitterly opposed any efforts to compromise the sovereignty of the United States. Wilson, who was more willing to cede some of this authority to achieve a larger goal, did not share Lodge's passion for American dominance. Neither was inclined to compromise on issues they felt were important. So long as Democrats controlled the Senate, Wilson had the ability to move forward many of his foreign policy initiatives. But the majorities enjoyed by the Democrats in 1913 would be short-lived. The stage was set for one of the bitterest battles in the history of United States foreign policy.

❦ ❦ ❦ ❦ ❦

Not long after Wilson began his first term, political observers began to ask whether or not he would seek a second term. The 1912 Democratic platform called for a constitutional amendment limiting a president to a single term. Some pundits turned to Marshall as a potential candidate.

Marshall was quick to douse the speculative fires. Marshall issued a statement saying that "Fair-minded democrats will recognize that he (Wilson) is entitled to a chance for a second term to prove the utility of his policies …"[219]

The statement took Wilson and his aides by surprise – and was probably just another illustration of the lack of communication between Wilson and his vice president. Joseph Tumulty, the President's secretary, denied he knew anything about Marshall's statement and did not make any public comments about Wilson's political plans for 1916.

Far from being disturbed by Marshall's statement, Wilson seemed genuinely grateful for the loyalty shown by his vice president. In September of 1914, he wrote to Marshall:

> *I have refrained from telling you how warmly I appreciated as a generous expression of your confidence in me what you are reported to have said the other day with regard to choice of a Democratic candidate for the presidency in 1916 only because I hesitated to risk misrepresenting myself by seeming to be thinking of my own political fortunes. But I am not at liberty to belie myself by seeming ungrateful for such confidence as you have expressed merely because of such a delicacy of scruple. I am sure you will believe me when I say that the performance of my duties is not connected in my mind in the least degree with calculations as to my own political future. I'm willing to let that take care of itself. I should be especially chagrined if my fellow-countrymen were to think that such personal matters played a part in my thoughts in these critical times when duty should be purged to the utmost of every thought of oneself, of every thought except the country's welfare and advantage. But since you have spoken so generously I cannot be churl enough not to tell you how grateful I am to be so believed in and supported.*[220]

Reporters asked Marshall about the conflict between the Democratic platform and the possibility of Wilson seeking a second term. Marshall replied that the Democratic Party was obligated to its platform, but that Wilson was not. The Party could still seek a constitutional amendment limiting a president to one term, but until then, Wilson was free to choose his own political future.

๙ ๙ ๙ ๙ ๙

William Gibbs McAdoo born on a farm near Marietta, Georgia, on October 31, 1863. In the late 1890s, McAdoo was given the task of building a railway tunnel under the Hudson River. Several earlier efforts at the project had ended in failure, but McAdoo combined his rudimentary background in engineering with his financial talents to make the project a success.

Tall and friendly, McAdoo's work came to the attention of the Governor of New Jersey, Woodrow Wilson. Soon after the tunnel was completed, personal tragedy struck when McAdoo's wife died. Seeing the potential for service by the young man, McAdoo was appointed by Wilson as Treasury Secretary. To keep his mind off his wife's death he worked long hours at his position, garnering the respect of many in the Wilson administration.

McAdoo was a good friend with Cary Grayson, and the two would go horseback riding through Washington. One day, Grayson brought along Wilson's youngest daughter, Eleanor, and she and McAdoo quickly formed a close relationship. In March of 1914, they announced their engagement.

Not everyone was happy with the announcement. Some of the stuffier socialites sniffed at the difference in age between McAdoo and Eleanor – he was fifty-one (and the father of six children), while she was just twenty-five. But Wilson was thrilled with the marriage, and the two were married in the Blue Room of the White House in May, 1914.

McAdoo wrote of Marshall:

> He was not a liberal, as many people thought when he was
> Governor of Indiana. He struck me as a decided conservative.
> I think he was an over-judicial man. As the presiding officer
> of the Senate, he sometimes disappointed his party because, on
> some crucial points, his rulings favored the opposition, when

they should have favored, and could very properly have favored, his own party. He was so anxious to appear impartial that he sometimes leaned back the other way.[221]

❧ ❧ ❧ ❧ ❧

Archduke Franz Ferdinand was the eldest son of Emperor Franz Joseph's younger brother Carl Ludwig. After the death of Crown Prince Rudolf by suicide in 1889, and his own father in 1896, Franz Ferdinand was next in line to become the Emperor of Austria-Hungary.

Prior to World War I, Austria-Hungary was a vast area stretching from Switzerland to Russia and from the Adriatic Sea north to Prague. Though large, the country was hardly united. Under an unwieldy agreement, Franz Joseph was the emperor of Austria, but the King of Hungary, a largely autonomous state.

The provinces of Bosnia and Herzegovina had been under the governmental administration of Austria-Hungary since 1878. Serbs in the area cherished their independence, but in 1908 Austria annexed the provinces. Serbian nationalists were outraged. A secret terrorist group, the Black Hand, was formed to gain independence from Austria-Hungary and form a Serbian state.

To strengthen the ties between Bosnia-Herzegovina and his empire, Franz Joseph sent Francis Ferdinand and his wife to visit the city of Sarajevo, in the heart of the Serbian region. The Black Hand group saw their chance. On June 28, 1914, as Archduke Ferdinand's motorcade made its way through Sarajevo, an assassin threw a grenade at the car carrying Ferdinand and his wife.

The grenade missed. The Archduke, remarkably unconcerned by the assassination attempt, continued with his itinerary. Upon arriving at City Hall, the Archduke interrupted the Mayor's welcoming speech. "What is the good of your speeches?", he said. "I come to Sarajevo on a visit, and I get bombs thrown at me. It is outrageous!"

Franz and his wife continued their motorcade, and shortly afterward a Bosnian member of Black Hand shot and killed them both.

The dominoes began to fall. Austria-Hungary used the assassination as an excuse to move its army into Serbia. Russia's alliance with Serbia led the Czar to mobilize his troops, leading Germany to declare war on Russia. But Germany's military strategy called for capturing Paris via Belgium before attacking Russia, which then brought England and France into the war. Turkey, Bulgaria, Rumania, Portugal and Italy soon followed.

Thanks to treaties both public and secret, eventually most of the world had aligned with one side or the other. Fighting would take place in Asia, Africa, the Pacific and the Middle East, but mostly this was a European war. The borders of Germany and Austria-Hungary were defined by muddy trenches, and men from countries ranging from Vietnam to Morocco to Senegal and, eventually, from America, would face each other with new implements of carnage such as machine guns and poison gas.

"The lamps are going out all over Europe," said Earl Grey, the British foreign secretary. "We shall not see them lit again in our lifetime."[222]

❧ ❧ ❧ ❧ ❧

The two years after the Election of 1912 proved to be a whirlwind of activity for Wilson and his wife Ellen. In addition to an immense domestic policy agenda and escalating international troubles, the Wilson's had presided over the wedding of their daughter Jessie to Francis Sayer in November of 1913, and that of Eleanor to the Secretary of the Treasury, William Gibbs McAdoo, less than six months later in May, 1914.

While the President might not have noticed due to his active schedule, those around Ellen Wilson saw that she was losing weight and becoming weaker. In March of 1914 she fell on the bedroom floor; by June, she was unable to retain food.

Woodrow thought his wife was suffering from exhaustion. Cary Grayson, the President's physician and a close friend to both of them, provided a collaborating diagnosis. "The chief cause of Mrs. Wilson's present critical condition," Grayson reported, "is a chronic kidney trouble ... developed as one of the results of a nervous breakdown."[223]

Perhaps Grayson was too close to the couple to provide a disinterested diagnosis; he may have felt the need to protect the President from emotional baggage as the world slipped closer to war. In any case, it was not Grayson but another physician, Edward Davis, who told the truth to the President. Ellen was dying from Bright's disease, incurable tuberculosis of the kidneys.

On Thursday, August 6, 1914, Ellen died. Perhaps because he failed to recognize the seriousness of the illness, Wilson was crushed. He had lost not only his wife of nearly thirty years, but his closest companion and advisor. Soon after the President returned from Ellen's funeral in Georgia, Grayson found him with tears streaming down his face. "It was a heart breaking scene, a sadder picture, no one could imagine," Grayson wrote, "A great man with his heart torn out."[224]

❧ ❧ ❧ ❧ ❧

Ferdinand de Lesseps, who was responsible for the construction of Egypt's Suez Canal, began work in 1882 for a canal that would connect the Atlantic with the Pacific through Panama, which was part of Columbia. But the geography of Panama was far different from Egypt. The Suez Canal was dug through soft sand, most of which was near sea level, in a hot but consistently dry climate. Most of Panama consisted of hard volcanic rock, some of which was several hundred feet high, and the entire country was bisected by the Chagres River, which often overflowed its banks during rainy season. The rain also brought mosquitoes, which spread yellow fever and malaria among the workers. Seven years after work was begun, at a cost of millions of dollars and thousands of lives, the French abandoned their project.

After Theodore Roosevelt became president, he began, in earnest, to begin again the project of completing a canal linking the Atlantic and Pacific oceans. Much of Roosevelt's motivation was grounded in military strategy. As the Assistant Secretary of the Navy during the Spanish American war, Roosevelt was painfully aware of the two months it took to move the battleship Oregon around South America in time to be used in a naval offensive against the Spanish. But some at the time were advocating that the canal be built through Nicaragua, rather than Panama. While knowledgeable engineers favored Panama, the French were asking $100 million to sell what remained of the effort they had abandoned in 1889.

The issue went to Congress, where the House of Representatives passed legislation authorizing the Nicaraguan option. But the Senate was more evenly divided among those who favored Nicaragua and those supporting Panama. In the end, the issue was decided on two factors. While the planned Nicaraguan canal was far from the nearest volcano, Panama proponents managed to convince many Senators that the country was rife with active volcanoes. (In fact, as the issue was being debated, a volcano erupted at St. Pierre on the

Caribbean island of Martinique, killing nearly thirty thousand people.) The Panama supporters also provided senators with copies of a Nicaraguan postage stamp that clearly showed an erupting volcano.

In the end, though, the issue came down to cost. The French lowered their asking price from $100 million to $40 million, and the economics of the issue made Panama the clear favorite. Congress approved the appropriation of the money to pursue the Panamanian option, and Roosevelt signed the legislation.

But acquiring the French assets in Panama was relatively easy; the United states also needed to negotiate a treaty with the government of Columbia for the rights to control the land that contained the canal. When the Columbian government proved difficult to deal with, some Panamanians, with assistance from the United States, engineered a revolution and declared Panama to be an independent country. While careful not to endorse the revolt, Roosevelt discreetly let it be known that the U.S. would view this as a positive development and would provide what assistance he could. At a key moment in the revolution, the American battleship Nashville arrived to keep away any Columbian troops that might want to suppress the revolution. The Country of Panama was formed, which was recognized by the United States the same day the insurgents announced the formation of a new government. (Years later, one Senator concisely described the transaction when he claimed that the Panama Canal belonged to the United States because "We stole it, fair and square".)

Many Americans were upset with the methods use to gain control of Panama, but Roosevelt was unperturbed. "There was much accusation about my having acted in an 'unconstitutional' manner," Teddy shrugged. "I took the isthmus, started the canal, and then left Congress -- not to debate the canal, but to debate me. . . . While the debate goes on, the canal does too; and they are welcome to debate me as long as they wish, provided that we can go on with the canal."

Opponents did, in fact, debate Roosevelt's methods, not the canal itself. Not long after the revolution had taken place, critics still questioned the President's methods. But Roosevelt both deflected the criticism and spoke to the country's optimism about the project when he responded, "Tell them that I am going to make the dirt fly".

But Marshall was concerned about the long-term consequences of the incident, particularly as it influenced American relations throughout Latin America.

> *Whatever may be said for or against the action of this government in the Panama Canal incident, I am quite satisfied it produced in the minds of all Latin Americans a feeling of uncertainty and insecurity. Whether we were or were not under treaty obligations ... to preserve the integrity ... of Columbia is beside the point. I am quite satisfied that Latin American governments believed what we were. You must now add to this the manifest irritation of the Monroe Doctrine as it would vision itself to one of those republics, in light of the Panama incident. ... one who felt America was in the wrong would look with a jaundiced eye upon what is known as the Monroe Doctrine. Such an eye would naturally construe it to be a doctrine which said to Europe: "Keep your hands off of the new republics of the new world, but remember that whenever we take a notion to interfere with them we shall do so." This is not an appealing doctrine. I felt, in the diplomatic atmosphere of Washington, that the kind of Monroe Doctrine these republics would like to have was a doctrine that said not only to Europe but also to the United States: "Keep your hands off our governments."[225]*

On August 15, 1914, the Panama Canal was officially opened. Plans had originally been made for a grand celebration to mark the event, but the onset of World War One resulted in a more modest affair.

There were no international dignitaries to witness the historic event. The chief engineer of the canal, Colonel George Goethals, declined the invitation to be aboard the first ship and, instead, followed the ship up through the Canal, thanks to the Panamanian railroad. He publicly turned away personal honors. "The real builder of the Panama Canal," said Goethals said, "was Theodore Roosevelt."

The extraordinary Sixty-Third session of Congress ended on March 4, 1915. The reforms they enacted stand out as some of the most remarkable in legislative history. The federal government would now rely on income taxes, not tariffs, to provide revenue. A central bank was created to provide rational monetary policy. Advances were made in antitrust policy and the regulation of commerce.

The overwhelming attitude among Senators was that Marshall had served as presiding officer with fairness and impartiality. He received the congratulations of many of them. In return, he stated:

> *May I be permitted to say that when I came here two years ago it was the first time that I ever stepped inside of a legislative body. I know that I have made mistakes, errors sometimes, of the head; but, thank God, I can look you in the face and say to you that there has never been an error of the heart.*[226]

The words were typical of Marshall – sincere, self-deprecating, and honest. At the end of two years in office, Marshall may not have established himself as a policy leader, but he had won the hearts of the United States Senate. Had Wilson recognized the value of the relationships that had been nurtured by his Vice President, the mistakes of the next four years might have been avoided.

❧ ❧ ❧ ❧ ❧

In May 1915, Major John McCrae was a surgeon with the Canadian 1st Field Artillery Brigade. Though he was a veteran of the Boer War in South Africa, the devastation he witnessed on the battlefield was appalling.

McCrae was particularly moved, however, by the death of a close friend from a shell burst. Artillery barrages were common during World War I. During the Third Battle of Ypres, for example, the preparatory bombardment alone consisted of 4,283,550 shells.[227] These bombardments often reduced a French village of limestone houses to wastelands of loose soil devoid of vegetation and rich in lime from pulverized buildings. The remains of McCrae's friend were brought to him in small sandbags wrapped up in an army blanket.[228]

The next day, while sitting in the back of an ambulance, McCrae noticed that wild, blood red poppies sprang up all around him. Poppies are a flower that can grow only under unusual circumstances. They require that the soil be loose and freshly churned. In addition, they thrive only when there are no other plants to compete with for moisture or nutrients. Finally, they require a high concentration of lime in the soil.

Surrounded by the flowers, McCrae wrote what has become perhaps the best know wartime poem.

> In Flanders fields the poppies blow
> Between the crosses, row on row,
> That mark our place; and in the sky
> The larks, still bravely singing, fly
> Scarce heard amid the guns below.
> We are the Dead. Short days ago
> We lived, felt dawn, saw sunset glow,
> Loved, and were loved, and now we lie
>   In Flanders fields.
> Take up our quarrel with the foe:
> To you from failing hands we throw
> The torch; be yours to hold it high.
> If ye break faith with us who die
> We shall not sleep, though poppies grow
>   In Flanders fields.

❧ ❧ ❧ ❧ ❧

Improvements in technology meant that in World War I new fighting machines were introduced that were frighteningly effective. Underwater boats, or U-boats as the Germans called their submarines, could deliver a torpedo to the most vulnerable portion of a ship – at the waterline. In the freezing waters of the North Atlantic, those who survived the detonation of the torpedo usually succumbed to the frigid water.

At the start of the War, German U-boats limited their targets to military vessels. But on February 4, 1915, Germany announced that the entire area around Great Britain was a war zone, and any ship attempting to travel within this zone would be destroyed. Five days later, President Wilson informed the

German government that they would be held "to a strict accountability" for "property endangered or lives lost".

Three months after Germany announced the war zone around the British Isles, the Cunard liner Lusitania was torpedoed and sank off the coast of Ireland. The passengers had been warned by the German Embassy not to sail on the ship. It was known, furthermore, that the ship was carrying munitions. On May 7, 1915, the Germans sank the ship without warning, and made no effort to rescue the passengers. Over 1,100 civilians died, including 128 American citizens.

Americans were outraged, but the Wilson Administration, at least initially, provided a subdued response. Secretary of State Bryan was the chief proponent of a cautious approach. Wilson declined to add fuel to the fires of passion. "There is such a thing", Wilson declared, "As a man being too proud to fight."

Marshall soon afterward gave a speech in Tupelo, Mississippi and reflected what he thought were the President's positions.

> *I trust my chieftain at Washington and not until he says "strike"*
> *will I speak in favor of war. The trouble with our civilization,*
> *especially northern and western States, is in not trying to follow*
> *the steps of "The Prince of Peace", instead of scheming to avoid*
> *the laws of the land and crying for war when war may not be*
> *the thing.*[229]

Along with his call for calm, Marshall also suggested that an American had responsibility for his own safety when he placed himself in a dangerous position by traveling on the ship of a belligerent nation.

The *New York Times* was outraged by Marshall's comments. The Vice President "should have sense enough not to embarrass the President by utterances at odds with his settled policy," the Times wrote, "and who will not spatter flippant epigrams on an international tragedy."

Marshall was angry at the remark, and directed some of his invective at Joe Tumulty, Wilson's secretary

> *I have been very much annoyed to see certain papers quoting me*
> *as not with the President on the war situation. I do not believe*

that he believes this. Still I want to tell you that everywhere I
was I urged everybody to trust him and pledged myself to await
his decision. These papers mix some comments on peace made
before the Lusitania incident with that incident. But nobody
who heard me doubts my loyalty and faith.[230]

Wilson was being urged by some advisors, particularly Robert Lansing of the State Department, to take a stronger tone with Germany in the official dispatches that crossed between the two countries in the wake of the sinking of the Lusitania. American public opinion was shifting decisively in favor of war, and Wilson felt he could no longer treat Germany and Great Britain as equals. Unable to support this policy shift, William Jennings Bryan resigned as Secretary of State on June 8, 1915. Wilson appointed Lansing in his place.

After Bryan's departure, Wilson took a firmer stance with Germany. He reiterated the American demand for recognition of the rights of neutrals, and that the belligerent nations were responsible for recognizing those rights. For Germany, which felt that unrestricted submarine warfare was critical to victory, Wilson's position put them in the untenable position of doing what they felt was necessary to win a military victory while at the same time endangering their relations with the United States.

Much of America applauded the tougher diplomacy. Marshall added to the chorus of congratulatory telegrams, and sent one to Secretary of State Lansing on July 24, 1915:

CONGRATULATIONS. YOU HAVE SAID IT. FOLLOW
WITH NOTE TO ENGLAND DEFINING THE
AMERICAN IDEA AND WE ARE IMPREGNABLE.[231]

Germany tried to maintain both their military options and their diplomatic relations. In early 1916, the semi-official German news agency, the Wolff Bureau, sought to obtain peaceful statements from American public opinion leaders. When asked for his views, Marshall said that the American policy was

... to uphold the recognized principles of international law
and maintain them impartially against all belligerents. We do

not want to humiliate Germany. Nothing is further from our thoughts. We do not want war; we want peace, but peace with honor, and all that our Administration is trying to accomplish is an amicable settlement, honorable to both sides.[232]

In the time before the United States committed to support the Allies, the German government used numerous methods to try to engender sympathy among Americans for the German cause. Marshall relays a story of one of these efforts.

One of the amusing incidents, to my mind, came out after (Count von Bernstorff, the German ambassador) received his letter of dismissal and we were entering the war. A girl from Indiana came into my office in great distress. She was a literary woman; had come to Washington to assist in the issuance of a society journal. It blew up when the count went home. Then she discovered that while it was ostensibly a society journal, in reality it was a magazine seeking favorably to mold public opinion for the German Empire. It had letters of endorsement from almost every leading woman, including Mrs. Wilson, in Washington, save and except Mrs. Marshall. It would contain an account of one of Mrs. Wilson's party gowns, and then below it would have some set of pretended friendship that the German Empire had shown to the American Republic. It was a shrewd move to mold public opinion in Washington, but it did not succeed.[233]

❧ ❧ ❧ ❧ ❧

On Sunday morning, July 5, 1915, Jack Morgan, the son of recently deceased financier J. Pierpont Morgan, and his wife Jessie, were finishing their breakfast when their butler, Henry Physick, answered a knock at the front door of their estate on the north shore of Long Island.

The man standing in the doorway presented Physick with a card indicating that he represented a firm that published society directories. Physick was skeptical and asked the caller to leave. The man forced his way into the house, and Physick raced to Jack and Jessie and yelled to them to run upstairs. Startled and uncertain what was happening, Jack and Jessie went upstairs, only to find the man carrying two pistols and holding their two daughters hostage at the top of the stairs.

The gunman calmly told the Morgans not to be frightened -- he only wanted to talk to them. As he spoke, Jessie saw her opening when the gunman was briefly distracted, and threw herself on him, knocking him to the ground. Jack jumped on the intruder who fired two shots, both of which struck him in the groin. Other servants rushed in and held the man to the ground while Physick smashed a chunk of coal over his head. As they subdued him they noticed a stick of dynamite in his pocket, which they placed under water until the police arrived.

As Jack Morgan was treated for his wounds, police identified the subject as Erich Muenter, a former instructor of German at Harvard who had disappeared in 1906 after being accused of poisoning his wife. Opposed to American arms sales in Europe, Muenter had planned to hold Morgan hostage until arms shipments were halted. He felt Morgan had the power to stop the sale of weapons. To make sure his plan was successful, he said, he also planted a bomb in the desk of Vice President Marshall.[234]

Several weeks after Congress approved the war resolution, Muenter had entered the Capital on the Friday afternoon before the long Fourth of July weekend. Carrying three sticks of dynamite, he tried to enter Senate chamber. Finding the chamber doors locked, he decided to place his explosives near the Vice President's office just outside the Senate gallery. After he set the timing mechanism he walked to Union Station and purchased a ticket for the midnight train to New York City. Just before midnight Muenter watched from Union Station when the bomb exploded.

Fortunately for Marshall, the bomb exploded when he was not in the office and no one was injured. Calls came for increased security for government officials, but Marshall was skeptical of their effectiveness. "If I am to be killed by an anarchist," he was quoted as saying, "I don't believe all of the Secret Service men in the country, if they were notified of the threat, could prevent it."[235] Marshall must have certainly had in mind President McKinley, who was surrounded by security men when he was shot.

Marshall received numerous death threats during his term as Vice President. He seldom took them seriously, and often threw away threatening letters rather than notifying the Secret Service. Muenter's bomb did not change Marshall's attitude. Though there were numerous assassinations of prominent leaders during Marshall's career – McKinley and Archduke Ferdinand were two recent examples – he remained unconcerned about the possibility of a violent death, and did not allow threats or intimidating letters to vary his daily schedule.

⤐ ⤐ ⤐ ⤐ ⤐

While the armies of European nations imposed ghastly carnage on their foes, plans continued for the Panama Pacific International Exposition in San Francisco. Scheduled long before hostilities broke out, the leading nations of the world prepared buildings and exhibitions designed to showcase technological advancements and world cooperation. Hoping the sessions might open up an avenue for peace negotiations, Secretary of State Bryan had declared in 1914 that the Exposition would proceed as planned, and each of the forty-one nations that had committed to the event continued their participation despite the war.

Wilson asked Marshall to represent the United States at the Exposition. Lois would accompany him, and his itinerary was developed with the help of Assistant Secretary of the Navy Franklin D. Roosevelt.

The Vice President and his wife planned several stops in their travels to San Francisco. One stop was Pittsburgh, where Marshall attended the funeral of a sailor who had been killed in Mexico. Marshall was always personally opposed to intervention in Mexico or any other Latin American country. His comments also touch on his pacifist views – a viewpoint that would be sorely tested:

> *(The sailor's) mother is a brave Irishwoman and she had draped her boy's picture with the Stars and Stripes. That woeful visit caused me to take a solemn oath that I would support no war movement by this country unless the alien invader's foot was placed on our shores.*[236]

The Vice President's entourage continued on to Chicago, were they were joined by more dignitaries, including Franklin Roosevelt's wife, Eleanor. She later wrote:

> *Vice President and Mrs. Marshall were to join us in Chicago; and, as I had never known either of them well, and the Vice President had the reputation of being extremely silent, I looked forward with some trepidation of being thrown with them on what must be rather intimate terms. I liked them both very much, and while I struggled through a number of meals with rather a silent gentleman, I discovered that he had a fund of dry humor and there was no pretentiousness about him. When he did not know a thing he said so. When he did not like a thing he said so, and usually had some amusing remark to make. We were on the back platform of the train when we crossed the Great Salt Lake. Everyone was exclaiming at the beauty around us. He removed the cigar which was rarely out of his mouth and remarked, "I never did like scenery".*[237]

When Marshall's party reached San Francisco, they were greeted with a parade through downtown San Francisco, including a band that played "On the Banks of the Wabash". That evening, Tom and Lois were the dinner guests of William Randolph Hearst and his wife.

The following Monday, a reception was held in the Vice President's honor at the California Building. Representatives from the leading nations of the world were present, as were the Governor of California, Hiram Johnson, and former Vice President Charles Warren Fairbanks.

Marshall's remarks were cordial and welcoming:

> *Shall I say welcome? Is it necessary? In a way, perhaps; but, my friends, you have but come into your brother's house. You are here on a friendly mission. There is nothing like looking a man in the eye, and clasping his hand, to know him. You may know that prejudices exist, but the gladness of my greeting today would be clothed in sackcloth and ashes if every Commissioner here, after he has met us to know us, could not go back to his own people knowing that he had been in a friendly land. I ask you, in the name of my Chief, to uphold his hand in this, the crucial hour of the world's history, and help make swords into plowshares and spears into knitting needles.*[238]

On Wednesday, the Exposition was dedicated by Marshall in the name of the President. Marshall speech on that day ranks as one of the finest of his career. Because there were no microphones, many in the crowd may have had difficulty hearing him. But those that were close enough heard the Vice President speak of high hopes for civilized men, of the beauty of the buildings at the Exposition, and for peace. He honored pioneers and pathfinders (perhaps he reflected on his own family's travels west in a covered wagon), and spoke glowingly of the recently completed Panama Canal.

In many ways, the speech was unlike Marshall's usual style. Rather than folksy stories and dry humor, he created a more glorious vision for his audience. Clearly he felt that he was speaking for the President and representing his country to the representatives of the world's leading nations who were gathered here in peace, while thoughts of war were uppermost in the minds of those present.

> *We believe that the whole world moves toward a far-off divine event and that our mission in that movement is to promote peace and good will. And we think the days here spent by those of other lands will greatly aid in that good work … Her men of every age and every clime behold the noonday of the world's accomplishment, the crystallization of the dreams and thoughts of genius and talent. May we not hope that here a thought-dawn will be born that shall not cease to broaden until, at its meridian height, all men around the world are one?*

Those present – including future president Roosevelt – could not help but have been moved by Marshall's eloquence. As one reporter noted, Marshall spoke …

> *… with an almost inspired tongue. Neither Woodrow Wilson nor any other man could have made on this day at the Exposition a greater speech than that of the second officer who represented the American government. History, prophecy, humanity, civilization, sentiment, idealism, imagination and logic all held place in the great heart and mind of this great American on this great occasion.*[239]

Later during the Exposition, the Vice President attended a reception held in his honor on the cruiser *San Diego*, which was anchored in the harbor. For the occasion, Franklin Roosevelt had designed the first vice presidential flag, which was flown when Marshall came on board.

> *Marshall came up the gangplank in the formal attire that the occasion required: silk hat, frock coat, gloves, and cane. He had forgotten to take the cigar out of his mouth. When the band struck up the "Star Spangled Banner," the vice president "realized his predicament" and took the cigar out of his mouth but was now trying to hold his hat, his cane and his cigar in one hand while saluting with the other. When the first gun of salute was fired, it so startled Marshall's 125-pound frame that the hat, cane and cigar went two feet in the air and scattered across the deck of the ship. "By that time," Roosevelt recalled, "the Admiral and I had sprinted across the deck and rescued the Vice President."*[240]

Later that week, Roosevelt and Marshall watched a motion picture that included the scene aboard the cruiser. "My God," said Marshall, "if I looked like that I will never go on board another ship as long as I live!"

ক ক ক ক ক

While the Marshalls were vacationing in Arizona in the fall of 1915, reporters began to circulate rumors that Wilson intended to drop the Vice President from the ticket in the 1916 presidential election. One story quoted Wilson as saying it was "unlucky to run the same team twice". Marshall told reporters he did not place any credence in the stories. Tumulty, speaking for the President, denied that Wilson had said he did not want Marshall for a second term.

Significantly, Tumulty did not directly address the question of whether or not Wilson wanted Marshall on the ticket in 1916 – he merely denied that Wilson had made any public statement about the question. But it soon became clear that Wilson would not be making a commitment to keeping Marshall on the ticket. Instead, he would leave that decision up to the 1916 Democratic Convention.

Rumors persisted that some Democratic leaders were recruiting candidates to take Marshall's place in 1916. Arizona Senator Henry Ashhurst, wishing to clear up the controversy, met with Wilson to ask him directly about his intentions regarding Marshall.

Ashurst asked Wilson to commit to Marshall as his running mate. "I have a very high regard for Vice President Marshall," Wilson replied, "and I wish you would tell him so." Does this mean, Ashurst asked, that he would support Marshall's renomination. "Why, Yes!" the President replied.

Ashurst immediately sent a telegram to Marshall in Arizona to inform him of his conversation with Wilson. Marshall was grateful for Ashurst's persistence:

> *I thank you for your telegram and kind letter, as much as for their contents. It pays a man for the little humiliations of life, to have such staunch friends as you and others are.*
> *You saw, of course, that I said I did not believe it. Whenever it is shown that I would be a burden to the President I would voluntarily withdraw, but I do not think I deserve to be kicked by men who lost their states while we carried Indiana.*[241]

Who Marshall was thinking of when he referred to "men who lost their states" is not clear. Since the southern states voted uniformly Democratic, reference must have been to a "northern" senator. About this same time, Senator James Hamilton Lewis of Illinois had indicated his interest in the Vice presidential nomination.

Surprisingly, the *New York Times*, known over the years for their editorials in opposition to Marshall, came out in favor of his renomination, but could not resist taking a swipe at some of his faults. "Even those who have been most impatient with his loquacity, his lack of wisdom, and his blunted sense of proportion," wrote the Times, "gladly admit his impeccable honesty, an honesty which is not limited to dollars and cents, but is an intellectual honesty as well."[242]

Edith Bolling was born October 15, 1872 in Wytheville, Virginia, one of eleven children born to William and Sally Bolling. While her family's roots traced back to early Virginia history, her early years were far from opulent as she and her family shared a small room above a retail store.

Her father's law practice eventually was successful, and he was appointed as a local judge. This put him in the position of sending his daughter Edith to school at Martha Washington College, but she disliked the academic rigors of a college education and withdrew after one year. She tried school again, but her good looks and slender figure caught the eye of many potential suitors. She dated many eligible bachelors and, four years after they first met, married Norman Galt, who owned a successful silver and jewelry store in Washington, DC.

Edith Bolling Galt showed little interest in her husband's business, and the couple remained childless after their son died in infancy in 1903. Edith, though, was fond of travel, especially in Europe, and the couple was one of the first in the Nation's Capital to own a new invention termed an "automobile", in which Edith could be seen as one of the first women to learn to drive in Washington.

In 1907, however, Norman developed a liver infection and died in January of the following year. Without the experience to run the jewelry store, Edith hired a manager to oversee the operations. Profits from the store enabled her to continue her travels, and during several trips to Europe acquired a large wardrobe of fine clothes.

Edith Galt had become a friend with the President's physician, Cary Grayson. Grayson had been dating Alice Gordon, a friend of Edith's – and who, within two years, Grayson would marry. One day, while Wilson and Grayson were driving in an automobile through Washington, Grayson spotted Edith and waved. "Who is that beautiful woman?", Woodrow is said to have asked.[243]

Woodrow and Edith would not meet until March of 1915. After walking with Wilson's cousin, Helen Bones, Edith was invited to tea at the White House. Edith protested that her shoes were too muddy; Helen persisted. As they entered the White House they happened to run into Wilson and Grayson who, as it happens, also had muddy shoes from a golf game.

The afternoon tea was followed several days later by dinner, and from that point on the widow and widower were inseparable. The fifty-eight year old

Wilson found a soul mate and confidant in the forty-two-year-old Galt, and they exchanged correspondence, presents, and affection. Within eight weeks, Woodrow had proposed marriage.

Despite Woodrow's infatuation with Edith, the timing of the romance could not have been worse from the perspective of policymakers close to the White House. Washington gossips were energized by the romance between the President the young widower seventeen years his junior. Wilson was incensed by a comment made by a British diplomat and quickly repeated among socialites in the nation's capital: "What did the new Mrs. Wilson do when the President proposed?" the story went. "She fell out of bed with surprise."[244]

Aside from the fact that Ellen had died just the previous August – a mourning period of a minimum of one year was considered proper – it became increasingly clear that the United States would be drawn into the conflict in Europe.

Mary Peck's relationship with Woodrow also resurfaced during the summer of 1915. In response to an appeal from Mary, Wilson had sent her a check for $7,500, ostensibly to set up Mary's son in a business. Word of the payment to Mary soon circulated among White House insiders including Grayson and Wilson's son-in-law, Treasury Secretary William McAdoo.

McAdoo and his wife Eleanor strongly opposed Wilson's remarriage. Hoping to postpone the engagement, McAdoo concocted a story which purported that Peck was sharing some of the intimate correspondence she had with the President with others, and that the revelations could hurt Wilson's reelection chances the following year. One version even suggested that the letters would be published. Though the story was a fabrication, many Washington insiders knew enough about the relationship to lend credence to the matter.

Wilson felt he had no choice but to share the details of his relationship to Peck with Edith, who was crestfallen on hearing the news. Despite the revelations of the relationship, Edith, after several days of soul searching, agreed to continue with the engagement. A wedding date was set for December of 1915.

In the fall of 1915, while Tom and Lois were vacationing in Arizona, they learned that the President would remarry. In Marshall's typical intimate fashion, he wrote to Edith Galt:

Now that you are about to become the Mistress of the White House, you will, I am sure, pardon the seeming unwarranted intimate tone of this letter. Out here upon the desert, Mrs. Marshall and I have heard of your happiness and that of the President. As we start back home we have wondered how best we could remember you upon your approaching marriage. We know that the gods, big and little, will lay at your feet the finer products of civilization. And so we thought and hoped something typical of the West might not be inappropriate. We have succeeded in procuring a blanket, woven of native wool, by an Indian woman for a Navajo chief. We send it to you as a sample of America's earliest "infant industry", hoping that what was intended to adorn the shoulders of an alleged noble red man, may be worthy to be trodden underfoot by the great White Chief, whom are (sic) democrats love and are loyal Americans. Believe that back of it there is the sincerest good wishes of Mrs. Marshall and myself.[245]

Marshall's warm and affectionate letter reflected his folksy personality and friendly manner. It would, however, do little to thaw the icy demeanor of Edith Wilson, or changer her thinly disguised disdain for Marshall and his wife.

On the journey back from Arizona, Lois became seriously ill. They decided to have her examined in Indianapolis, where it was determined that Lois would need abdominal surgery. The surgery was performed successfully just before Thanksgiving Day, but, as a result, Marshall was not present for the convening of the Sixty-Fourth session of Congress in early December.

Lois Marshall made a full recovery, and she and Tom were back in Washington for the start of the new year, 1916. The Vice President must certainly have looked back proudly at the Wilson administration's accomplishments over the previous three years, and the role that he played as goodwill ambassador and Democratic party supporter.

But the quadrennial election calendar showed 1916 as a presidential election year. Wilson had not yet announced his election intentions, though Marshall knew he would be Wilson's running mate should he seek a second term.

In Europe, advancing technology was resulting in a death toll unprecedented in human history, with no end in sight. And the next four years would bring Marshall political, ethical and personal challenges that he could not have imagined.

✍ ✍ ✍ ✍ ✍

In the early part of 1916, Kaiser Wilhelm II was convinced by his advisors that the key to winning the war was to force the French to capitulate. Russia was on the verge of revolution and would soon cease being a threat; the British, it was reasoned, would not pursue the war against the Germans without the French as strong allies.

Cannily, the Germans chose the launch a major offensive against the fortifications at Verdun. While of dubious strategic value, Verdun had represented the patriotism and nationalism of the French. It was the last fortress town to fall to the Prussians in the Franco-Prussian war of 1870-71, and since that time Verdun's fortifications had been significantly boosted so that they would never again be overrun by the Germans. The Germans knew, then, that the French would relentlessly defend Verdun if only because of its symbolic value. Surrounded on three sides, German forces had the strategic advantage and thought they could "bleed France white" in its defense of the town.

The German offensive began on February 21, 1916 with a 21-hour bombardment by 1,400 guns along an eight-mile front. Each hour, 100,000 shells poured into Verdun, as the Kaiser hoped to kill the majority of the French defenders before the infantry even started their advance into the fortress. When the shelling had stopped, one million German troops advanced against 200,000 French defenders.

The Germans had correctly predicted that the French would defend Verdun at all costs, but they overestimated their ability to overcome the defenders. A second offensive was launched in early March, and a third in April. When little ground had been gained by June, the Germans introduced phosgene gases, which, when inhaled, formed hydrochloric acid in the lungs of the French soldiers. They died gasping for air as the acid burned through their lung tissue.

The French poured reinforcements into the battle until their casualties were estimated at over half a million, including 250,000 dead. German dead exceeded 200,000. By late summer it was clear that neither side would gain any military advantage from the carnage. The French army avoided complete decimation only because the British had agreed to launch a new offensive at Somme.

Comprising the main Allied attack on the Western Front during 1916, the Battle of the Somme is famous chiefly on account of the loss of 58,000 British troops (one third of them killed) on the first day of the battle, 1 July 1916, which to this day remains a one-day record. The attack was launched upon a 30-kilometer front, from north of the Somme river between Arras and Albert, and ran from 1 July until 18 November, at which point it was called off.

On Saturday, June 24, 1916, the British Army began a bombardment of the forward defense of the German lines along a twenty-mile front just north of the Somme river. The artillery shelling, from 1,500 British guns, would eventually result in 1.8 million shells exploding among the German front lines.

The British plan called for the shelling to continue until July 1. At that time, planners had concluded, the front line of the German army would be decimated, and British troops, loaded with supplies, would move into the recently shelled area. Cavalry on horseback would speed ahead and clear any remaining German survivors. With the barbed wire blasted to pieces by the shells, it was reasoned that the troops should move forward in military marching order, so as to remain organized to set up the new British camps where the Germans had stood.

Most of the British soldiers were volunteers. Motivated by patriotism and the promise that groups of friends could be kept together, they had little understanding of the technological advances in the science of military weaponry. Inspired by a publicity campaign at home, the British forces went into action together with their peers: Boys enlisted together from Oxford and Cambridge, the sons of miners from Wales, farm boys from the north country. Entire sports teams joined together under the promise of being kept together in the army units.

When the shelling stopped on the morning of July 1, the British moved forward in tightly packed lines. Laden down with provisions for several weeks, they moved slowly past the muddy shell craters. But the British artillery barrage had failed not only to incapacitate the German soldiers, it also did little to disrupt the barbed wire. The Germans, warned of the advance by the incessant shelling, stepped from the bunkers when the bombing stopped and quickly set up machine guns. With heavy packs, tangled in the wire, the British made easy targets. The horses of the cavalry found themselves mired in mud and they, too, were riddled by machine gun fire. On the first day of the offensive, 19,240 British soldiers died – the most to die on a single day in any war before that day or since.

Despite carnage, the British leadership was convinced the Germans were on the point of exhaustion and that a breakthrough was imminent. British troops continued their advance from July through November. Despite the introduction of a new fighting vehicle called a "tank", the British gained little ground. Finally, in mid November, British leaders called a halt to the offensive. British forces moved forward just seven miles, the taking of which resulted in 420,000 estimated British casualties, plus 200,000 French casualties. The Allies, then, lost 88,000 men for each mile they advanced. The Germans had lost half a million men.

Days before, Woodrow Wilson had been re-elected as President of the United States. It could not have been a comfort to the British or French to hear what Wilson had said the previous May during a speech in Philadelphia. "There is such a thing as a man being too proud to fight," Wilson said, "There is such a thing as a nation being so right that it does not need to convince others by force that it is right."

⋞ ⋞ ⋞ ⋞ ⋞

Charles Evans Hughes was born in upstate New York in 1862. Extraordinarily bright, by the age of twenty-two he had earned a baccalaureate at Brown and was first in his class in the law school at Columbia University.

After two decades building a successful law practice, he turned to public service and developed a reputation as honest, hard working and incorruptible. Though repelled by many aspects of politics, he was elected Governor of New York in 1906. When a vacancy occurred on the Supreme Court in 1910, he was nominated by President Taft and most observers thought his political career was over.

But while Hughes was serving on the high court the Republican Party was painfully split by the Roosevelt-Taft schism of 1912. Few Republicans emerged from that debacle unscathed, and when party leaders looked for a strong candidate their eyes turned to Hughes, who had not been forced to cast his lot with either side in the 1912 contest.

The Indiana delegation to the 1916 Republican National Convention supported Charles Warren Fairbanks as a "favorite son" candidate, hoping to put his name forward as a compromise candidate. When Hughes obtained the nomination, the Indiana delegation was successful in naming Fairbanks as his running mate. At first Fairbanks opposed the appointment but, in the interest of party unity, he accepted.

The election of 1916, then, would pit two Hoosier Vice Presidential candidates against one another. But political pundits were unimpressed by either running mate. As the New Republic put it, "Mr. Marshall is an argument for the election of Mr. Hughes. Mr. Fairbanks is an argument for the re -election of Mr. Wilson."

Hughes spoke in Richmond, Indiana on a campaign swing through the Hoosier State. He attacked Wilson for signing the Adamson Bill which provided for an eight-hour workday for workers on interstate railways and required time and a half for working overtime. Neither Wilson nor Marshall liked the measure, but the President signed the bill in order to ward off a threatened Labor Day strike.

Marshall publicly supported the Adamson bill. "Solomon worked his men eight hours a day in building the Temple," he noted, using his characteristic humor and historical reference, "and Solomon was a pretty wise man for his generation." The Vice President tried to move the campaign rhetoric away from the Adamson bill, stating that the "paramount issue" of the campaign was Wilson's leadership in foreign policy. Writing to the President in late September, 1916, Marshall noted:

> *I am saying nothing upon the 8-hour law other than to make fun of it as an issue until the Republican candidates for President, senators and Representatives will join in a written statement to the American people that will repeal the law if elected. I hope to keep away entirely from it, but this is the best I can do – to deny that any body can make an issue by mere criticism. If you*

want me to accept it as an issue, please let me know and I will then take it up in detail before my audiences.

Am not scared yet though Brother Hughes is blushing for his country all over Indiana. He says so. Nobody has seen the blush.

"I think you are taking the right attitude towards the so-called issue he is making on the 8-hour day," Wilson responded, "For a little while I feel that in some quarters he is making some impression, but it will prove to be a broken reed in his hand, as everything else has".[246]

Hughes spoke often of how his decisions would differ from Wilson if he were chief executive. In an era before the prominence of sound bites and continuous news channels, Marshall's response was sure to delight readers in newspapers across the country:

He doesn't know what he would have done. He only thinks he knows. I think if I had been in the Garden of Eden I would not have eaten the apple. But I don't know – I never met that charming soubrette Eve. I might have eaten two apples.[247]

◈ ◈ ◈ ◈ ◈

As the presidential election of 1916 drew to a close, Wilson's advisors were grim in their predictions of the electoral outcome. The first results in the nation – from Maine, which voted in September – went decisively for Hughes. Though a traditionally Republican state, Democratic strategists were disappointed in the results. Gambling bookies in New York made Hughes the slight favorite.

Colonel House kept one eye on the election and the other on the carnage in Europe. Particularly problematic to House was the long lag between the results of the election in November and inauguration the following March. Could a lame duck American President adequately manage foreign policy? If not, would the soldiers in the trenches suffer while the United States waited until the new President assumed his duties?

House developed a plan to give presidential power to Hughes before inauguration day. The Constitution called for the Secretary of State to assume the powers of the Presidency in the event of the death, disability or resignation of both the President and Vice President. Under House's plan, in the event of a Hughes victory, Secretary of State Lansing would resign, and Wilson would appoint Hughes in his place. Soon afterward, both Wilson and Marshall would step down, giving the powers of the presidency to Hughes.

House presented his plan to Wilson, outlining the political and legal ramifications of the transfer of power. He was confident he could persuade Wilson and Hughes to move forward with the plan, but also knew that he needed one more vote of approval. "The course I have in mind," House wrote, "is dependent upon the consent and cooperation of the Vice President."

Was Marshall ever informed of the plan? The historical record is unclear. No mention is made in his memoirs. In addition, even if Marshall was briefed ahead of time, it is entirely possible that he would decline to agree with the proposal, given his strong affinity for the will of the electorate. He and Wilson were elected in 1912 for four-year terms, Marshall may have thought, not to resign before their responsibilities were complete.

John E. Brown, in his dissertation on Marshall, concluded that the Vice President was informed of the plan but declined to participate. He cites an interview that Charles Thomas, Marshall's biographer, had with a close friend of Marshall's from Columbia City, J.C. Sanders. In that interview, Sanders said Marshall told him of a time when Wilson had asked Marshall to resign. Sanders thought that the request came during the League of Nations debate, but Brown thinks that is unlikely. Based on his interview with Sanders, Thomas also believes Marshall knew of the plan but refused to go along. "The one thing certain was that he had refused to resign," Thomas wrote, "Marshall emphatically explained to this friend that the people had elected him for a four-year term and he had intended to serve out his entire term."[248]

But a comment Marshall made in September of 1916 makes it clear Marshall had agreed to the plan. During a campaign stop in Terre Haute, Indiana, he told his audience that he would resign rather than become president should "a calamity" overtake Wilson:

> *If I believed the European war would last during the remainder of the present administration, and there was a likelihood of a calamity befalling President Wilson that would shift the burden of responsibilities to my shoulders, I would resign my office.*[249]

Why would Marshall make such a statement, apparently without prompting, with the election only six weeks away? He could have avoided the issue, but his devotion to honesty and candor would not allow him to mislead the public. The only explanation for Marshall's comments are that Colonel House had communicated his plan to Marshall, and Marshall agreed to go along.

With the partisanship of the election in full bloom, it is not surprising that that Republican-leaning newspapers squarely condemned Marshall's comments:

> *It is highly regrettable ... that (Marshall) indulged in an utterance so radical, for the reason that those who do not know him, and this is something over ninety-nine millions of Americans, will take him at his word. And taking him at his word they will wonder what sort of a wild and woolly fool he is. They will believe that he is lacking in backbone, nerve, and manhood, and they will naturally conclude that one who is so lacking is unjust both to his party and his country in assuming an office that is removed only one place from the presidency and which any hour may thrust the presidency upon him. They will conclude, and very logically, too, that if he feels that way about his office he should never have accepted a renomination and that it is not yet too late for him to retire. They will say that he lacks moral courage, stamina and a good many other things that should pertain to the position which he holds. And Mr. Marshall himself because of his weird words will be directly responsible for all of the unkind things thought and said about him. He will merit the censure, for he is old enough, in all conscience, to come down to earth and talk common sense.*[250]

With the election of Wilson the issue was moot. Wilson won by slim margins in both the popular vote and electoral college. The solid Democratic vote in the southern states was enough to give Wilson the victory. That was fortunate, because neither Wilson nor Marshall could carry their home states.

Hughes proved to be a poor campaigner. In an era when voter impressions were formed at speeches and political rallies, Hughes had a speaking style that was lackluster and uninspiring. Teddy Roosevelt referred to Hughes as "the bearded iceberg", and one aid to Taft felt he had the magnetism of a potato.[251]

Worse still for the Republican ticket, Vice Presidential candidate Fairbanks became ill in September, and didn't campaign for the remainder of the election.

But perhaps the most damaging mistake came when Hughes snubbed California Governor Hiram Johnson while visiting with dignitaries in western states. Johnson had reluctantly served as Roosevelt's running mate with the Progressive Party in 1912. Mainstream Republicans, including Hughes, still seethed at Johnson's role in that debacle. But Hiram Johnson remained popular among the electorate in California.

As a result, while Johnson nominally supported Hughes, he did little to promote his presidential campaign. Johnson's inaction may have been decisive. While Johnson won a Senate seat by almost 300,000 votes, Wilson beat Hughes in California by less than 4,000 votes. A victory in California would have given Hughes the presidency. Instead, Wilson garnered 277 electoral votes versus 254 for Hughes.

In Indiana, Hughes and Fairbanks won by seven thousand votes out of nearly seven hundred thousand cast. Republicans won both Senate seats, as well as the governorship.

Marshall soon received congratulations from his friend Fairbanks, and he returned the favor.

> As a partisan it is worth much to know that we have won. As a man it is worth more to know that the years of personal friendship have not ended with this campaign, and to feel that there are left a few men at least who may differ in politics and yet wish each other well. I rejoice to believe that you always have been of that chosen few. Long life and serene content for you.[252]

Though the margins were slim and his party fared poorly, Marshall knew that a victory was a victory regardless of the numbers. Thomas Marshall became the first Vice President to be re-elected since John C. Calhoun had done it in 1829. Marshall would also become the first Vice President to serve two full terms since Daniel Tompkins had done so in the period from 1817 to 1825 (Calhoun resigned before his second term was complete.)

Marshall quoted Shakespeare in his congratulatory telegram to Wilson:

> *'TIS NOT SO DEEP AS A WELL*
> *NOR SO WIDE AS A CHURCHDOOR:*
> *BUT 'TIS ENOUGH. 'TWILL SERVE.*[253]

CHAPTER EIGHT:

She Can Do No Other

(1917-1918)

The elections of 1916 would produce a split in control of Congress. Republicans held a slim majority – 217 to 213 – in the House, while the Democrats had a majority of twelve seats in the Senate.

But the mood was far different than four years previously. The sense of progressive reform that had permeated both sides of the aisle was gone, replaced by increasingly partisan rhetoric. In addition, it was clear that the Republicans were gaining the political momentum.

Soon after the elections, Tom and Lois hosted a reception for Senators and their wives at their residence in the Willard Hotel honoring the President and Mrs. Wilson. The evening was filled with friendly conversation until Henry Cabot Lodge's name was mentioned. The President's face became grim, and he firmly announced that he would not shake hands with Senator Lodge.

Passions for and against the war were high, and the debate would take an ominous turn when the content of a letter written by German Foreign Minister Arthur Zimmermann to the German Minister in Mexico in mid-January were released to the press.

*ON THE FIRST OF FEBRUARY WE INTEND TO BEGIN SUBMARINE WARFARE UNRESTRICTED. IN SPITE OF THIS, IT IS OUR INTENTION TO ENDEAVOR TO KEEP NEUTRAL THE UNITED STATES OF AMERICA.
IF THIS ATTEMPT IS NOT SUCCESSFUL, WE PROPOSE AN ALLIANCE ON THE FOLLOWING BASIS WITH*

MEXICO: THAT WE SHALL MAKE WAR TOGETHER AND TOGETHER MAKE PEACE. WE SHALL GIVE GENERAL FINANCIAL SUPPORT, AND IT IS UNDERSTOOD THAT MEXICO IS TO RECONQUER THE LOST TERRITORY OF NEW MEXICO, TEXAS AND ARIZONA …

President Wilson was shown the note, which had been intercepted by British intelligence, on February 24th. He released it to the world press a week later. Americans – even those who had opposed the United States entering the war – were incredulous. The resumption of unrestricted submarine warfare was chilling enough, but for the Germans to propose an alliance with the Mexicans to enable them to "reconquer" Arizona, New Mexico and Texas shocked the nation and jolted it out of what remained of its commitment to neutrality. The reaction was swift and virtually unanimous – war was now inevitable.

✄ ✄ ✄ ✄ ✄

Wilson's inauguration for a second term in March of 1917 was perhaps the most somber in the nation's history with the exception of Lincoln's inaugural in 1861. With the publication of the Zimmerman Telegram the prior week, it was clear that the nation was heading for a war in which the outcome was not at all certain. "The inauguration was not a festival," wrote the *New York Times*, "it was a momentary interlude in a grave business, and it must be got over with as briefly and simply as possible."

Marshall understood the solemnity of the day. His inauguration for a second term would also be brief and subdued. Upon the conclusion of his oath, he responded, "I do, so help me God, in whom I believe."[254]

The inauguration was wrapped up quickly, and all eyes turned to Wilson. He huddled with his closest advisors (Marshall, of course, was not included) who, to a man, called for war.

To Marshall, it was clear that war against Germany was inevitable.

The submarine warfare grew in intensity during the early months of 1917. I was out making a few speeches in the South, and I think I am the first person who declared that regardless of

whether there was a declaration of war, there was a state of war
existing between the government of the United States and the
Imperial German Government. For many times in the history
of man a state of war has existed without there having been a
declaration thereof.[255]

Barely a month after the start of Wilson's second term, and despite the fact that he ran for reelection on the theme that "He kept us out of war", the indecision of the previous four years was over. The Senate chamber was packed with congressmen, Supreme Court justices, cabinet members, diplomats and prominent national and international leaders in the gallery. Wilson's speech to Congress on April 2, 1917, stands not only as one of his finest, but as one of the great Presidential speeches in American history.

It is a fearful thing to lead this great peaceful people into war,
into the most terrible and disastrous of all wars, civilization
itself seeming to be in the balance. But the right is more precious
than peace, and we shall fight for the things which we have
always carried nearest our hearts – for democracy, for the right
of those who submit to authority to have a voice in their own
governments, for the rights and liberties of small nations, for a
universal dominion of right by such a concert of free peoples as
shall bring peace and safety to all nations and make the world
itself at last free. To such a task we can dedicate our lives and
our fortunes, everything that we are and everything that we
have, with the pride of those who know that the day has come
when America is privileged to spend her blood and her might for
the principles that gave her birth and happiness and peace which
she has treasured. God helping her, she can do no other.[256]

Finally, Wilson was unable to maintain his neutral stance. Marshall had nothing but admiration for his President's decision.

Then came the day when he appeared before the Congress of
the United States to deliver what was known as his famous
war message. I never had the opportunity to penetrate his inner

consciousness, but I felt then as I feel now, that it was the most abhorrent duty he ever performed.[257]

❦ ❦ ❦ ❦ ❦

Jeanette Rankin was born on June 11, 1880, on a ranch near Missoula, Montana, the oldest of seven children. After graduating from the University of Montana in 1902, she began her career as a social worker and also became active in the suffrage movement. In 1912, she returned to Montana to lead the fight for a women's suffrage law, which was passed two years later.

Building on her popularity among the newly-franchised women voters, Rankin was elected to the House of Representatives. She took her seat on April 2, 1916 – on the same day that Wilson had asked Congress for a declaration of war. Four days later, in the predawn hours of April 6, after months of mounting pressure, she told her colleagues in a moment of high drama: "I want to stand behind my country, but I cannot vote for war."

Rankin stood against the declaration of war. She was joined by forty-nine of her colleagues, as the final House vote to declare war was 373 to 50. Her position was unpopular, and in 1918 she lost in her bid for the Republican nomination for the Senate.

Thirty-two years later, seeing war clouds gathering in Europe, she again ran for the House of Representatives. She ran on a pacifist platform, and was successful based, in part, on her vote against entering the declaration of war in 1917.

Pearl Harbor did not change her stance. Despite the pleadings for unanimity by congressional leadership, and the eloquence of Franklin Roosevelt, Rankin cast the only dissent in the 388 to 1 House vote on the Declaration of War against Japan. "I voted against it", she said, "because it was war."[258]

❦ ❦ ❦ ❦ ❦

On April 6, 1917, Speaker of the House Champ Clark, Vice President Thomas Marshall, and President Woodrow Wilson signed the Joint Resolution of the Sixty-fifth Congress declaring war.

The months of the European war dragged on with leaden feet. In the main, blood became thicker than water. The neutral position of the American government became more and more difficult. People would talk about the war, and notwithstanding all the charges that we were a money-grubbing people, the great majority looked on what they believed to be the offences of the British government in violation of international law, as less reprehensible than those of the German government. For the allies turned their attention to property while the German submarine turned its attention to life; and the attitude of the American people slowly was being crystallized into one friendly to the allies.[259]

Marshall saw World War I as a moral crusade to preserve the dignity of the state for the rights of individuals.

The World War was not entered, in reality, because a few of our ships were sunken and a few of our citizens were lost upon the high seas. It was because the soul of America could no longer yield its assent to the doctrine that there were two measures of conduct – one for the individual and one for the state – and that the state could order the individual to break every moral law and the individual go Scot free in the courts of man and God because he had obeyed constituted authority.[260]

Subsequent evaluations of America's role in World War I would declare that it was the business interests and the quest for profits that resulted in America's participation in the war to end all wars. Marshall strongly disagreed.

The American people have been accused of money-grubbing and money-loving. Their sympathies up to that time were quite largely with the allied governments, it is true, but not to the extent of condoning what they believed to be a breach of international law, nor in joining the fight with those who were guilty of this breach. But there is something the American loves more than money – he loves humanity. And when he realized the attitude of the Imperial German Government, it was immaterial to him how many of the laws of neutrality had been violated by the allies or how much of the property of America had been, as he saw it, unjustly seized. He is not willing to sacrifice a single human life for the collection of an American dollar, but he is willing to sacrifice every American dollar to avenge the ruthless destruction of a single American life by a government which pretends to be and which ought to be a civilized government.[261]

⚜ ⚜ ⚜ ⚜ ⚜

One afternoon in May of 1917, Marshall asked for an appointment with the Wilson. So soon on the heels of the declaration of war both the Commander in Chief and his Vice President must have certainly had many issues to deal with, but Marshall felt bound by duty to inform his President of an event in the life of he and his wife. Tom and Lois were going to bring a child into their family.

By the spring of 1917, Tom and Lois had been married nearly twenty-five years. Their love and devotion were without question, and despite the Vice President's heavy travel schedule the two were almost never apart. With only a few exceptions their active life had been integral for Tom's career and exhilarating for Lois. But by 1917 Tom was in his mid-sixties while Lois was in her mid-forties. The tensions that were natural with this type of age discrepancy were exacerbated by their childless marriage.

The reason for their lack of fertility is unclear. It is unlikely that they had intentionally avoided children. No record exists to confirm whether he or she had any type of medical condition which resulted in infertility, but by this time in their marriage it would be reasonable to assume that Lois could look to a time when she would be alone. It is likely that it was she who was looking for an opportunity to bring a child into their life.

As part of her charitable work, Lois helped create a nutrition center in Washington. The Diet Kitchen Welfare Center was created to provide nourishing meals for young children. While helping to operate the center, Lois met a young mother of twins. While the daughter was healthy, the baby boy suffered from chronic illnesses. There was little money in the family – the father served as a church janitor – but the boy would need better health care than the family could afford.

Lois formed a close bond with the baby, and it was she who first approached her husband with the idea that, perhaps, they could bring the child into their home. Knowing that even a curmudgeon like Tom could hardly resist the little boy's angelic features, she held the child in her arms when she asked him if they could raise him as their son.

> *With that brutality which marks the man, I had said to her that she might keep him, provided he did not squall under my feet. He grew out of his crib; but he never walked with as sure a certainty on the streets of Washington as he walked into my heart.*

The Marshalls did not adopt the little boy, who was named Clarence Ignatius Morrison. In correspondence he was referred to as Morrison Marshall, but within the household he was known as Izzy. "Beautiful as an angel; brilliant beyond his years; lovable from every standpoint," was how Tom described the boy. To go through the formal adoption proceedings with the parents still living and actively raising Izzy's twin would have certainly proved, at best, awkward. When President Wilson congratulated the couple, the note said simply, "With congratulations to the baby."

They made an informal arrangement with Izzy's parents to keep the child in their household for an indeterminate period of time. Mrs. Marshall arranged for a job for Izzy's mother at the Willard Hotel, and even installed a special kitchenette and play room for the child's use. Tom and Lois, devoted faithfully to each other through nearly a quarter of a century, now had another fresh, young face toddling through their apartment and their lives. "He came to be the sun and center of Mrs. Marshall's life," Tom wrote, "and of mine."[262]

⧸ ⧸ ⧸ ⧸ ⧸

Marshall had developed a political philosophy that embraced the Democratic party but could not be neatly pigeonholed as either liberal or conservative. His stance on organized labor and corporate regulations marked him as a liberal. Yet he opposed suffrage for women and was adamant in his conservative fiscal viewpoint. He was aptly described as "a Progressive with the brakes on." But when Izzy entered his life he developed a new appreciation for charitable organizations and the role they played in provided a safety net for the downtrodden.

> *Throughout America today, under the Children's Bureau, there is going forward the work of weighing and measuring and examining all children under six years of age. Statistics show that 300,000 of them die every year, and that, humanly speaking, with proper advice, attention and care, one-half of this number can be saved. This work is being done gratuitously all over the Republic and is a very serious strain upon charitably disposed people.*

Marshall recognized that Washington, D.C. faced a special hurdle, in that it was not a self-governing municipality but was under the authority of Congress. The Vice President saw the need do more for indigent children in the Nation's Capital, and with an understanding of the political process, he knew that an issue like this would have a good chance of success if he could obtain a strong endorsement from the President:

> *Mrs. Marshall and other good women here in Washington are spending three hours a day three days a of each week in the making of this health census under the auspices of the Washington Diet Kitchen. When this census is completed it will be about as valuable as last year's bird nest unless some plan is devised to follow it up to see that proper care and attention are given these children. It is doubtless true that throughout America where local self government still reigns, if it does anywhere, the duty is incumbent upon a locality to look after its children but in the City of Washington there is neither an autocracy nor a democracy. The District government can make no appropriation for the carrying on of this work without the consent of the Congress and the Congress is too much interested in the boll weevil and San Jose scale to appropriate for children. Nothing*

but your strong hand and forceful and emphatic approval of
some appropriation to follow up this work will avail.[263]

With Wilson's support, a bill that was pending before the Committee
on the District of Columbia was amended to include an appropriation for a
Bureau of Infant Hygiene. The following year, the new bureau was established
within the Health Department and provided help for many of the children of
the city – children just like Izzy.

❧ ❧ ❧ ❧ ❧

After the United States entered the First World War, Marshall spent much
of his time speaking at rallies to sell Liberty bonds, and also hosting social
meetings with visiting diplomats. But Marshall felt that America was not
prepared for war.

> *At last the declaration of war was made. The solemn instruments*
> *which made legal the condition, were all signed, and then we*
> *found ourselves, as English-speaking people always do, wholly*
> *unprepared for the event. In the beginning it was thought we*
> *might safely rely on the embattled farmers to enlist in such*
> *numbers as to render conscription unnecessary. But we had*
> *no training stations for officers; no cantonments for troops; no*
> *military supplies, to speak of; no ships. We were in a war with*
> *naked hands.*[264]

Despite the general feeling of patriotic fervor across the nation, Edith
Wilson's patrician background and personal ambition mixed poorly with
Marshall's Midwest roots and wry humor. The President's wife viewed the
responsibilities of her position as similar to royalty; Marshall showed little
inclination for pomp and aristocratic airs.

Soon after the declaration of war, the President and Vice President
welcomed a British delegation led by Foreign Secretary Arthur Balfour. To
the right of the First Lady was seated Lord Balfour; to her left was Marshall.
Edith Wilson was charmed by Balfour, and viewed him as a prime example of
an English aristocrat. Marshall made less of an impression. "The Vice President

was at his worst," the President's Wife noted, "saying all the things you hoped he hadn't."[265]

❧ ❧ ❧ ❧ ❧

As America prepared for war, Treasury Secretary McAdoo needed a method of raising funds quickly and then repaying the loans using reasonable revenue sources.

Rather than ask for loans from large banks and rich investors, McAdoo proposed the idea of Liberty Bonds which would be sold in small enough denominations so that an average family of some means could afford to buy them. Noted personalities – such as Vice President Marshall – would travel across the country promoting the bonds. These efforts were extraordinarily successful, as some estimates show that at least half of American families purchased a Liberty Bond.

To repay the bonds, McAdoo was the beneficiary of one of the more fortunate accidents in American financial history. As Abraham Lincoln had discovered, the most effective way to repay a war debt would be through the imposition of an income tax. But the Supreme Court decision in *Pollock* in 1895 made such a tax impossible without a constitutional amendment – a lengthy and time-consuming process. But just five years before Archduke Ferdinand was assassinated, Congress had passed the enabling legislation to adopt such an amendment. Formal ratification came in February of 1913, and the first income tax law was signed by President Wilson that October.

Now the law was in place, as well as the mechanism to collect the tax. To finance the war, tax rates would soar and the number of families paying the tax would need to rise, as well. The 1913 income tax legislation had a top rate of seven percent, and exempted the first four thousand dollars of income. Two months before the election of 1916 President Wilson signed into law an increase in the top rate to thirteen percent. On October 3, 1917 – four years to the day after he signed the first income tax bill – President Wilson signed into law the War Revenue Act. The exemption fell to one thousand dollars – meaning that five million families would start paying the tax for the first time – and the top rate soared to sixty-seven percent for incomes above two million dollars a year. Even that would not be enough. Before the war was over, the top rate would be pushed to seventy-seven percent.[266]

ক ক ক ক ক

As part of the process of managing international relations during the world conflict, European delegations visited the United States, and Marshall helped to welcome them. Visiting dignitaries would also be permitted to address Congress, as Rene Viviani, the French Minister of Justice, did in late April.

Unable to speak English, Viviani addressed the Senate in French – a language understandable by only a few Senators.

> *It was quite interesting to me to watch the countenances of certain senators; observe them shaking their heads in affirmation when to my certain knowledge they knew less of the French tongue than they did of Choctaw. I, myself, nodded and smiled, although what the distinguished gentleman said conveyed to me no more information than a menu card in French, but I could not afford to allow the galleries to imagine that I was not at least High Lingo.*[267]

While Marshall may not have been able to address the delegations in their native tongue, his welcoming speeches were no less eloquent. Perhaps no greeting provides a better illustration of Marshall's ability to convey warmth and profound meaning than his words to the Belgian delegation:

> *To me, in all profane history, there is no sadder, sweeter, sublimer character than Sidney Carton. Dreamer of dreams, he walked his lonely, only way. In all the history of nations here is no sadder, sweeter, sublimer story than the story of Belgium.*[268]

Marshall's reference to Sidney Carton referred to the Charles Dicken's story *Tale of Two Cities*, in which Carton, like the Belgians, walked sorrowfully to face execution by the Germans.

ক ক ক ক ক

Vladimir Ilyich Ulyanov was born April 30, 1870, in a small town about 500 miles east of Moscow. While his early life was comfortable, he developed an interest in revolutionary causes after his brother was hung for his participation in a plot to assassinate Russian leader Alexander III. After studying law he began to spread propaganda calling for the overthrow of the tsar. For this, he was exiled to Siberia in 1895 and, when his exile ended in 1900 he left Russia to continue his revolutionary activities abroad.

He lived in a variety of countries, waiting for an opportunity to return to Russia and overthrow the government. With the start of World War I, his opportunity would arise. The poorly organized government of Nicholas II was ill equipped to muster the forces required to fight the Germans and properly feed and house their country's citizens. Unrest was growing not only among the starving populace but with the disenchanted soldiers, as well. By 1917 neither the Axis powers nor the Allies could claim an advantage in the fighting across Europe. Seeking to exploit any reasonable advantage they could muster, the German government looked for ways to remove Russia from the fighting. It was clear by this time that Russia was in disarray, as widespread famine led to starvation in the cities and the effectiveness of the Russian army was crumbling.

The Germans were aware of Ulyanov and his desire for revolution. By this time, he was living in Switzerland, observing the events taking place on Moscow and elsewhere. On April 3, 1917, German authorities provided a special railroad car to take Ulyanov to St. Petersburg. By this time, also, Vladimir Ilyich Ulyanov had come to be known simply as Lenin.

Through the spring and summer of 1917, civil unrest had led to strikes, marches and, in some cases, violence. Soldiers fired into crowds on numerous occasions, and by the end of summer it was clear that the municipal authorities were incapable of preventing further violence. In the middle of October, Lenin and his supporters saw their chance. The Russian army began to disintegrate, and mutinies were widespread. On October 25, Bolshevik troops loyal to Lenin took control of bridges, railroad stations, the telegraph office and power stations.

On November 7, 1917, the Bolsheviks seized power. Just as the Kaiser had hoped, they signed an armistice with Germany a month later. Hundreds of thousands of German troops were now released from their duty on the eastern front and could be moved to positions in France. It would be another six months before American troops would arrive in sufficient numbers to make a difference in the outcome of the war, and the question of the ultimate victor of the conflict was still uncertain.

᷍ ᷍ ᷍ ᷍ ᷍

Athletes who play at a high level will tell you about "slumps" – periods of time when the years of practice, training and experience seem to be for naught and nothing goes right. The bat comes around too slow; the three point jumper misses badly; the pass to the receiver is beyond his reach. Even the best players suffer slumps, but they work harder, focus on their goal, and soon emerge to their prior excellence.

In sports terms, both Wilson and Marshall suffered a slump in 1918. The year was one of poor decision-making, bad judgment and political setbacks for the two men and their party. Though great triumphs were realized – such as what occurred in the eleventh month, on the eleventh day, at the eleventh hour – the year was disastrous for the presidency of Woodrow Wilson. The stage was set for the fateful year 1919 – the consequences of which the world is still dealing with today.

By the early months of 1918, Wilson and Marshall were exchanging cordial communications on relatively low-level issues, but Marshall was generally kept out of strategy and planning sessions and, as a result, often found out about new policies and positions from the Wilson administration the same way everyone else did – by reading about them in the newspaper. But as Vice President, Marshall was expected to echo the viewpoint of the President and, when the two made contradictory statements – as often happened early in their first term – the result could be embarrassing backpedaling. By the time of the second term, Marshall was experienced enough to recognize what he did not know, and sought advice from either Wilson or his advisors before making important speeches.

The wartime elections of 1918 presented a unique challenge for political strategists. With millions of men facing each other in muddy trenches across Europe, should the political parties set aside their partisan differences and unite behind a common policy to win the war and return the troops home safely? Or, should one party try to seek a political advantage by positioning themselves as the party with the superior policies for winning the war and saving lives, and ask voters for support not just for political gain but as their patriotic duty?

Neither Wilson nor Marshall could be considered brilliant political strategists. Both benefited from the support of much stronger political bosses who supported the two men based on their electibility before they were in office and their malleability once in office. Both also proved to be disappointments for political bosses seeking favors. While neither of the men developed strong skills in implementing electoral strategies, it was Marshall, based on his background and personality, who had a much better sense of the mood of the voters and the needs of the common man. No one could surpass Wilson for his idealism, his vision, and his academic background. But, among the two, it was Marshall who understood voter sentiment.

Early in his political career Wilson relied on advice from seasoned professionals. Colonel House and Joe Tumulty understood voting patterns, paid attention to the needs of local political bosses, and developed policies with one eye on the political consequences. But by the early part of 1918 both House and Tumulty's stature as political advisors had fallen, and Wilson's decision-making was mainly influenced by his wife Edith. Early in their relationship, Edith had raised doubts with Woodrow about the qualifications and effectiveness of both House and Tumulty. Edith said House looked like a "weak vessel", and "he writes very like one very often". While raising mild objections to Edith's characterizations of House, Woodrow noted that House might not have the intellectual qualities a presidential advisor might need. He agreed that House might take the "short and personal view when he ought to be taking the big and impersonal view, thinking not of my reputation for the day, but of what is fundamentally and eternally right, no matter who is for the time being hurt by it."

"I know he is fine and true," Edith responded, "But I don't think him vigorous and strong. Am I wrong?"[269] By early 1917 Edith was aggressively lobbying her husband to appoint House as the ambassador to England. She knew House's influence with her husband would be significantly reduced if the Colonel was in London rather than Washington. House declined the appointment, but his stature and position in the Wilson administration fell significantly.

As for Tumulty, Edith's patrician upbringing made her much less sympathetic towards the Irish Catholic from Jersey City. The President's wife raised objections to Tumulty similar to her chagrin over Marshall. Edith preferred gentlemen with more refined upbringing and greater deference to the manners developed by America's aristocrats.

Wilson agreed. He wrote to Edith that Tumulty "is common ... he was not brought up as you were; you feel his lack of our breeding." Wilson pointed out that many of the politicians in Washington were not of "our kind", nor "I need hardly add, are a majority of voters in the country".

Soon after Wilson was reelected, Edith more aggressively sought Tumulty's removal from the President's administration. Assisted by some of Wilson's other advisors, Edith helped to arrange for Tumulty to be offered a position outside of Washington. Tumulty saw the ruse for what it was – a move to lessen his influence while cementing Edith as the President's primary political advisor. Tumulty tearfully begged Wilson to keep him as part of his administration, and Wilson relented. Tumulty kept his position, but his access to the President was greatly diminished.

❧ ❧ ❧ ❧ ❧

Marshall was asked in the Spring of 1918 to make the keynote address at the Democratic State Convention in Indianapolis. Wanting to make sure his comments reflected the policy of his President, he arranged to meet with Wilson.

> *In accordance with my custom of taking orders from my chief, I called on the President and apprised him of this fact. I said I desired to consult him whether I should not make a speech announcing that the only question before the American people was winning the war and standing behind the president. Should I not propose that both Democrats and Republicans nominate men pledged to these two objects and let the people make a choice between them, promising that in the event the war closed prior to the expiration of their terms of office, they would resign and go back to the people on local issues. I also suggested proposing to the Republican party to close up all political headquarters and to expend the money saved thereby in Red Cross and other war activities.*[270]

While Marshall's ideas might not have been wholly practical, it is clear that he was advocating a strategy which set aside partisan differences and placed victory as the paramount goal. But Wilson's supreme confidence in his own intellectual abilities, and low regard for Marshall's, meant the nonpartisan strategy would not move forward.

> To this he answered that it would not do; that he expected to issue a call shortly before the election for a Democratic Congress, and had no doubt that the people would give it to him because they had refused him nothing so far. I then said: "Is it your desire for me to make an old-fashioned Democratic speech at the convention?" He said: "Yes." I told him he was my commander-in-chief, and his orders would be obeyed.[271]

Marshall knew the partisan strategy would not be successful, but his sense of loyalty overrode his inclination to advocate for a different position. "It was perfectly apparent," Marshall wrote, "that he had a rocky road to travel, and that the definite end was not in sight."

Edith was opposed to Wilson's decision to take a fiercely partisan political strategy in the elections of 1918. But her objections were muted, for she probably was unable to understand the ramifications of the strident policy the way House or Tumulty might have. But with the two of them playing a lesser role in policy decisions by 1918, Wilson was free to make his own mistakes without a trusted, experienced advisor to argue otherwise.

∾ ∾ ∾ ∾ ∾

In March of 1918, Colonel House was feeling ill, and returned to his home where he was bedridden for two weeks. After a brief recovery, the illness struck again, and, since he was too ill to travel, he spent the next three weeks in bed at the White House until he was well enough to resume his duties.

A few weeks earlier, Dr. Loring Miner, a physician in Haskell County, Kansas, had taken note of flu-like symptoms of unusual intensity in several of his patients. The victims had violent headaches and body aches, and a high fever. What was particularly troubling to Dr. Miner was the physical health of those who were the sickest. Rather than taking a toll on the elderly and feeble, this flu was at its most destructive with an improbable population – strong, healthy, and robust young people.

Concerned by this seeming inconsistency, the doctor contacted the U.S. Public Health Service. They, too, were alarmed, but the country at the time had other priorities. Across the nation, thousands of strong, healthy and robust young men were gathering in military camps for training and shipment to Europe. Because of the speed with which the camps were constructed, they often consisted of thousands of young men in cramped tents, eating, sleeping and bathing together.

Camp Funston in Kansas was one such camp. The winter of 1917-1918 was one of the coldest on record, and the trainees were stacked in bunk beds within poorly-heated barracks. Many naturally gathered around wood stoves for warmth. On March 4, a cook at Camp Funston reported ill with flu-like symptoms. Within three weeks, eleven hundred soldiers were ill. Of those, thirty-eight would die.

Public health officials warned that conditions were ripe for a major influenza outbreak. Camp Funston, they feared, was just the first of many military encampments that could encourage the spread of the disease.

But the nation was preparing for war. Building larger military facilities with adequate health safeguards would slow down the flow of troops to Europe. Worse still, a major influenza outbreak would hurt the morale of both enlisting troops and families at home. In order to keep the war efforts moving forward, authorities issued public statements minimizing the extent of the epidemic and reassuring the public that the situation was under control.

In late November, Colonel House again became ill with influenza. By now, with the wartime censorship lifted, it was clear that the influenza outbreak first reported in Haskell County, Kansas the previous March was far more than a simple outbreak of the flu. As it turned out, the influenza virus made a relatively minor appearance in the Spring of 1918 – when House first became ill. Over the next few months, the epidemic appeared to subside. When the flu reappeared, however, its intensity was much more violent and destructive. The influenza outbreak of 1918 is now generally recognized as the deadliest epidemic in human history. Spread by the movement of young soldiers around the globe and hidden by wartime censorship, the disease killed at least fifty million people worldwide. A full-scale influenza pandemic was beginning.

The pattern was repeated from nation to nation. One infected victim would travel to a healthy town. Within a few weeks, at least a third of the population would be ill, and death rates among the infected commonly exceeded twenty percent.

Even for those who recovered, many exhibited symptoms that would remain for the rest of their lives. Doctors often pointed to changes in the emotional state of influenza survivors – more irritable, quicker to anger and less patience. In addition, autopsy reports of victims of the virus often noted damage to blood vessels in the brain.

Doctors and nurses would treat patients with flu-like symptoms such as high fever and headaches. The disease would then attack the lungs, and air sacks in the lungs would be unable to transfer oxygen to adjacent blood vessels. Blood containing oxygen is red, but without oxygen veins turn to blue. Patients would often exhibit dark blue skin, a common sign that death was near. Furthermore, because the mechanism for the spread of the disease was not fully understood, the medical staff would often fall ill, as well, leaving no one to care for the sick.

Disease and death spread all around the world. The urban and heavily-populated areas suffered most, but even in isolated settings the effect of the outbreak was catastrophic. In a remote corner of Alaska, local officials found it difficult to bury bodies in the permanently frozen ground. Lacking an alternative, graves were dug deep into the permafrost, and the bodies were covered with several feet of dirt. Nearly 90 years after the influence outbreak of 1918, in 2005, scientist dug up the grave of an Alaskan woman who had been buried eighty-seven years earlier and, using modern scientific methods not available in 1918 they found and analyzed the genetic material of the virus.

The researchers discovered that the virus that had spread so quickly in 1918 had actually originated in birds. The virus was composed of about 4,400 amino acids, and attacked its victims by adhering to the lining of the cells that made up air sacs in lungs. While infecting the bird, less than 1% of the amino acids underwent a genetic change. Like shuffling a deck of cards, in many cases these genetic changes would result in a harmless new virus.

In 1918, however, these small changes in the amino acids resulted in a virus that was extraordinarily lethal to humans. The most effective carriers, moreover, were the young healthy soldiers heading for the front lines. Both the Ally and the German armies were greatly affected – but, of course, neither side could share that information with the enemies they stared at across no man's land.[272]

− − − − −

Democrats had reason to be concerned with the congressional elections of 1918. Traditionally, the party in the White House did poorly in midterm elections, particularly in the second term of a presidency. The political effects of the war created additional uncertainty.

Wilson wrote to Marshall:

> *I have no doubt that you have been following, as I have, with a good deal of anxiety, the critical Senatorial contest in Wisconsin. The attention of the country will naturally be centered upon it because of the universal feeling against Senator Lafollette and the question which will be in every patriotic man's mind whether Wisconsin is really loyal to the country in this time of crisis or not.*
>
> *Personally, I do not doubt that the great body of the citizens of Wisconsin are thoroughly loyal, but there is some danger of the issues being obscured. The election of Mr. Lenroot would, I am afraid, by no means demonstrate that loyalty, because his own record has been one of questionable support of the dignity and rights of the country on some test occasions.*
>
> *It is, therefore, of the utmost importance, I think, that we should secure the election of Davies, and I am wondering if you would not add to your many generous acts in such matters by going out there to make some speeches for him. It would greatly hearten everybody and I am sure it would be most effective.*[273]

Marshall opposed the strategy, but grudgingly complied – perhaps too well. He may have been fatigued from his crowded schedule; or, he may not have understood what Wilson was proposing. Though known as an orator who could easily draw in his listeners, Marshall blundered badly. He began the early part of his talk with comments that went well beyond acceptable boundaries for political discourse.

"The world was amazed when German bayonets entered Belgium," he said. "America was aghast when German ballots entered Wisconsin". The audience was stunned. Did they hear the Vice President correctly? Marshall characterized Republican Senate candidate Irvine Lenroot as a German sympathizer and a traitor to his country. The entire state was home to a multitude of traitors, and the Republican party support the German government.   Marshall continued:

> *Your State of Wisconsin is under suspicion… If the vote at the primary is based on the charges and counter-charges which you have made, each against the other, you are about half for America, half for the Kaiser, and all against Wilson.*[274]

The speech failed miserably. Lenroot beat Davies by 15,000 votes, and the Senate came one step closer to a Republican majority.

✌ ✌ ✌ ✌ ✌

In late October, with the results of the elections of 1918 still in doubt, Wilson released a statement which many feel was the greatest mistake of his career. With military victory at hand, and the job of negotiating the peace facing the country, Wilson issued to the press his appeal to the nation's voters:

> *I have no thought of suggesting that any political party is paramount in matters of patriotism. I feel too deeply the sacrifices which have been made in this war by all our citizens, irrespective of party affiliations, to harbor such an idea. I mean only that the difficulties and delicacies of our present task are of a sort that makes it imperatively necessary that the Nation should give its undivided support to the Government under a unified leadership, and that a Republican Congress would divide the leadership.*
> *The leaders of the minority in the present Congress have unquestionably been pro-war, but they have been anti-administration. I need not tell you, my fellow country men, that I am asking your support not for my own sake or for the*

sake of a political party, but for the sake of the Nation itself,
in order that its inward unity of purpose may be evident to all
the world. In ordinary times I would not feel at liberty to make
such an appeal to you. In ordinary times divided counsels can
be endured without permanent hurt to the country. But these
are not ordinary times.[275]

Reaction to Wilson's partisan appeal was swift and uniformly negative. Republicans were indignant over their implied anti-patriotism; even many Democrats thought the President had gone too far. Wilson's enemies knew his strategy would backfire. "I am glad Wilson has come out in the open," Teddy Roosevelt wrote to Senator Lodge, "I fear Judas most when he can cloak his activities behind the treacherous make-believe of nonpartisanship."

Wilson's blunders resulted in Republican majorities in both the House and Senate after the elections of 1918. Republican support would be required for any significant legislation over the next two years. Importantly, Senator Henry Cabot Lodge was now the Chairman of the Senate Foreign Relations Committee, through which Wilson would need approval for any foreign treaty. It is ironic, then, that Wilson, the consummate visionary, could not look far enough ahead to understand the end product of his partisanship.

Winston Churchill, looking back on the long-term consequences of the mistakes of 1918, would see in Wilson's actions the seeds of the foreign policy disasters that were to follow.

A tithe of the fine principles and generous sentiments he lavished
upon Europe, applied during 1918 to his Republican opponents
in the United States, would have made him in truth the leader
of a nation. His sense of proportion operated in separate water-
tight compartments. The differences in Europe between France
and Germany seemed trivial, petty, easy to be adjusted by a little
good sense and charity. But the differences between Democrat
and Republican in the United States! Here were really grave
quarrels.

Churchill understood what Wilson's missteps meant for the new world order after the fighting stopped. "Peace and goodwill among all nations abroad, but no truck with the Republican Party at home. That was his ticket," Churchill wrote. "And that was his ruin, and the ruin of much else as well."[276]

Marshall agreed with Churchill. If Wilson had thought enough of his Vice President to genuinely ask his advice, much of what followed might have been avoided. As Marshall wrote:

> *I have sometimes thought that great men are the bane of civilization; that they are the real cause of all the bitterness and contention which amounts to anything in the world. Pride of opinion and pride of authorship, and jealousy of the opinion and authorship of others wreck many a fair hope. I saw the time when the President had the Republican part in the Senate so split as to be, himself, in absolute control and domination of American affairs. I saw this split knit together with bands of steel, by the letter he wrote preceding the election of 1918.*[277]

◈ ◈ ◈ ◈ ◈

On November 11, 1918, fighting ceased across Europe. When war broke out in the summer of 1914, each side no doubt thought that hostilities would be over quickly and, for their cause, successfully. But the scorecard of dead in each participating country numbed the senses: 1.8 million Germans, 1.7 million Russians, 1.4 million from France, while Austria-Hungary lost 1.3 million. As compared to the base populations the numbers are even more astounding. France lost one in every five men between the ages of eighteen and thirty.

Woodrow Wilson addressed a joint session of Congress, read the terms of the armistice, and announced that the war was over. Exhausted and thankful, Marshall reflected the attitude of the nation and the world when he wrote:

> *It did come to an end at last; partly, of course, by arms and munitions and military strategy, but a large factor in bringing it to a close was the confidence of the world in the desire of the president to have the contending forces come to an armistice, to bring about a peace without victory. So overwhelming was his influence in the councils of the world, that at last the glad dawn*

of Armistice Day showed on a war-weary and war-wrecked world.[278]

Later that month, the Sixty-fifth session of Congress came to a close. A resolution was passed thanking Marshall "for the dignified, impartial and courteous manner in which he has presided over its deliberations." For his part, Marshall must have been relieved that the difficult year was over. Resorting to his personable manner which he found more comfortable than bitter partisanship, Marshall returned the thanks of the Senate:

Senators of the United States, I thought that we were to wind up one session of the Senate without this usual, ordinary, gracious but wholly perfunctory resolution on behalf of the presiding officer of the senate. Nevertheless, as the years go by I find myself more and more under obligations to the Senators of the United States for the patience they exercise in the moments of irritation upon my part, for their generous judgment of my conduct, and for something that is far deeper to me than even the record of a presiding officer over the great and illustrious body – the feeling which I have and which, if I ought not to have it, I beg you will not take away from me, that regardless of politics and politicians, regardless of the ebb and flow of party sentiment and party ideas in America, up to this good hour I have had practically the unanimous individual and personal friendship of the Senators of the United States. For this I thank you. I hope that in the days to come I may be worthy of a continuance of that friendship.[279]

CHAPTER NINE:

The Parliament of Man

(1919)

Soon after the armistice, Theodore Roosevelt and his Republican colleagues put Wilson and the European leaders on notice that their party would play a significant role in the peace negotiations.

> *Our allies and our enemies and Mr. Wilson himself should all understand that Mr. Wilson has no authority whatever to speak for the American people at this time. His leadership has just been emphatically repudiated by them. The newly elected Congress comes far nearer than Mr. Wilson to having a right to speak the purposes of the American people at this moment. Mr. Wilson and his Fourteen Points and his four supplementary points and his five complementary points and all his utterances every which way have ceased to have any shadow of right to be accepted as expressive of the will of the American people.*[280]

Roosevelt was not only advancing his Republican Party's legitimacy in playing a significant role in the peace negotiations. He was also reaffirming the Senate's Constitutional role in the approval of treaties.

Article II, section 2, of the Constitution states that the president "shall have Power, by and with the Advice and Consent of the Senate, to make Treaties, provided two-thirds of the Senators present concur." The Senate can either approve the treaty outright, or approve it with conditions. One option is

244

to approve the treaty "with reservations", which are amendments which would vary the legal effect of one or more of the provisions of the treaty.

The Constitutional language presents a logistical challenge for presidents as they negotiate treaty terms. Before the age of global telecommunications, treaties often were negotiated far away from Washington, with delicate discussions and compromises carried out with foreign governments. This made it difficult to fulfil the "Advice" portion of the constitutional provision, as it often meant that the Senate was viewing treaty terms for the first time after an agreement had been reached with a foreign government.

As might be expected, tensions between the role played by the President and the Senate in treaty negotiations began in the Washington administration. In August of 1789, George Washington asked for a meeting with the Senate to discuss the terms of a newly-negotiated treaty with an Indian tribe, and Senators willingly offered their opinions. The period of relative harmony continued when Washington established the precedent of asking Senate approval for treaty negotiators. In 1794, when Barbary pirates seized American sailors in Algiers, Washington asked for Senate approval before securing their release through the payment of ransom.

But not long after that, the relationship between the President and the Senate over treaty negotiations began to chill. Relations with Great Britain were strained as British warships continued to capture American seamen as part of their efforts to cut off shipping to France. In addition, the British still threatened peace in the Northwest United States through the forts that they still maintained in places like Detroit and on the Maumee River outside Toledo.

With the approval of the Senate, Chief Justice John Jay was appointed to negotiate a treaty with the British. Jay's Treaty, signed in London in November of 1794, required England to vacate her posts in the Northwest, and permitted American seamen to continue their trade unmolested by the British navy. But American public opinion strongly opposed the Jay Treaty, and before passing the measure by a narrow margin the Senate passed significant amendments.

More than a hundred years later, the friction between the President and the Senate over the treaty approval process was still being debated – this time among the principals who would clash again in the near future.

In 1898, soon after the end of the war in Cuba, President McKinley asked his Secretary of State, John Hay, to negotiate with the British to secure the

246 | David J. Bennett

rights for the Americans to construct a canal in Central America linking the Pacific with the Caribbean. Under a treaty approved in 1850, Great Britain and the United States had agreed that the canal would be a joint project of both countries. After nearly two years of discussions, Hay proudly announced in February of 1900 that the British had agreed to allow the Americans to proceed on their own with the construction of the canal.

But the treaty was opposed by a potent political faction dedicated first and foremost to ensuring that America's military might become the most powerful in the world. Led by Senator Henry Cabot Lodge, the group opposed the Hay-Pauncefote Treaty on the grounds that it specified that the new canal should be free of military fortifications and equally open to all ships.

Lodge was joined in the debate by an unlikely source for treaty dissension: the Governor of New York, Theodore Roosevelt. "I do not see why we should dig the canal," wrote Roosevelt, "if we are not to fortify it so as to insure its being used for ourselves and against our foes in time of war."[281]

Though Roosevelt and Hay were friends, the latter was angry that a governor would inject himself into treaty negotiations. "Et Tu?", wrote Hay, "Cannot you leave a few things to the President and the Senate, who are charged with them by the Constitution?"[282]

The Senate rejected the first Hay-Pauncefote treaty, and in doing so continued a pattern that had existed since the Civil War. Aside from their disagreement over the terms of the treaty, Senator Lodge was leading his colleagues in reasserting the power of the Senate to control treaty relations with foreign governments. America had not had a strong president since Lincoln, and in rejecting the Hay-Pauncefote Treaty Congress was asserting its dominance over the executive branch in treaty negotiations. This power struggle between the presidency and Congress had been described by none other than Woodrow Wilson, in his 1879 senior thesis at Princeton. After writing the article he submitted it for publication to the editor of the International Review – the twenty-nine-year-old Henry Cabot Lodge.

John Hay seethed over the rejection by the Senate of the treaty (a relationship that was certainly complicated by the fact that he was having an affair with Lodge's wife). But McKinley insisted that the negotiations be reopened, this time with Lodge as a key part of the discussions. Because he was intimately involved with the new talks, Lodge obtained congressional approval less than a month after the second Hay-Pauncefote treaty was finished. Wilson would have been wise to have heeded a comment made by Hay during the debate.

> *The worst of all is the uncertainty about what the Senate may do in any given case. You may work for moths over a Treaty, and at last get everything satisfactorily arranged, and send it into the Senate, when it is met by every man who wants to get a political advantage, or to satisfy a personal grudge, everyone who has asked for an office and not got it, everyone, whose wife may think mine has not been attentive enough – if they can muster one-third of the Senate plus one, your Treaty is lost without any reference to the merits.*[283]

As an academician who had written about congressional power, Wilson was acutely aware of the importance of Senate passage of the peace treaty. Nevertheless, when it came time to send the American delegation to Paris to craft the terms of the peace, Wilson named a five-man team that did not include any Republican senators. Wilson was adamantly opposed to asking Lodge to be part of the peace contingent; similarly, he knew he could ask no other Republican senator if he did not invite the Chair of the Foreign Relations Committee. His lone Republican appointment was Henry White, a competent career diplomat but hardly the right person to sway Republican decision makers. No less an observer than comedian Will Rogers understood that Wilson had made a mistake by snubbing Republican leadership. "I tell you what", Rogers said, "We will split 50-50 ... I will go and you fellows can stay."[284]

Lodge and the Foreign Relations Committee were outraged by their exclusion from the formal discussions. They proposed a resolution that would have added eight Senators to the negotiating team in Paris. The resolution was defeated, but not before one cynical lawmaker suggested that the proper number of Senators sent to Paris was not eight; it should, in fact, be all ninety-six.

Wilson also shocked observers by his fifth appointment to the negotiating team – himself. His self-appointment to the Paris peace conference was probably to be expected, given that other leaders of the major powers – David Lloyd-George of Great Britain and Georges Clemenceau of France, would represent their countries.

Wilson's mission would present another issue, as well. No sitting American president had ever gone to Europe. Who would govern the country in the President's absence? Did the Constitution require that Wilson divest the powers of the presidency to Vice President Marshall?

Article II, Section 1 of the United States Constitution would never be tested as thoroughly as it would be in the year after the armistice was achieved. The section in question read, at that time:

> *In case of the removal of the President from office, or of his death, resignation or inability to discharge the powers and duties of the said office, the same shall devolve on the Vice President, and the Congress may by law provide for the case of removal, death, resignation or inability, both of the President and Vice President, declaring what officer shall then act as President, and such officer shall act accordingly, until the disability be removed, or a President shall be elected.*

Marshall was in Boston when a reporter for the *New York Times* called. In a speech to the Council on Foreign Relations in New York City, former Attorney General George Wickersham was discussing President Wilson's impending departure for the peace negotiations. In the opinion of Wickersham, under Article II, Section 1 of the Constitution, while Wilson was outside the United States Marshall would have the duties of the President. What, the reporter asked, was Marshall's reaction to Wickersham's statement?

Marshall was taken by surprise. Not only was he unaware of the Constitutional question – he was not even informed that the President would be part of the delegation to the peace conference in Paris. Despite his lack of foreknowledge of the question, Marshall provided a well thought-out answer. Under no circumstance would he assume the presidency based just on a reasoned legal opinion. He was noncommittal should Congress ask that he become Acting President. Should a court having jurisdiction ask him to assume the Presidency, however, he would "unquestionably" do so.

> *It is the duty of every American citizen to obey the judgments of courts, and I would obey them, not because I want to but, as a law-abiding citizen, would feel compelled to do so. I hope the controversy will be stopped, as I have not the slightest desire nor intention of interfering with the President, unless I am forced to, and that will be of infinite regret to me.*[285]

The *Times* pressed harder. As an attorney, what was Marshall's opinion of his responsibilities relative to Article II of the Constitution once Wilson had left the country?

> *I have made no investigation of this subject. I saw no reason to. The President decided it was right and proper for him to go to the Peace Conference, and I supported his decision heartily and cordially. Most certainly I do not want his job while he is away. That does not mean that I am dodging responsibility. I am not. If the question should arise, I would meet it squarely and accept whatever responsibility was placed upon me. I am most reluctant to become involved in any academic discussion of the constitutional or other questions involved, because I am fearful that my participation in such a discussion might give the President the impression that I am in some way opposing his going. I am not. Furthermore, as I said, I have not studied these questions for the reason that I did not anticipate anything arising which would force them upon me.*[286]

While Wilson was the first President to visit Europe, he was not the first President to leave the country. His predecessor, William Howard Taft, visited Panama – and no one, at that time, raised the constitutional question. While many felt it was unwise for Wilson to leave the country at this time, few raised the constitutional question posed by Wickersham.

Wilson was preparing for his departure when Mark Thistlethwaite, Marshall's secretary, received a phone call from the White House. Could

Marshall meet with the President – at someplace other than the White House? That evening, Wilson came to Marshall's apartment at the Willard Hotel. While no written record exists of the meeting, Marshall immediately afterward cancelled both a speaking trip out west and his vacation in Arizona. It is likely that Wilson was being cautious. It might not be prudent to have the President's successor far away from Washington while Wilson traveled to Europe. In addition, heads of state such as a delegation from Japan were scheduled to be in Washington over the next few weeks, and Marshall could serve in as host in the President's absence. What is clear is that Wilson had considered the consequences of his absence – whether temporary or permanent. Regardless of the President's view of Marshall, he was the Vice President and was constitutionally mandated to assume the power of the Presidency should something unfortunate befall Wilson. Within a year, the question was no longer academic.

On December 4, 1918, President Wilson sailed for France. While the President received an enthusiastic send-off when he sailed from the United States, he could not have anticipated the adulations he would receive once he arrived in Europe.

In Paris, more than two million French turned out to welcome the man who they viewed as not only the "savior of humanity" and the "Moses from across the Atlantic"[287] but as the leader of a new world order. When Wilson traveled on to England and then to Italy, the response was no less enthusiastic.

"As I have conversed with the soldiers, I have been more and more aware that they fought for something that not all of them had defined, but that all of them recognized the moment you stated it to them." Wilson told a crowd assembled in London. "They fought to do away with an old order and to establish a new one." No longer would brute force and power be used by one nation to bully another. The new order would be overseen by "single, overwhelming, powerful group of nations who shall be the trustee of the peace of the world."[288]

Soon after the President's departure, Marshall welcomed the Japanese delegation. The Japanese Ambassador, Viscount Sutemi Chinda, looked at Marshall. "I know you, though you have forgotten me," said the Ambassador. " I was a student at DePauw University, in Indiana, when you were at Wabash College, and I met you several times at one or the other of those institutions." As it turned out, two members from the Japanese delegation had been students at DePauw University at the same time Marshall was at Wabash. The two schools are only thirty miles apart, and even though they had graduated more than forty years before, they had remembered meeting Marshall.

Marshall was moved by his conversation with his visitors from Japan.

> *They called to my attention the fact that as we had a certain population on the western shores of our country that was never-endingly talking about the yellow peril, we should not forget that they had a like population in their own country who never ceased to talk about the white peril; that as our people on the western slope viewed with alarm the increase in Japanese, so over there they looked at us in the Philippines, and they saw France and England holding the balance of power in China. And they reached the same conclusion I have reached: that there will be no danger of any trouble between Japan and the United States unless the yellow peril criers on the Pacific Coast, or the while peril criers in Japan, shall succeed in getting hold of the reins of government.*[289]

❧ ❧ ❧ ❧ ❧

In addition to his social responsibilities while Wilson was away, Marshall also presided, for the first time, over cabinet meetings. On December 10, 1918, Marshall called to order the first cabinet meeting over which he – or any other Vice President – had presided. He began with a brief statement:

> *I am here and am acting in obedience to a request preferred by the President upon the eve of his departure and also at your request. But I am here informally and personally. I am not undertaking to exercise any official duty or function. I shall*

preside in an unofficial and informal way over your meeting out of deference to your desires and those of the President.[290]

It is likely that the decision for Marshall to preside at cabinet meetings, as well as the outline of his statement, were discussed in the meeting between Marshall and Wilson the week before. Wilson may have wanted to counteract Republican criticism that little would occur in his absence; at least, it could be shown, the cabinet continued to function.

Marshall was upbeat speaking with reporters afterward. In the banter after the meeting, he told reporters that he had written a friend from Indiana asking his opinion of the legal consequences of the President's absence. "The President by leaving the country," his fictional friend wrote back, "loses his office but retains his salary." Marshall said that, since he was not going to get the salary of the President, he would not exert himself in that capacity.[291]

❧ ❧ ❧ ❧ ❧

In the middle of January, 1919, news came of the death of Theodore Roosevelt. In many ways including politically, Roosevelt and Marshall were very different, and they had faced each other in the battlefield of politics. But Marshall clearly respected Roosevelt, and released a statement to the press:

I am not one of those who have no feeling of regret over the death of a man who occupied so large and prominent a place in the political affairs of American life as did the late President Roosevelt simply by reason of the fact that I did not agree with him in his political views nor approve of his theories of statesmanship. The greatest safety to the Republic arises from the sharp clashes of men whose ideas are as far apart as the poles. This clashing of ideas enables the common people at large to pursue a middle course. The late President undoubtedly will leave a permanent impression upon American life. He was a born fighter.[292]

Wilson was overseas when he learned of Roosevelt's death, and asked Marshall to attend the funeral on his behalf. Thomas and Lois attended the small ceremony in Oyster Bay, Long Island. The Vice President continued to relay his respect for the former President. "Death had to take him sleeping," Marshall was later quoted as saying, "for if Roosevelt had been awake, there would have been a fight."[293]

⌘ ⌘ ⌘ ⌘ ⌘

The Paris Peace Conference of 1919, which opened on January 12, was an international gathering of unprecedented proportions. Nearly every nation in the world, whether victor or vanquished, was represented. While many delegations gathered, only a handful had significant influence. Most decisions were made by the "Council of Four" – France, England, Italy and the United States. Most other nations, particularly from the defeated nations, could only ask and hope that Lloyd-George, Clemenceau, or Wilson would respond to their pleas.

Yet while Wilson clung to an idealistic view of the new world order, the other principals had different goals. The British were interested primarily in preserving and expanding their empire, no longer the world's premier colonial power but seeking significant foreign dominions nonetheless. France sought to make sure that Germany would no longer menace her Eastern border, and would also be forced to pay reparations for the cost of the war (much of which was fought on French soil).

Marshall had a low opinion of the Paris peace negotiations:

> *I was not at all proud of our conduct over there, after the war. It reminded me of a man going to the relief of his neighbor who was being assaulted by a burglar. After he had assisted in throwing the burglar out of the house, although his neighbor was wounded and in sore stress, he picks up his hat, says good night and goes home.*[294]

Some delegations played a minimal role for other reasons. The Korean delegation, hoping to shake off control by Japan, underestimated the distance to Paris. They set out on foot from Siberia in February, 1919, and by June had reached only as far as the Arctic port of Archangel.[295]

❧ ❧ ❧ ❧ ❧

Scholars, historians and even poets had for centuries dreamed of a utopian organization that could monitor the nations of the world, mediating disputes, serving as a forum for discussions and, ultimately, advancing the cause of world peace. Just when Woodrow Wilson first took up the cause is not certain, but as war raged in Europe the idea grew in his mind and the outlines of the organization took shape. He mentioned American participation in an organization of nations in his January, 1917 address to Congress. As the war drew to a close, and the nations of the world began to look to the world order when peace had been achieved, the idea of a world peace-keeping organization took shape in Wilson's plans.

In January, 1918, Wilson addressed a joint session of Congress and presented what history has come to call his Fourteen Points. He viewed these ideas as the basis of a long-lasting peace, and the principals on which the world would operate after the guns for this war were silenced. Wilson called for the abolition of secret diplomacy – which he knew had contributed to the rapid escalation of hostilities after the assassination of Archduke Ferdinand. In addition, he asked for freedom of the seas, reductions in armaments and self-determination for nations.

But perhaps his most important point was saved for last, as Point 14 called for "a general association of nations ... affording mutual guarantees of political independence and territorial integrity to great and small states alike." It is with this concept that Wilson captured the imagination of much of the world. Many had dreamed of an organization devoted to the end of all war; now, with much of Europe in ruins, the time had come. It is likely that Wilson was familiar with Alfred Tennyson's famous poem "Locksley Hall", which called on mankind to abandon war and form a political federation that spanned the globe; a parliament of man.

> *Till the war-drum throbb'd no longer,*
> *and the battle-flags were furl'd*
> *In the Parliament of man, the Federation of the world*
> *There the common sense of most shall*
> *hold a fretful realm in awe*
> *And the kindly earth shall slumber, lapt in universal law*

Woodrow Wilson's ambitious plans were not universally well received. "Even God Almighty," Georges Clemenceau said of Wilson's famous Fourteen Points, "only has ten!" Henry Cabot Lodge read the document, and was told that it had been drafted by Wilson himself. "As an English production it does not rank high", Lodge sniffed. "It might get by at Princeton but certainly not at Harvard."[296]

While the concept of an international league to enforce peace had been widely discussed, the details of such an organization remained unclear. Wilson himself was unwilling to discuss more fully the structure of such an organization, even with his own negotiating team. "There must be a League of Nations," he publicly stated, "and this must be virile, a reality, not a paper League." Beyond that, the details were uncertain.

On January 25, the Peace Conference officially set up the Commission on the League of Nations, with Wilson as the chair and including two representatives apiece from Great Britain, France, Italy, Japan and the United States. Wilson moved quickly to make his idea a reality. The first meeting of the Commission was held on February 3, and they met almost daily. By February 14 the first draft was prepared. The document was sweeping in scope but short on details. All nations that were part of the League would meet as a general assembly, with voting powers distributed so that the Big Five nations (Great Britain, France, Italy, Japan and the United States) would hold a majority of the votes. In addition, any of the Big Five would have veto power over any resolution. The League was charged with establishing an international court. In addition, the organization was pledged to work against arms trafficking and the spread of slavery. The document also established the International Labor Organization, which would seek international standards on working conditions.

The question of military powers possessed by the League proved difficult to negotiate. The French, who probably suffered the most during the war, argued for the League to have its own army which could be used to stop aggression against any member nation. But most nations balked at giving the newly-created organization such power, and it was finally agreed that all League members would pledge themselves to respect the independence and territorial boundaries of other members.

While there were numerous portions of the peace treaty which were controversial, none drew more attention than Article X, which stated:

The Members of the League undertake to respect and preserve as against external aggression the territorial integrity and existing political independence of all Members of the League. In case of any such aggression or in case of any threat or danger of such aggression the Council shall advise upon the means by which this obligation shall be fulfilled.

This section of the document would, in Wilson's view, be critical for the success of any League. Hostility against any League member would be treated as an act of aggression against all members. As a united body, the entire League would then use its collective power to maintain the "territorial integrity" and "political independence" of its members. Weak nations need not fear the hostility of stronger neighbors under the new League, as all members would pledge to support any other member that was threatened.

The true meaning of Article X was open to debate. Treaty opponents argued that it would force American troops to be called out incessantly each time tensions grew on a border involving a League member. Supporters countered that, unless the actions of the League could be backed up by force, any stand taken against aggression would be meaningless.

Thomas Marshall was less enthusiastic about any type of enduring commitment on the part of America to remain involved in European disputes. He did, however, see the need in 1919.

I really never wanted a permanent alliance with the peoples of Europe but I felt it was our duty to join in this most altruistic idea of the president for the furtherance of world peace and to stay until Europe had been restored to normality.

Marshall took a different viewpoint regarding Article X, asserting that no treaty could override the provision in the United States Constitution regarding the authority to declare war:

Every country that sat at the table at Versailles well knew that the president and the Senate could not plead the American people to make war. That was the business of the Congress of the United States. The Treaty did not bind the American people legally to make war, nor did it bind them morally, because the other countries knew the limitations of authority which rested with the president and the Senate. In addition to this, treaties from the beginning have been abrogated by the Congress of the United States, and this Treaty might have been abrogated in fifteen minutes if there were ever any attempt on the part of any other nation of the earth to do anything that was not in the best interests of the American people. I was always with the president in his insistence that Article X was the heart of the covenant.[297]

Several years after the League fight was over, Marshall wrote that he supported Wilson's decision to fight any attempt to dilute Article X.

In my humble opinion President Wilson was right when he said that Article X was the heart of the Covenant of the League of Nations. Great lover of humanity and protagonist of peace that he was, he was not deceived about the human heart or the ambitions of men, and he believed that the time had not yet come when a law without power to enforce it would amount to very much under stress of circumstance.[298]

As the conference focused on the structure of the League, other vexing issues were ignored. The Japanese dearly wanted the document to address racial equality, but Wilson feared the language would provide support for equal treatment for American blacks. The borders of defeated Germany, Austria-Hungary and Ottoman Empire needed to be redrawn. Still looming also was the question of German reparations.

But Wilson was adamant in pushing the League forward, in part to address these questions. For him, the League of Nations was the core of any peace settlement, as it was the vehicle that could be used to settle any lingering disputes not resolved at the negotiating table. The new international organization would serve as the final arbiter for maligned ethnic groups, nations disputing boundaries with neighbors and any conflict that threatened the peace. The League would support peace-loving nations and punish those that pursued a course of war. In the eyes of Wilson, the League of Nations was not only a tool to bring peace to Europe, it would be a covenant that the nations of the world would make with all of humanity to preserve the peace now and in the future.

On the evening of February 14, having presented a draft of the League covenant to the members of the Peace Conference, Wilson left Paris for a brief return to the United States. "Many terrible things have come out of this war," he stated, "but some very beautiful things have come out of it."[299]

ᦕ ᦕ ᦕ ᦕ ᦕ

Despite the fact that the world's attention was focused on the war and subsequent treaty negotiations, other reforms based in the Progressive movement moved their way through the American political system. Changing public attitudes caused by World War I culminated Thomas Marshall's involvement in two constitutional amendments during Wilson's second term.

The prohibition movement gained strength after the turn of the century and reached its peak around the time of Wilson's presidency. By 1917, twenty-seven states prohibited the sale of alcohol (termed "dry") and many other states – such as Indiana – allowed local communities to vote themselves dry. But dry states complained that enforcement was difficult when drinkers could simply drive to a neighboring state to purchase liquor. In addition, the war encouraged a spirit of sacrifice – particularly towards beer, a drink closely associated with Germany and the Kaiser. Despite significant campaign contributions from brewers, the Anti-Saloon League was able to tie drinking to crime, prostitution, gambling and general degeneracy. Congress passed the Eighteenth Amendment to the Constitution, prohibiting the "manufacture, sale or transportation of intoxicating liquors", and Marshall signed the amendment on December 3, 1917.

Marshall had strong opinions about one of the more prominent issues of the day, extending voting privileges to women.

> *One of the most annoying things was the everlasting clatter of the militant suffragettes. I think the adoption by the Senate of the Nineteenth Amendment was portrayed in the Scriptures by the unjust judge who got tired of hearing about it. The amendment really was submitted to the people in self-defense,*

to get rid of these women in order that some business might be transacted. They did not call on me very often, however, because it was quite well understood that while I was not opposed to an intelligent woman voting, I was distinctly opposed to universal woman suffrage, and still more strongly opposed to transferring the question of suffrage to the general government.[300]

The movement to extend voting privileges to women can be traced to 1848 at the first Women's Rights Convention, held in Seneca Falls, New York. At that time, the issue of women's suffrage was closely related to the anti-slavery efforts made by abolitionists. When the 15th Amendment – extending the vote to black men -- was proposed after the civil war, the movement was split. Some equal rights supporters favored the Amendment as a step towards voting rights for all; others opposed the measure because it excluded women. When the Amendment was approved, supporters of voting rights for women – knowing the difficulty of enacting constitutional amendments -- knew they had missed out on a chance to achieve their goal.

An amendment extending voting rights to women was offered in the Senate in 1868, but it failed to move forward. In 1872, Susan B. Anthony became a leader in the suffrage movement when she was arrested after she and fifteen other women tested New York laws by voting in a national election. Her trial attracted a great deal of national attention, and leaders of the movement began working with state legislatures to enact voting rights for women through referenda. Soon after that, the Senate Committee on Privileges and Elections held hearings on a renewed proposal. It was clear, however, that the senators present had little interest in the bill, and it failed to get out of committee.

Several years later, the Senate appointed a Select Committee on Woman Suffrage, which recommended passage of the amendment. But the opposition included southern senators and those opposed to prohibition, who feared that newly enfranchised women would use their votes to outlaw the sale of alcoholic beverages.

Even though by 1890 the separate activist groups were merged into a single National American Woman Suffrage Association (NAWSA), the cause of voting rights for women advanced very little over the next twenty years. By 1912, nine states allowed women to vote -- mostly in the West. In January

1913, a delegation of suffragists presented to the Senate petitions signed by 200,000 Americans.

The strategy changed when leaders organized a march on Washington, DC on the day of Woodrow Wilson's inauguration in March, 1913. In a sight the nation's capital had seldom seen up to that time, 5,000 women marched through the streets. This was followed up by silent picketing in front of the White House. More radical members of the movement carried anti-Wilson banners, which at times led to violence and arrests. Leaders of the NAWSA officially disapproved of the tactics, but also knew that, for the first time, the issue was gaining support.

When protesters sought to establish a presence near Congress, however, they received a chilly response from the presiding officer of the Senate:

> *While the picketing of the president was going on these enthusiastic women became desirous of adopting the same tactics towards the Senate of the United States. They had some knowledge, however, of the fact that they might find themselves in the capital lock-up, if they did so without permission. Two of them called on me, therefore, to obtain permission to picket the Senate. I responded by saying that the Congress of the United States had created a Fine Arts Commission; that this commission had exclusive jurisdiction over the erection of works of art in the city of Washington; that nothing could be erected in the public parks and grounds of the city until the commission had certified that it would beautify and adorn the landscape. I told them if they would take their proposed picketers to the Fine Arts Commission and the commission would certify that they would beautify and adorn the landscape, I would sign a permission therefore; but I warned them that they would have to be better-looking women than those I saw standing in front of the White House, before they could ever hope to obtain this permission. They were good sports; laughed it off; went away, I think, satisfied and the Senate of the United States was saved from marching through an army terrible with banners.*[301]

Perhaps the most important factor which gained victory for the suffragists occurred in Europe. The role of women in World War I – in military hospitals, canteens and in activities like scrap collection and bandage production on the home front – diminished the arguments of opponents. Soon after the armistice of November, 1918, Woodrow Wilson took action that would lead to legislative victory for suffrage supporters. In a fifteen-minute address to the Senate on September 30, 1918, he urged adoption of a constitutional amendment that would allow American women the right to vote. The House had approved the amendment months earlier, but Senate observers predicted that without the president's help, they would miss the required two-thirds majority by two votes. In his speech to the Senate, Wilson cited the role of women in supporting the nation's involvement in World War I. "We have made partners of the women in this war," he said, "Shall we admit them only to a partnership of suffering and sacrifice and toil, and not to a partnership of privilege and right?"

Surprisingly, it was the elections of 1918 – during which the Republicans gained control of Congress – that brought an increase in the ranks of the amendment's supporters, permitting adoption of what would become the Constitution's 19th Amendment. On May 20, 1919, the House of Representatives passed the woman suffrage amendment, followed by Senate action on June 4. Woodrow Wilson and Thomas Marshall signed the legislation, and the action shifted to the states, with approval from thirty-six states needed for ratification. Marshall was resigned to the eventual passage of the new law.

> *Well, it's all over. The amendment has been adopted as a part of the organic law of the land, and woman now has her rights. It is to be hoped that she will realize that having obtained this right there is a duty superimposed upon it – the duty to maintain not only the old-fashioned government in America but the great ideals upon which that government was founded: The duty to make a home, from out whose portals there will pass strong and courageous men and brave women, who will dare to stand for the right regardless of mere personal advantage. It is to be hoped that she will take a greater interest in informing herself about public questions than the average man has done; but, above all,*

it is to be hoped that this amendment will remain a question of suffrage and not a question of sex; that the ballot will sweeten rather than sour the mothers of our land.[302]

Final ratification came with the vote of the Tennessee legislature on August 24, 1920. Two days later, without fanfare, the Secretary of State signed the 19th Amendment into law.

History is filled with ironies, and certainly Marshall's involvement with amending the United States Constitution is one of them. Visitors to the National Archives in Washington can view an original copy of the Eighteenth Amendment, which enacted prohibition, and the Nineteenth, which extended suffrage to all regardless of sex. On those documents, they will see the signature of Vice President Thomas Marshall, who abused alcohol during most of the early years of his adult life and opposed voting rights for women.

∽ ∽ ∽ ∽ ∽

President Wilson returned from Paris in February, 1919, and immediately began to lobby for support of the League of Nations. Stopping first in Boston, Wilson tried to generate enthusiasm for the draft covenant of the League. He urged support from Americans, and said that those opposed to the new international organization were selfish and shortsighted. To help the audience understand the document, copies of a draft of the covenant for the League were placed on the seats of each one in attendance.

Once again, Wilson showed an appalling lack of understanding of domestic politics or the delicacies of dealing with the Senate. Had he sought the advice of his Vice President, Marshall could have counseled Wilson regarding the most effective way of gaining Senate support. As it was, Wilson's trip to Boston proved to be a serious blunder. The President erred when he used such harsh language to characterize his opponents. In addition, members of the Senate Foreign Relations Committee should have been the first to receive copies of the covenant for the League, rather than each attendee at a political rally. Finally – and perhaps the most egregious error – Wilson chose to begin his public relations effort in the hometown of the Chairman of the Senate Foreign Relations Committee, Henry Cabot Lodge.

On March 5, Lodge circulated a Republican "round robin", which was a letter signed by thirty-nine senators, declaring that "the constitution of the League of Nations in the form now proposed to the peace conference should not be acceptable to the United States." The document was significant in that the opposition of 39 senators would be enough to defeat the passage of the treaty in the Senate, which would require the vote of at least 64 of the 96 senators. Marshall watched as the President refused to back down.

> (The President) was presented with a round robin from a sufficient number of Republican senators to insure its defeat, notifying him that they would have nothing to do with it if he attempted to insert it into the Treaty of Peace. To this he very promptly replied that he would make it the backbone of the Treaty of Peace and that they would have to take it.[303]

While Wilson had hoped that he could get the Peace Conference to approve the February 14 draft of the League covenant, it was clear that he needed to resolve the tricky question of the effect of the document on the Monroe Doctrine.

First described by James Monroe in 1823, the Monroe Doctrine was designed to keep European powers away from north and south America.

> The American continents, by the free and independent condition which they have assumed and maintain, are henceforth not to be considered as subjects for future colonization by any European powers ... we should consider any attempt on their part to extend their system to any portion of this hemisphere as dangerous to our peace and safety.[304]

Thomas Marshall was concerned about the potential nullification of the Monroe Doctrine should America adopt the League covenant. Marshall endorsed the ideas behind the covenant, but like many Senators he would prefer that certain concepts be enacted before the United States became a party to the treaty.

The Vice President set forth four principals which he felt were necessary in order for the Senate to approve the treaty. Marshall wrote:

1. *The validity and binding force of the Monroe Doctrine should be admitted by all other parties to the League;*

2. *It should be clearly stated that none of the penalties of the League should be compulsory for the purpose of preserving the political integrity of any nation from internal revolution.*

3. *No nation shall be required to proceed further in the maintenance of the principles of the League than the constitutional theory on amendments thereof may subsequently warrant. When a nation now has no such constitutional authority, it will submit to its people amendments to its organic law vesting it with such authority.*

4. *In discharging the duties of a mandatory (action by the League, as described by Article X), no nation shall be compelled to send its army into foreign territory.*[305]

In part to address concerns raised by Marshall and others, Wilson felt compelled to seek an amendment to the draft which would specifically address the Monroe Doctrine. Despite opposition from the French, the Commission adopted language which stated that nothing in the League covenant would nullify existing international agreements designed for peaceful purposes, such as the Monroe Doctrine.

With that, in late April the Peace Conference approved the covenant of the League of Nations. Wilson was elated. For him, his reasons for personally attending the Peace Conference had been vindicated. The League of Nations was in place; from here, he felt, all other questions could be resolved. "One by one the mistakes can be brought to the League for readjustment," he told Edith, "and the League will act as a permanent clearinghouse where every nation can come, the small as well as the great." [306]

❧ ❧ ❧ ❧ ❧

As Colonel House gathered with Wilson and the other delegates in Paris, he was attacked by the influenza virus for a third time, and his condition was grave. Some newspapers had reported that he had, in fact, died. While the obituaries were premature, there is no doubt the disease had reduced his effectiveness. "When I fell sick in January," he wrote in his diary, "I lost the thread of affairs and I am not sure that I have ever gotten fully back."[307]

Earlier the month of January, Congressman William Borland of Kansas became the third congressman to die of influenza. Borland had been in France, and by now the virus was taking its toll on Paris. After peaking at 4,574 deaths of Parisians in October of 1918, by February 1919 the monthly death toll was nearly half as large, as 2,676 died. The decline to 1,517 deaths in March told local authorities that the disease was in decline.

But on April 3, Cary Grayson was with Wilson around dinnertime when the President became violently ill. He at first feared the chief executive had been poisoned, he soon diagnosed that Wilson had the influenza virus. Falling into a familiar pattern, Grayson tried to hide Wilson's illness from most of the world, and particularly the other delegates at the Paris conference. This secrecy was made more difficult when a young staff member with the delegation, who became ill the same day as Wilson, died four days later. Despite Grayson's efforts, within a week it was clear to the other delegates that Wilson was ill. Clemenceau and Lloyd-George came to his bedside for negotiations.

Astute observers noticed a change in Wilson after his bout with influenza. Herbert Hoover, who had been in Paris as part of the relief effort, could see the change in Wilson after his illness:

> *Prior to that time, in all matters with which I had to deal, he was incisive, quick to grasp essentials, unhesitating in conclusions and most willing to take advice from men he trusted ... (Now) others as well as I found we had to push against an unwilling mind. And at times, when I just had to get decisions, I suffered as much from having to mentally push as he did in coming to conclusions.*[308]

Putting his faith in the problem-solving powers of the League, Wilson put only minimal effort into influencing the outcomes of the remainder of the Peace Conference. While others in the American delegation seethed, Wilson was consistently outmaneuvered by Lloyd George, Clemenceau and others who viewed the conference as their means of rearranging the world order.

Article V of the Fourteen Points presented high-minded language intended to govern the redrawing of national boundaries:

> *A free, open-minded, and absolutely impartial adjustment of all colonial claims, based upon a strict observance of the principle that in determining all such question of sovereignty, the interest of the populations concerned must have equal weight with the equitable claims of the government whose title is to be determined.*[309]

But lofty language regarding the interests of populations soon collided with of ethnic and nationalistic realities. Wilson called in his Fourteen Points for the "freest opportunity of autonomous self-development" of the peoples of Austria-Hungary, and that Serbians would have access to the sea.

For Serbians to have a seaport, land would need to be taken from Bosnia or Montenegro. A Bosnia route would require additional ceding of land by the Croatians. And what, exactly, bound people of the Balkan region together? Boundaries would look significantly different if they were based on common language, or religion, or ethnic similarities. And mapmakers needed to satisfy the demand for land from the victorious nations of Italy and Greece. The result was the country of Yugoslavia carved, almost arbitrarily, out of sections of southern Austria-Hungary and Serbia. Disappearing into the newly-created amalgamation of once-autonomous regions were Croatia, Bosnia, Serbia, Montenegro, Kosovo and Macedonia. The new nation combined peoples with a bitter hatred for each other, kept from slitting each other's throats only by a dictatorial government.

The Middle East provided another opportunity for some at the Peace Conference to move national boundaries like chess pieces, hoping for an advantage in the new world order. Britain and France would covet lands stretching from the Dead Sea to the Caspian, carved into pieces by the Sykes-Picot Agreement of 1916. At the end of the War, with Russia distracted by internal revolution, it was up to the British and French to draw the new boundaries. By 1919, it was clear that oil would provide an important strategic asset to whoever owned it. While coal was the primary energy source for the Industrial Revolution, by the end of World War I cars, tanks and ships all increased the demand for oil. Though the extent of the oil reserves in the Middle East were unknown at the time, both Britain and France knew they wanted to control whatever lay under the sands of the desert.

Like the Balkans, however, the people of the Middle East defined themselves in a variety of ways. The Muslim religion was dominant, though significant pockets of Jews and Christians were intersperse in the area. Even among the Muslims, some considered themselves Sunni Muslims and others Shia Muslims, a distinction lost among those making decisions in Paris. The Arab population dominated the southern sections, while those in the north considered themselves Kurds, Persians or Assyrians.

Adding to the tension was a growing movement to convert the country of Palestine into a homeland for the world's Jewish population. The British provided their support for a Jewish homeland, declaring in the Balfour Declaration:

> *His Majesty's Government views with favour the establishment in Palestine of national home for the Jewish people, and will use their best endeavours to facilitate the attainment of this object.*[310]

Despite the fact that 700,000 Arabs already lived in Palestine, Wilson added his voice in support of the Balfour Declaration. "To think that I the son of the manse should be able to help restore the Holy Land to its people," Wilson wrote.[311]

In the end, the French and British carved out arbitrary boundaries that would create the nations of Syria and Lebanon, controlled by the French, while Iraq, Transjordan and Palestine would be overseen by the British. The British reaffirmed their belief that Palestine should welcome Jews from around the world, despite strong opposition from Arab leaders. In the next twenty-five years Palestine would become a safe haven for Jews fleeing the persecution of the Third Reich. But the safety of Palestine proved fleeting, as the large Jewish population would put the newly-named state of Israel on a collision course with the larger Arab population who could not forget that, not that long ago, they were their own masters in a nation called Palestine.

⁊ ⁊ ⁊ ⁊ ⁊

The work of the Peace Conference was done without the presence of a delegation from Germany. The German people waited anxiously for the terms that would be imposed on their defeated nation. They had come to believe that Woodrow Wilson would protect Germany from the most severe peace terms. They had convinced themselves that the language in the Fourteen Points – including self-determination – would protect them from significant loss of land. In addition, Wilson must surely understand, they thought, that onerous treatment in areas such as payment of reparations could push Germany into the arms of the Bolsheviks, as had occurred in Russia.

In May, the German delegation was summoned to Paris to hear the details of the peace treaty. The delegates were shocked by the vindictiveness of the terms. Germany alone was forced to accept responsibility for causing the war. Germany would lose the Saar basin, Poland and Silesia, amounting to over ten percent of its population. The Rhine would remain a part of Germany but would be occupied by France for at least fifteen years. The Germans would be forced to disarm, as their army was limited to 100,000 men and was forbidden to have submarines or military planes. Most importantly, Germans would be forced to pay $33 billion in reparations – the only defeated country required to do so.

Rather than bring Germany to her knees, however, the Treaty of Versailles would serve as the scapegoat for all that was wrong in Germany over the next twenty years. High prices and unemployment were traced directly to the payment of reparations – even though Germany ended up paying only about ten percent of the reparations requested. Former residents of Germany in the ceded territories such as the Sudetenland were convinced that their ultimate destiny lay in a reunification with the mother country. When the German leader who had signed the Treaty of Versailles was murdered, the assassins were hailed by some as heroes.

The Germans never forgave Wilson for what they viewed as his acquiescence to French and British demands for harsh peace terms against Germany. After Wilson's death in 1924, the flags of all the foreign embassies in Washington flew at half-staff, except for those at the German embassy.

◈ ◈ ◈ ◈ ◈

On June 28, 1918, delegates gathered in the Palace of Versailles to sign the treaty ending World War I. Both the date and place were significant, as the ceremony took place on the fourth anniversary of the assassination of the archduke and his wife at Sarajevo, and it was in the Palace that the German empire had been proclaimed in 1871.

Historians now know what many in the Palace on that day suspected: the Treaty of Versailles was a flawed document that would settle little and would, in fact, lead to tensions that would result in violence and war over the next hundred years. The amalgamation of the Balkan states into Yugoslavia would do nothing to reduce the fighting between its diverse population, and would ultimately lead to "ethnic cleansing". Arbitrary boundaries created in the Middle East would force rival factions together into countries unified in name only. The immigration of large numbers of Jews, and the discover of vast resources of oil, would create a tinderbox that would be ignited with frustrating regularity. And the imposition of harsh geographic and financial terms on the Germans would provide fodder for radical nationalists who would use the terms of the treaty to call for the creation of a Third Reich. "This is not a treaty of peace", French Field Marshall Ferdinand Foch would remark, "This is a twenty year cease fire."

Woodrow Wilson, who certainly must rank as one of the most intelligent of America's presidents, knew that the Treaty was imperfect. He also knew that the problems raised and issued ignored in the document could probably not be resolved in a few weeks by leaders gathered in Paris. To face the conflicts that would almost certainly appear, the world needed an organization of states, a parliament of man, a League of Nations. Throughout history, nations had shown a proclivity for violence and war. It was the League of Nations that would provide the last, best hope for mankind to live together in lasting harmony and peace.

CHAPTER TEN:

The First Great Shock

(1919-1920)

On July 8, 1919, President Woodrow Wilson returned from Paris after signing the Treaty of Peace by the United States and her allies with Germany in the Hall of Mirrors at Versailles. The Navy sent a fleet of nearly fifty ships, and thousands were there to meet the returning President at Hoboken, New Jersey.

Before the President's ship docked, Vice President Marshall sent him a message using the new "wireless" technology, clearly crafted to appear the next day on the front pages of newspapers across the country:

> *Mr. President: We, who now salute you, are only the advance guard of that vast army of your fellow-countrymen who joyfully welcome you to the homeland, not to the hours of rest which your arduous duties so justly entitle you to, but in health of body and strength of mind to assist in the solution of those vexing and intricate internal problems arising out of the world war so happily now concluded; to congratulate you upon the auspicious ending of your epoch-making mission and your position while at the Peace Table of that rare blending of vision and common sense which enabled you to get all you could see and not to see anything you could not get; and to renew our pledge of loyalty and service so long as you shall continue to stand for the glory, the perpetuity and the manifest destiny of the Republic.*[312]

On July 10, Wilson became the first President to formally deliver a treaty in person to an open session of the Senate. He was met by a five-man delegation, including Lodge, who escorted the President to the Senate chambers. Looking at the large and bulky document under Wilson's arm, Lodge joked, "Mr. President, can I carry the Treaty for you?" "Not on your life," was Wilson's retort, to the amusement of those present.

Wilson's testimony, while inspired in parts, did little to persuade key senators. By this point, the Senate was split into four distinct groups. The largest voting block was a group of Democratic senators who would support the treaty in its current form. Close behind philosophically were the "mild reservationists" – senators who were generally inclined to vote in favor, but wanted to see some changes before final passage. Opponents knew they needed to have the votes of only one-third of the Senate to defeat passage of the treaty. They were led by Lodge, who was viewed as part of a group of "strong reservationists". This group would support the Treaty only if significant changes were made – particularly to Article X.

Finally, a group of senators were dubbed by the press as the "Irreconcilables". This group, led by William Borah of Idaho, opposed passage of the Treaty in any way, regardless of amendments or reservations. Included with this voting block were not only fourteen Republicans but four Democrats as well. During the Treaty debate, Senator Borah made a speech in opposition to the League of Nations covenant that has often been cited as the turning point which galvanized opponents of the measure. Even Marshall was moved; after Borah's speech the Vice President sent him a note saying that "even a mummy on a pedestal could not remain silent after such a speech".

Marshall considered Borah to be one of his closest friends in the Senate.

> *For no man in America have I greater admiration and for few greater affection. I have many times heard fall from his lips specimens of oratory which, if they had been uttered by Cicero, or Webster, or Burke, would have become the common heritage of the schoolboy of today for declamatory purposes. No man has higher motives for public good than he has. A Republican, he advocates about two-thirds of the time, what I consider to be Democratic principles.*[313]

Marshall's friendship with Treaty opponents such as Borah, along with his open willingness to seeking a compromise which would allow the League of Nations covenant to be approved by the Senate, could only have acted to drive a further wedge between those in power in the White House – most notably, Edith Wilson – and the Vice President.

From a political standpoint, Wilson would have had his best chance of passage if he had assembled a coalition of supporters and mild reservationists. Together, these groups probably amounted to the sixty-four votes needed for passage. His address to the Senate on July 10, however, did little to draw votes to the Treaty. Rather than discuss detailed questions asked by the Senators, Wilson couched his delivery in lofty phrases and appealed to the legislators to adopt his vision of the new world order. "Shall we or any other free people hesitate to accept this great duty", Wilson asked. "Dare we reject it, and break the heart of the world?"[314]

During the summer of 1919, viewpoints from all sides were expressed as the Senate debated passage of the Treaty of Versailles. Marshall was once again called upon to use his oratorical skills to promote the position of the Wilson Administration. While Marshall was happy to comply with the President's request, some reports indicate he was less than enthusiastic about Wilson's position.

> *The long and weary months of discussion over the Treaty, after he returned in June and laid it before the Senate, was to my mind simply a waste of raw material. There never was a moment when those who had said they would not stand for the League of Nations could have been induced, under any circumstances, to vote for the ratification of the Treaty. No difference what the effect might be upon the world; no difference how public opinion might have changed; no difference what new light they had upon the subject, they had said they would not stand for it, and they did not. It was pride of opinion, as I saw it.*[315]

It was clear that Wilson would be unable to persuade the Senators. The idea was raised – probably by Joseph Tumulty – to go on a cross-country speaking tour to garner public support. Dr. Grayson advised against the trip, but Wilson's mind was made up.

The League of Nations is now in its crisis, and if it fails, I hate to think what will happen to the world. You must remember that I, as Commander in Chief, was responsible for sending our soldiers to Europe. In that crucial test in the trenches they did not turn back – and I cannot turn back now. I cannot put my safety, my health in the balance against my duty – I must go.[316]

In twenty-two days the President traveled over eight thousand miles and gave close to forty speeches. By any measure, the trip would have been strenuous even for someone much younger and healthier than Wilson. Edith could see the toll that the western trip was taking on her husband. At what would his last stop, in Pueblo, Colorado, Wilson's headaches intensified. He mounted the speaker's platform despite his discomfort, and delivered what may have been his best speech of the western trip. He recalled his visit to Suresnes, France on Memorial Day of that year, where he dedicated a monument to 974 American war dead. How he wished, he said, that his opponents could visit that spot. "I wish that the feeling which came to me could penetrate their hearts", he told the assembled crowd. The American people, he said, have seen "the truth of justice and of liberty and of peace." He closed with words made more poignant because they would be the last words Woodrow Wilson would utter in a public speech:

We have accepted that truth, and we are going to be led by it, and it is going to lead us, and, through us, the world, out into the pastures of quietness and peace such as the world has never dreamed of before.[317]

After the Pueblo speech, Grayson noted that Wilson looked "very tired". That evening, Mrs. Wilson woke Grayson at two o'clock in the morning, where the doctor found the President unable to sleep, nauseous, and with a twitching in the muscles of his face. An asthma attack also made it hard for Wilson to breathe. More ominously, the President's left side appeared to sag, and he moved his left arm only with difficulty. In addition, he had trouble speaking and his words were often mumbled. Edith and Joseph Tumulty knew his condition was serious; to Grayson, it was clear that Wilson was suffering from the effects of a stroke.

Grayson had no other choice but to insist that the remainder of the trip be cancelled. He woke Tumulty who agreed, but convincing Wilson was more difficult. The President awoke the next morning and began to shave in preparation for another round of speeches, but Grayson and Tumulty were adamant that the trip was over. "I don't seem to realize it, but I have gone to pieces," Wilson said. "The Doctor is right. I am not in condition to go on. I have never been in a condition like this, and I just feel as if I am going to pieces."[318]

With that, Wilson turned, looked out the window, and wept.[319]

᭟ ᭟ ᭟ ᭟ ᭟

President Wilson's train arrived in Washington early on the morning of September 28. By this time, he had recovered sufficiently to walk under his own power through the station to a waiting vehicle. When a group of wounded soldiers cheered him as he walked past, he acknowledged their greeting with a nod and a smile.[320] Though no one knew it at the time, never again would the 28th president acknowledge public acclaim from a group of well-wishers.

Safely ensconced back at the White House, Edith, Tumulty and Grayson developed a plan to allow the President to get the rest he needed without the burden of managing the affairs of state. By this time word had quickly spread that the President was ill, though his walk through the Washington train station and reassuring reports from Dr. Grayson helped to minimize speculation on Wilson's health. But when ten reporters who had been part of the western trip were invited to the White House on the day after the train had returned to Washington, it was Edith, without her husband, who entertained them.

Official business those last days of September was limited to dictating letters and signing bills. Visitors were kept only to those closest to the President. When the head of British intelligence asked for a meeting to convey what he described as important information, he only got as far as Edith, who assured him that she would relay the information to her husband.

Despite public assurances to the contrary, the President's physician knew his boss was gravely ill. Grayson suspected Wilson might have suffered a stroke on September 25, or more ominously a transient ischemic attack. Though less serious, the latter could be a precursor for a more serious stroke to follow.[321] Grayson discreetly asked several specialists, including a neurologist, Francis Dercum, from Philadelphia, to come to Washington.

On Wednesday evening, the first day of October, Edith and Woodrow watched a movie in the East Room, and afterward the President felt well enough to read aloud to his wife several passages from the Bible. Only partially reassured by her husband's newfound strength, she nonetheless slept only with short naps and awoke frequently to check on Wilson's condition. Early in the morning on October 2, she found her husband deep in a restful sleep.[322] But when she entered Woodrow's room shortly after eight that morning, she found the President sitting on the side of his bed trying to take a drink but unable to hold a water bottle. His left arm had again gone limp, and he walked only with great difficulty. She helped him into the bathroom and closed the door.

Sometime in the next few minutes, Wilson suffered a serious stroke and passed out. When he fell from the stool, he struck his head on the bathtub and opened two large lacerations-- one across the bridge of his nose, the other near his temple. He lay stricken on the floor for an unknown period of time that could have been as long as thirty minutes. At ten minutes until nine, as Edith returned to the bedroom, she went to the bathroom and, upon opening the door, found her husband unconscious on the floor. The President's wife grabbed a pillow from the bed and placed it under her husband's head, while also covering him with a blanket. Knowing that the White House switchboard could not be trusted to keep the information confidential, Edith went to a phone down the hall from the bedroom and phoned White House Usher Ike Hoover on a private line. "Please get Dr. Grayson,", Edith said, "The President is very sick".[323]

Grayson arrived soon after nine o'clock, and he and Edith moved the President to his own bed. Wilson had suffered an occlusion of the right middle cerebral artery – a massive stroke. He was completely paralyzed on his left side, and in addition was diagnosed with a left homonymous hemianopia, which is a loss of vision in the left half fields of both eyes.[324] Because he had already lost his central vision from a previous stroke, the President was effectively blinded except for a small field of vision in his right eye. In addition, the paralysis on the left side of his face also limited the movement of his tongue, jaw and pharynx, making both swallowing and speaking difficult. Ike Hoover waited outside the bedroom while Edith and Grayson made the President comfortable. When Grayson emerged from the room, he was visibly shaken. "My God," Grayson told Hoover, "the President is paralyzed."[325]

Soon after the President was stricken, three noted medical specialists arrived at the White House. Along with Dr. Dercum from Philadelphia was Dr. E.R. Stitt of the Washington Naval Hospital and Dr. Sterling Ruffin, who in addition to being a physician was also a close friend of Edith's. The physicians quickly determined that the President's situation was grave. The medical prognosis pointed to a recovery that was likely to be neither quick nor certain. Complete rest was the only solution, but the professionals were unable to determine when or if the President would again regain his speech, vision, or movement on the left side of his body.

By that evening it was clear even outside the President's closest advisors that the situation had deteriorated. The bustle of activity, the arrival of the medical specialists, and the lack of information from the Oval Office led many to speculate on Wilson's condition. Grayson understood that he needed to release some type of official announcement. Not wanting to either minimize the gravity of the situation or precipitate a constitutional crisis, the first bulletin was serious in tone but otherwise short on factual information. At ten o'clock that evening – more than thirteen hours after the stroke occurred – came the first official bulletin:

> *The President is a very sick man. His condition is less favorable today, and he has remained in bed throughout the day. After a consultation with Dr. F.X. Dercum of Philadelphia, Drs. Sterling Ruffin and E.R. Stitt of Washington, in which all agreed as to his condition, it was determined that absolute rest is essential for some time.*[326]

The bulletin was posted on the front page of newspapers across the country, though had editors known the extent of the crisis they would have certainly made the news a more prominent headline. Even the usually perceptive *New York Times* missed the gravity of the illness. The largest headline in that newspaper on the day after Wilson's stroke announced the drubbing of the Chicago White Sox by the Cincinnati Reds 9-1 in the first game of the World Series. Usually-dependable Eddie Cicotte, Chicago's starting pitcher, got the

"Worst Drubbing Received By Any Pitcher In History Of Baseball Classic", as the headline read, after he started the game by plunking the Red's second baseman in the back with his first pitch. Marshall, a lifelong baseball fan, must have kept one eye on the box scores for a championship that pitted two teams so close to his native Northeast Indiana.

The official bulletin on the next day, Friday, was a mix of optimism and caution. "The President had a fairly good night," the press release said, "But his condition is not at all good this morning." White House watchers could not overlook the fact that both of the President's daughters had been summoned to be with their father.

Due to Wilson's illness, Marshall was asked to fill in for the President as the head of state. On the day of Wilson's stroke, Marshall traveled to Hoboken, New Jersey to greet the King and Queen of the Belgians along with their seventeen-year-old son, Prince Leopold. After the visiting royalty had been greeted by Secretary of State Robert Lansing, as well as various ambassadors and military leaders, Marshall provided the welcome:

> *Your majesty, the head of this government, worn in body, is unable to meet and welcome you on behalf of the American people and himself. He has delegated this pleasing duty to my less competent hands.*[327]

Within twenty-four hours the triumvirate of Edith, Tumulty and Grayson had created a tight cordon around the President. Secretary of State Lansing – third in line of succession under the wording of the Constitution in 1919 – hurried back from greeting the Belgian royalty in Hoboken to learn more about the situation. He phoned Grayson, who divulged to Lansing that the President's condition was "bad" but also indicated that no one was permitted to visit him.

But while many felt confident of the Vice President's abilities, those closest to the President were far less willing to see Marshall assume any presidential authority. Edith, Tumulty and Grayson chose to keep the extent of Wilson's disability a secret, rather than risk elevating Marshall to the presidency.

Edith Wilson's memoirs, written more than a decade after the events of late 1919, paint the picture of a presidential wife trying to balance the advice of doctors with the needs of the country. Mrs. Wilson contends she consulted with Dr. Francis Dercum, the neurologist, who told her that Woodrow could make a full recovery if Edith helped to shield him from problems that might upset him. "How can that be," Edith asked, "when everything that comes to an Executive is a problem? How can I protect him from problems when the country looks to the President as a leader?"

The President's wife claims that she and Dr. Dercum jointly developed a plan of action to prevent the President from further stresses that could retard his recovery. Dercum was said to have advised:

> *Have everything come to you. Weigh the importance of each matter, and see if it is possible by consultations with the respective heads of the departments to solve them without the guidance of your husband. In this way you can save him a great deal. But always keep in mind that every time you take him a new anxiety or problem to excite him, you are turning a knife in an open wound. His nerves are crying out for rest, and any excitement is torture to him.*

Edith's reconstruction of events contends that she raised the possibility of presidential succession. "Then", responded Mrs. Wilson, "had he better not resign, let Mr. Marshall succeed to the Presidency and he himself get that complete rest so vital to his life?"

"No", said Dr. Dercum.

> *Not if you feel equal to what I have suggested. For Mr. Wilson to resign would have a bad effect on the country, and a serious effect on our patient. He has staked his life and made his promise to the world to do all in his power to get the Treaty ratified and make the League of Nations complete. If he resigns, the greatest incentive to recovery is gone; and as his mind is clear as crystal he can still do more with even a maimed body than any one else.*[328]

Edith's version of events in the days following October 2 are likely only partially correct, and probably intended to rebut contrary versions written by White House Usher Ike Hoover and others. She knew her husband's commitment to an unamended Treaty of Versailles, and had little respect for the Vice President, whom she viewed with disdain. Joseph Tumulty was more than willing to back his one-time adversary Edith, probably in the hope that should the President recover his place as a close advisor to the President would be restored.

As for Dr. Cary Grayson, his responsibilities as the President's personal physician bound him to abide by the wishes of his patient's wife. Dr. Grayson was in the unique position of being both Wilson's friend and his physician. Lois Marshall stated, years later, that Grayson had told her that he urged Wilson to resign, but the President refused. Knowing the President and understanding the risk to his health from continuing in office, Grayson's advice was probably sound. But he also knew Woodrow and Edith well enough to support their decision, and once it was clear that the President would not resign Grayson was bound both personally and professionally to abide by their wishes.

It was Secretary of State Lansing who was the first to seriously raise the question of presidential disability. The United States Constitution at the time said that the vice president could assume the duties of president in case of the president's *"Inability to discharge the Powers and Duties of the said Office,"* but until the Twenty-fifth Amendment was adopted in 1967, the Constitution said absolutely nothing about how the vice president should assume the duties of the presidency. The question had actually been publicly debated months before, when Wilson left the country for an extended period of time during the negotiations over the Treaty of Versailles. Other presidents had been ill, but death usually came quickly and the nation never faced the prospect of a long period of presidential disability.

Lansing met with Joseph Tumulty, who was still clearly shaken by the events of the last twenty-four hours, on the day after the stroke. Tumulty told Lansing that Wilson's condition was worse than had been public admitted. "In what way?", Lansing asked. Rather than respond, Tumulty moved his right hand down the left side of his body. The message was clear; the stroke had left the left side of the President paralyzed.

While accounts of meetings held the day after Wilson's stroke conflict, several events seem clear. The two men gathered in the Cabinet Room near the Oval Office. While both Lansing and Tumulty were aware of the constitutional provision on presidential disability, Lansing produced a copy of the constitution and read it to Tumulty. Perhaps taken aback by Lansing's arrogance, Tumulty's demeanor shifted from visibly shaken to defiantly agitated.

> *Mr. Lansing, the Constitution is not a dead letter with the White House. I have read the Constitution and do not find myself in need of any tutoring at your hands of the provision that you have just read.*

"You may rest assured," Tumulty continued, "that while Woodrow Wilson is lying in the White House on the broad of his back I will not be a party to ousting him. He has been too kind, too loyal, and too wonderful to me to receive such treatment at my hands." At this point, Dr. Grayson entered the cabinet room. Tumulty – still outraged by Lansing's constitutional lecture – turned to the doctor and said, "And I am sure that Dr. Grayson would never certify to his disability."[329]

Grayson concurred with Tumulty. Should Lansing or anyone else try to certify the president's incapacity, Tumulty continued, he and Grayson would together deny such an attempt. Grayson's immediate affirmation of Tumulty's statement make it clear that the message had been agreed upon ahead of time, probably at the urging of Edith Wilson.

Neither Lansing nor Tumulty were swayed by their Cabinet Room discussion. It is also likely that both were looking ahead to their prospects in a Marshall administration. Lansing may have been positioning himself for a key appointment – perhaps Vice President – under President Thomas Marshall. Tumulty probably knew that his relationship with Marshall was not strong, but that didn't mean that he couldn't take steps to tie himself closer to the Vice President over the next few weeks. Later that Saturday, Tumulty met with Secretary of Agriculture David Houston. While the meeting has been described as having occurred "by chance", Tumulty shared the true nature of Wilson's illness with Houston. Probably not by chance, Houston would have lunch with Marshall the following day.

That Sunday, October 5, Marshall was growing increasingly anxious. It was clear to Marshall that the President's condition was grave, that press accounts were obfuscating the nature and extent of the illness, and that many in the government knew a lot more than they were sharing with the Vice President. Also at this time, in addition to Wilson's family and physicians, the true nature of the President's illness was known to Tumulty, Josephus Daniels, Secretary of State Lansing, Secretary of Agriculture Houston, and numerous White House staff. When Marshall spoke with Daniels after church that morning, no mention was made of the President's illness – even though one might expect the President's advisor to talk with the Vice President about the topic that was engaging the rest of the nation's attention.

It was bad enough that no knowledgeable official had relayed any meaningful information; now, with Daniels' silence it was clear that the lack of communication with the Vice President was intentional. Marshall and Daniels had enjoyed a cordial if not close relationship during Wilson's administration. Daniels, in his memoirs, would describe Marshall as "a real statesman of patriotism, ability, originality and devotion to the public weal".[330] For Daniels to avoid mention of a topic that was riveting all of Washington was a clear signal to Marshall that Daniels was under orders to avoid discussing the topic with the Vice President.

By the time Houston met Tom and Lois for lunch at the Shoreham Hotel that Sunday, Marshall's usual upbeat demeanor had given way to a rare bout of anger. Houston's own memoirs provide the only account of the meeting, and they indicate that, based on his promise to Tumulty, Houston did not share the full extent of the President's illness with the Vice President. That account may not be entirely accurate, however, as it seems likely that Houston met with Marshall at Tumulty's request.

Houston's account of the meeting describes Marshall as angry, disturbed and vocal in his displeasure with the lack of reliable news. Marshall

> *Was evidently much disturbed and expressed regret that he was being kept in the dark about the president's condition. He asked me if I could give him the real facts, which I was unable to do. I could not even repeat what had been told to me, because it had been said in confidence. The Vice President expressed the view that he ought immediately to be informed; that it would be a tragedy for him to assume the duties of the President, at best; and that it would be equally a tragedy for the people; that he knew many men who knew more about the affairs of government than he did; and that it would be especially trying for him if he had to assume the duties without warning.*[331]

Lansing, for his part, felt he needed to seek a resolution of the disability question. Without the president's knowledge or approval, Lansing called a cabinet meeting for Monday, October 6, which had been reported in the papers that Sunday morning. Tumulty may have sent Houston to give Marshall the message that he should avoid public comment until after Monday's cabinet meeting. In any case, despite Houston's lack of details, Tom and Lois must have come away from that meeting knowing that the eyes of the world would, over the next few weeks, focus on the Vice President.

The meeting of the Cabinet took place as scheduled on the morning of October 6. It was clear from the start, though, that Tumulty, Grayson and the President's wife had avoided giving Lansing any ammunition to use with the other Cabinet members. The official press bulletin was very upbeat on Sunday, noting that the President "had a very good night", and that, "if there is any change in his condition it is favorable." For good measure, it was noted that his appetite was improving and that he was sleeping better. Grayson added to the optimistic reports by stating that he had difficulty persuading the President to stay in bed. The story was even released that the President had asked for a stenographer but was reminded that it was Sunday and no good Presbyterian would do work on the Sabbath day.

Lansing probably knew when the meeting started that the Cabinet would take no action on that day. After opening the meeting, Lansing turned to Dr. Grayson for an update on the President's condition. To the surprise of no one, the doctor's report was positive. Grayson "gave a very encouraging report on the President's condition, which, he said, showed decided improvement and seemed to indicate a speedy recovery." There being no one in the room to say otherwise, Lansing asked Grayson to "convey to the President our felicitations and best wishes." After a discussion of routine matters, the meeting was adjourned.

But while the Cabinet would take no action on that day, the issue was certainly not resolved. Despite public statements to the contrary, Wilson was not out of danger. The question of whether or not Marshall would assume the presidency would be decided by Wilson's health, not in the Cabinet Room of the White House.

Later, Marshall acknowledged the importance of that cabinet meeting in his own humorous way, telling the story of an overheard conversation on a train ride:

A couple sitting immediately in front of us had been reading the latest news from Washington and they were discussing it very earnestly. The man seemed to believe President Wilson had acted for the best, but his companion heatedly expressed the view that Secretary Lansing could have followed no other course than he had throughout. "Why, what else could Mr. Lansing have done?" the woman asked with some asperity. "Here the President was sick. A lot of big questions had to be talked over and there was the Vice President, who doesn't amount to anything. The only thing Mr. Lansing could do, I tell you, was to call these Cabinet meetings, and I think he did the right thing." There you have it in a nutshell. The woman was right. I don't amount to anything.[332]

૭૭ ૭૭ ૭૭ ૭૭ ૭૭

Along with the rest of the country, Vice President Marshall read with alarm reports of the President's health after Wilson had cut short his trip to the western states. Had the Vice President and congressional leaders known the true severity of Wilson's illness much of the activity in Washington over the next few weeks might have been deferred until the President's condition stabilized. But official reports were optimistic, and while the truth would slowly unfold to an ever-widening circle over time, in the first few weeks of October the official business of Washington continued. The nation divided its attention between the excitement of the World Series and concerns about the President's health. With the Senate in session during and after Wilson's trip, Marshall remained busy presiding over floor debate, most of which focused on the ratification of the League of Nations covenant.

With the fate of the League in jeopardy, emotions ran high on the Senate floor. At one point Senators Borah and Hitchcock exchanged especially angry words regarding a point of debate on the Versailles treaty. As tempers rose, Marshall interrupted the debate to read what he described as an important communication to the Senate. Expecting some type of announcement, perhaps from Wilson, the Vice President instead read a letter he had received from the father of a newborn boy. The new dad was looking for a name for his son, and hoping for a little more as well. "The man who will give the baby the biggest prize can have the name," the letter said, "Mr. Marshall, see what you can do for me." The letter produced the effect Marshall had hoped. The laughter from the Senators was genuine, tempers cooled, and debate resumed.

◆ ◆ ◆ ◆ ◆

The elevation of the Vice President and his wife to the status of primary contact for visiting dignitaries proved to be a strain on Tom and Lois. The arrangements for the arrival of the King and Queen of Belgium were poorly organized, and on the same day of Lansing's cabinet meeting the Vice President wrote the Secretary of State a tersely worded letter:

> *What becomes of me as Vice President is very unimportant but, when I travel in the name of the President, I expect to be treated as the President would be treated. In view of the experiences I had when going to New York to represent the President in the welcome of King Albert, I desire to notify your Department that, if called upon to represent him again, a complete schedule of the way in which I am to be treated as his representative must be furnished to me. This is official and not personal.*

Marshall received immediate replies from both Lansing and the undersecretary of state. Yet the problem was not wholly resolved; in the confusion of Wilson's illness, no funds had been allocated to Marshall for entertaining foreign dignitaries. Knowing that it would be an insult to the King to entertain he and the Queen in the Willard hotel where they lived, the Vice President's dilemma was finally resolved when the wife of a Denver mining millionaire offered her home on Massachusetts Avenue for the official dinner.[333]

◆ ◆ ◆ ◆ ◆

The President's wife, secretary and physician may have been able to manage the flow of information from the President's bedside, but they could not control speculation among Washington's elite, nor could they alter the President's true condition. About two weeks after the stroke, Wilson developed a severe urinary blockage. Unless the blockage abated, the President would suffer fatal poisoning. In a younger and healthier patient surgery would be the recommended course of action. But in Wilson's condition, Edith was advised that the chances that her husband would survive such an operation would be slim. Edith decided against an operation. For several hours, Wilson's life hung in the balance. With all of Washington keeping watch on the White House, and as the President's fever rose, it was clear from the actions of the President's closest advisors that their Commander in Chief was facing a critical point in the medical crisis. To the great relief of those who stood watch in the presidential bedroom, after a few hours the urinary blockage dissolved naturally and, for now, the latest crisis had passed. But the experience had made it clear to the three persons who controlled access to the President that they could no longer withhold the truth from the Vice President.

Such an action was without historical precedent. Would any type of communication from a White House official trigger the constitutional mechanism for Marshall to assume the presidency? If so, how could Marshall be informed in a manner that would put him on notice of a potential transition of power without actually beginning the process of presidential ascension?

It was likely Tumulty, an attorney, who developed a method for informing Marshall. They asked a trusted intermediary, J. Fred Essary, a correspondent with the Baltimore *Sun*, to brief Marshall on the president's condition. Essary was a journalist who was fully aware of the true nature of the President's disability. He also had the advantage of being able to visit the Vice President as part of his daily routine without triggering speculation as to the nature of his visit.

Essary made an appointment with Marshall at his office. He got quickly to the point, explaining who had sent him and informing the Vice President that Wilson's condition was so grave that he might die at any time. A stunned Marshall sat speechless, staring at his hands clasped on the desk. It was the first time that the Vice President has received a clear, unambiguous and truthful report of Wilson's condition. David Houston's lunchtime conversation the Sunday after the stroke had put Marshall on notice that the President was sicker than the public bulletins had revealed. But two weeks had passed without any further discouraging news, and like most of Washington Marshall would have understandably assumed that the prognosis was improving. For the first time, Thomas Marshall was aware that he might, at any moment, become the leader of the nation.

Marshall's first reaction was stunned silence. Essary waited for a reaction from Marshall, but saw none. After hesitating for a moment, he rose and left without any additional conversation. Many years later, Essary and Marshall were reunited in Indiana. Marshall was apologetic. "I did not even have the courtesy to thank you for coming over and telling me," he said, "It was the first great shock of my life."[334]

By the middle of October it was clear to most of official Washington that the President was far sicker than the official bulletins intimated. The inability of anyone other than family and close advisors to see the President did little to dampen the speculation; official business was also conducted in a manner that gave clues to the acuteness of the President's condition. Procedures called for the President to either sign or veto a bill within ten days of its passage by Congress. In the absence of any action the bill would become law without the President's signature. Wilson only rarely allowed this to happen; yet, in the first two weeks of October, four bills became law in this manner. On October 16, Congress passed the Volstead Act, which provided a mechanism for the enforcement of Prohibition. Wilson's signature presumably vetoed the act (and the veto was promptly overridden by Congress), but many lawmakers carefully scrutinized the signature and expressed doubts that it was actually that of the President.

Other matters desired the President's attention at this time. Presidential appointments were left unfilled; another crisis was emerging in Mexico; negotiations in Europe between the Allies and belligerents regarding various aspects of the negotiated peace required an official decision by the United States. But the nation's – and the world's – attention was focused on the ratification of the Treaty of Versailles and the League of Nations.

The pressure on Marshall came from several sources. There were various efforts by legislators from both parties to elevate the Vice President. While Marshall publicly supported President Wilson's position against any amendments to the Treaty, in private conversations he let it be known that he favored the mild reservations that could lead to the congressional votes necessary for passage. As a result, the "mild reservationist" faction attempted to get Marshall to assume presidential powers.

The Vice President was notified by a small group of Democratic senators that they would support him should he seek to gain presidential powers. More surprisingly, a group from the Republican Party said that they, also, would support such a move. Calls for succession came from other quarters, as well. A former Attorney General, Republican George Wickersham, had proposed a transfer of power even before the President's serious stroke.

Few men in history have had to wrestle with the decision that faced Vice President Thomas Marshall in October of 1919. Those who knew the truth were aware that President Wilson was undoubtedly suffering from the type of disability contemplated by the framers of the Constitution, and that according to both the spirit and intent of the law Marshall should have assumed the powers of the presidency. He had reason to believe that he would have had the support of a coalition of concerned Democrats, moderate Republicans, mild reservationists, and political leaders from the states that enthusiastically cheered Wilson on his western trip. Many leaders in the international community – particularly those who had been enthralled by Wilson's vision – watched anxiously as American leaders struggled with the succession question.

The decision would have clear international repercussions, as well. President Marshall may have chosen to pass the Versailles Treaty with reservations and then lead the United States into meaningful participation in the League of Nations. The League, backed by the strong support of the United States, might have been able to help the world avoid the coming conflagration.

ക്ക ക്ക ക്ക ക്ക ക്ക

Two weeks after Wilson's stroke, on October 16, 1919, a young former German soldier addressed a meeting of the German Workers Party, which at the time was a small and ineffective group of just seven members. But the young man saw the Party as his vehicle to deliver his message to his fellow countrymen.

Born on April 20, 1889, the young man had enlisted in the German army and served until October 1916, when he was wounded by a shell fragment at the Battle of the Somme. He quickly reenlisted after his recovery, but was blinded by British chlorine gas in October, 1918 near Ypres. He was lying in a hospital bed recovering from that episode when news came that the Kaiser had abdicated and the war was over. But like many Germans, he felt his country had been defeated not on the battlefield but by unscrupulous politicians and, more importantly, by the Jews. "There followed terrible days and even worse nights," he would later write, "in these nights hatred grew in me, hatred for those responsible for the deed."[335]

At the meeting in the beer cellar, those present – about a hundred – were spellbound by the young man's very emotional method of speaking. At times firm and resolute, at other times nearly hysterical, the young man delivered his strongly nationalistic, and anti-Semitic, message. His short speech had its intended effect on those present.

> *I spoke for thirty minutes, and what before I had simply felt within me, without in any way knowing it, was now proved by reality: I could speak! After thirty minutes the people in the small room were electrified and the enthusiasm was first expressed by the fact that my appeal to the self-sacrifice of those present led to the donation of three hundred marks.*[336]

The young man's reputation as an orator grew. Four months later, two thousand people crowded into a meeting hall in Munich to hear him speak. Within a year the crowds had grown to six thousand at a single gathering.

Those present were enthralled by what they heard and the young man's vision for his country. He called for the rejection of the Treaty of Versailles, the union of all Germans into a single country with a strong central government, and citizenship to be determined by race and to exclude Jews. The German people, bitter at the loss of land and payment of reparations, shouted enthusiastic support for the young man and his message.

By early 1921, the popular speaker would be the overwhelming choice to become the leader of the German Workers Party. By this time, the name of the party was changed to the National Socialist German Workers' Party (Nationalsozialistische Deutsche Arbeiterpartei, or NSDAP), which name was abbreviated to the Nazi Party. In July of 1921, the war veteran was elected by acclaim as the new leader of the Nazi Party. After the vote, members present were introduced to their new leader, or Führer, Adolph Hitler.

Thomas Riley Marshall would never know the consequences of his decision, nor the course that history would take in the two decades after Wilson's stroke. Years after ratification of the Covenant of the League of Nations was defeated by the Senate, Marshall wrote:

> *It is idle to speculate about what might have happened had we entered the League of Nations. Much good has been accomplished by it, but a thoughtful man will pause before he says of a certainty that the kings and emperors have not been succeeded by autocrats.*[337]

"The bitter irony," wrote historian Samuel Elliot Morison, "is that if (Marshall) had become President at this juncture he would have made the necessary concession and the treaty would have been ratified."[338] Arthur Link, Wilson's biographer, also saw Marshall's decision as one of the great turning points in history. "In a world with the United States playing a responsible, active role," he wrote, "The possibilities of preventing the rise of Hitler were limitless".[339]

Marshall weighed the information he had, and naturally turned to his closest friend and confidant, his wife Lois, as they debated the situation. "I could throw this country into civil war", he told Lois, "but I won't."[340]

> *Those were not pleasant months for me. The standing joke of the country is that the only business of the Vice President is to ring the White House bell every morning and ask what is the state of health of the president. If there were a soul so lost to humanity as to have desired his death, I was not that soul. I hoped that he might acquire his wonted health. I was afraid to ask about it, for fear some censorious soul would accuse me of longing for his place. I never wanted to have his shoes. Peace, friendship and good will have ever been more to me than place or pomp or power.*[341]

Marshall told his decision to Mark Thistlethwaite, who pressed the Vice President for further clarification. Would Marshall assume the office if asked to do so by a joint resolution of Congress, or if the President was declared incapacitated by the Supreme Court? Both were unlikely, Marshall replied. The only circumstance which would cause him to assume the presidency, he said, would be a joint resolution of Congress, a written affirmation from the president's physician, and the approval of Mrs. Wilson. Of those, perhaps the last was the most unlikely. Marshall's decision was shared with the leadership in Washington, and talk of presidential succession ceased.

☙ ☙ ☙ ☙ ☙

Though speculation on presidential succession had abated, the need for international diplomacy continued. In mid-November the Vice President's patience would be tested by a visit from the heir to the throne in England, the Prince of Wales.

> *And then came notice of the intended visit of the Prince of Wales. And then my troubles began! To receive and welcome and to be hospitable to a king of mature years, whose wife accompanied him, was mere child's' play to acting as host for an upstanding, unmarried young fellow. Throughout all the years of my life, as I had read history from King David down, I had not been much impressed with the conduct of royal families. But after I finished my experiences with the Prince of Wales I am ready to go on record and say that I am amazed at the restraining which these so-called blue bloods put upon their personal conduct.*[342]

Prince Edward Albert Christian George Andrew Patrick was born June 23, 1894, the eldest son of the Duke of York -- who would later become King George V – and the great-grandson of Queen Victoria. The world got its first good look at the future King when his grandfather, Edward VII, died and his father took the throne. Tall, blond and handsome, the Prince of Wales was just sixteen years old when his picture was spread around the globe from his father's coronation service. He immediately became the world's most eligible bachelor.

When England declared war against Germany, David, as his family called him, was eager to serve on the front lines and sought an assignment with the infantry. But military strategists were more concerned with his possible capture than the risk of his death, and they, along with his father, kept him far from the line of battle. But he was not completely removed from danger. One day he had taken only a few steps away from his car when it was struck by an artillery shell, killing the driver. Despite having never fired a shot, he still forged close ties with other men in his regiment, and by war's end David was popular both in his country and around the world.

To capitalize on this popularity and his movie-star good looks, he was sent on a tour of friendly nations soon after the hostilities ended. To mark the first anniversary of Armistice Day, his first stop would be the United States.

> It was no sooner definitely settled that the Prince was to visit us, than every fooling mother of a fool daughter, who could raise the necessary railroad fare, started for Washington. Beauty parlors put on aristocratic airs, and one of the common herd was unable to get a shampoo. Everybody was being dolled up to meet the prince.[343]

Marshall met His Royal Highness at Union Station and accompanied him on his tour of official Washington. While at first piqued by the media attention paid to the twenty-five year old prince, the Vice President soon developed affection and respect for the man and the role he played in the British Empire. The Vice President's story of their trip to Mount Vernon showed Marshall the reverence his subjects held for their future King.

> He insisted, with the wind blowing fifty miles an hour, on going in an open car. His reason was that some woman had sent him a bouquet and that she had said she and her husband would be along the road to greet him. I did not dare rail at royalty, but that was one of the mornings when I regretted my prohibition tendencies. I wished I were drunk enough to forget the state of the weather. But I let my temper warm up to a point where it kept my body in fair condition, and away we went! Sure enough, about halfway to Mount Vernon there was a woman with her husband. The prince stopped, got out and discovered that the man had been a member of his regiment in France.

> *I lost all my irritation when I saw the genuine good will with*
> *which he greeted one of the privates in his regiment.*[344]

At one point during the visit, Lois became ill and was unable to attend the public ceremonies for the Prince. As a courtesy to Mrs. Marshall, his Highness asked to come to the Willard Hotel so that he could pay his respects in person. Lois and Izzy were waiting.

> *Well, when the prince came this little fellow toddled in and*
> *looking with the eye of trust and confidence into his eye, said:*
> *"Who are you?" Then I knew that the faith and trust of*
> *childhood are as essential to democracy as they are to entrance*
> *into the Kingdom of Heaven. When all mysteries were solved,*
> *all doubts removed, then I knew that what we each should look*
> *for in each other, ask for at the hands of each other, receive out of*
> *the lives of each other, were friendship and good will. Pomp and*
> *place and circumstance crumble into dust before friendship and*
> *good will. It glorified this heir to the throne of Great Britain;*
> *it raised to kingship this little child from a humble American*
> *home.*[345]

The Prince of Wales went on to make successful world tours in Canada, New Zealand, Australia and India. But the Prince had apparently learned more from his philandering grandfather than his faithful father, as the royal family became increasingly concerned about his extravagant lifestyle and peculiar affection for women who were already married. When he at last thought he had genuinely fallen in love, it was not with an acceptable member of the British aristocracy but, instead, with an American divorcee estranged from, but still married to, her second husband.

The Prince of Wales would become King seventeen years after his trip to the United States. The happiness that he must have felt during his afternoon with Tom, Lois and Izzy eluded him, however, as he would abdicate his throne barely ten months after his father died. "I have found it impossible to carry the heavy burden of responsibility and to discharge my duties as King as I would wish to do," he said in a radio broadcast, "without the help and support of the woman I love."

Fearing a constitutional crisis should his new wife have a child, and also disturbed by reports that he had reached an agreement with Adolf Hitler to return to the throne if Germany won the second world war, the Prince of Wales, who became King Edward VIII, was banished from his homeland for the rest of his life.[346]

❦ ❦ ❦ ❦ ❦

Senator Gilbert Hitchcock visited President Wilson on November 7. Hitchcock was the first person outside of Wilson's inner circle to see the President since his stroke, and it was clear that Wilson was gravely ill. "I was shocked to see that he had become an old man", the Senator later wrote. "As he lay in bed slightly propped up by pillows with the useless arm concealed beneath the covers I beheld an emaciated old man with a thin white beard which had been permitted to grow. But his eye was clear and his resolve strong."[347]

The status of the League vote in the Senate was the primary reason for Hitchcock's visit, and Wilson was anxious for news. Hitchcock told him that he could only muster about forty-five votes for the League without reservations. "It is possible, it is possible," whispered Wilson. Afterward, Hitchcock met with reporters. Was the President, the reporters asked, still committed to passage of the League without reservations, even if it meant defeat in the Senate?

> He did not say outright whether he would favor rejection rather than acceptance of the majority reservations. He said he would accept any compromise the friends of the treaty thought necessary to save the treaty, so long as it did not destroy the terms of the pact itself. He made it plain that the Lodge reservations would kill the treaty.[348]

On November 17, a letter was completed by the White House and sent to Hitchcock, who passed it along to the rest of the Senators.

> You were good enough to bring me word that the Democratic senators supporting the treaty expected to hold a conference before the final vote on the Lodge resolution of ratification

and that they would be glad to receive a word of counsel from me. I should hesitate to offer it in any detail but I assume that the senators desire my judgment only upon the all-important question of the final vote on the resolution containing the many reservations by Senator Lodge. On that I can not hesitate, for in my opinion the resolution in that form does not provide for ratification, but rather for the nullification of the treaty. I sincerely hope that the friends and supporters of the treaty will vote against the Lodge resolution of ratification. I understand that the door will probably then be open for a genuine resolution of ratification. I hope therefore that all true friends of the treaty will refuse to support the Lodge resolution.[349]

By early December the problem of the President's inaccessibility had grown more acute. In addition to the debate over the League treaty, Mexico had once again become the focus of international interest, as the government of Venustiano Carranza had seized an American citizen, William Jenkins, and clamor again grew for military intervention.

On December 4, while being questioned by the Senate Foreign Relations Committee, Secretary of State Lansing admitted that neither he nor anyone else from his department had spoken with the President since August. Startled by the revelation, the Committee went into closed session and decided, in a six-to-five party line vote, to send a subcommittee, consisting of Hitchcock and Senator Albert Fall, to go to the White House to meet with the President. The stated reason for the visit was to inquire regarding the President's view of the Mexican situation, but it was clear that the real reason for the visit was to check up on Wilson's health. Irreverent Washington observers called it the Smelling Committee.

Cary Grayson knew that he could not keep the President isolated forever, and he carefully staged the meeting. While lights were on in the room, Wilson himself was in a shaded area. Knowing Wilson's left side was paralyzed, he positioned the President so that important papers were within easy reach of his good right arm. Wilson's humor also eased the gravity of the moment.

"I hope you will consider me sincere." Fall began the meeting, "I have been praying for you, Sir."

Wilson shot back, "Which way, Senator?"

Grayson's stage management continued. To the good fortune of Wilson, the Mexican Government had earlier in the day released William Jenkins. Grayson found the perfect way to deliver the news. He returned to Wilson's bedroom and announced, "Pardon me, gentlemen, but Secretary Lansing had asked me to tell you immediately that Jenkins has been released."

The meeting of the Smelling Committee could not have gone better for Wilson and his supporters. "Senator Fall did most of the talking," Hitchcock told reporters afterwards, "And presented a very good summary of conditions to which the President gave his deepest attention." More importantly, Fall reported back to both his Republican colleagues and to the rest of the nation: "In my opinion, Mr. Wilson is perfectly capable of handling the situation."[350]

❧ ❧ ❧ ❧ ❧

Alarm over events in Russia, and the mobilization of the propaganda efforts for the war, led the passage of the Espionage Act in June, 1917. The law called for $10,000 fine and prison terms of up to 20 years for interfering with the recruiting of troops or the disclosure of information dealing with national defense. Additional penalties were included for the refusal to perform military duty. Before the end of 1917, nearly a thousand people were jailed under the Espionage Act.

The Sedition Act of 1918 made it a federal crime to criticize the government or Constitution. Despite constitutional safeguards on freedom of speech, under the law any spoken or published form of writing expressing negative opinions about the war effort, or opinions against the draft, could lead to the imprisonment. Eugene Debs, the presidential candidate of the Socialist party in three previous elections, was jailed for comments he made during a speech in Ohio and stripped of his citizenship. On May 1, 1919, a May Day parade in Cleveland, Ohio, protesting the imprisonment of Debs erupted into violent riots. After one of the organizers of the parade was arrested, 36 bombs were sent by mail to prominent politicians and judges.

Alexander Mitchell Palmer was appointed Attorney General of the United State by President Wilson on March 5, 1919. In addition to having to deal with the May Day riots and the subsequent bomb scare, large strikes, which some felt were backed by Bolshevik leaders, were staged throughout the country. On September 9, the Boston police force went on strike, and later that month 275,000 steelworkers walked off their jobs. Most of Pittsburgh's steel mills were shut down, and in Gary, Indiana, the unrest was so prevalent that martial law was declared on October 5.

With President Wilson's health at its most perilous, the politically ambitious Palmer used the leadership vacuum to strike what he felt would be a decisive blow against the threat of a Bolshevik revolution in America. On the night of November 7th, 1919, the second anniversary of the Russian Revolution, over 10,000 suspected communists and anarchists were arrested. While the vast majority of those arrested were eventually released, nearly 250 were deported to Russia.

In the national fervor to root out the threat of a communist revolution in the United States, a group was formed in St. Louis on May 8, 1919 "to uphold and defend the Constitution of the United States of America; to maintain law and order; to foster and perpetuate a one hundred per cent Americanism." By the end of 1919 the group had over one million members. The organization, which would be named the American Legion, garnered widespread support and the phrase "Leave the Reds to the Legion" soon became the response to threats of Bolshevism in America.

Eugene Debs would remain in jail until pardoned by President Warren Harding. His citizenship would not be restored until 1976, fifty years after his death.

❧ ❧ ❧ ❧ ❧

As President Wilson's condition appeared to stabilize, Marshall felt more comfortable accepting speaking engagements outside of the Washington area. In late November, he traveled to Atlanta to address a convention of the Loyal Order of the Moose.

As Marshall was addressing the crowd, a phone call came into the auditorium office. When asked if the Vice President was available to come to the phone, the speaker noted that he was on the stage in the middle of his speech. "Well, I guess he'll come now," the speaker on the other end of the telephone said. "President Wilson has just died in Washington and Mr. Marshall is wanted at once on the long distance." Officials at the auditorium felt they had no choice but to notify the Vice President. Midway through the speech, an employee walked onto the stage and whispered to Marshall that Wilson was dead.

Silently, Marshall bowed his head for a moment. When he again looked at the crowd, he shared the news with them. Many instinctively bowed their heads; some women could be heard crying. "I cannot bear the great burdens of our beloved chieftain," said Marshall, "unless I receive the assistance of everybody in this country."

As the organist began to play the hymn "Nearer My God To Thee", Tom and Lois left the stage. He immediately called the White House to determine his next course of action. It was only then that he learned that the call, in fact, was a hoax, and the President was still alive.

"There was no sense of elation but rather the contrary," Marshall later told Josephus Daniels. "I was stunned, first by grief for my dead chieftain and second by the awful responsibility that would fall upon me. I was resolved to do my duty but I can truly say that I dreaded the great task."[351]

❧ ❧ ❧ ❧ ❧

The World Series of 1919 pitted the Chicago White Sox against the Cincinnati Reds. Because of the popularity of the game after the war, the Series was extended to best of nine, rather than best of seven. Prior to the series, the White Sox were heavy favorites, led by the popular "Shoeless" Joe Jackson. Just before the first game, however, Cincinnati became the betting favorite. The first game was played in Chicago on October 1, 1919. Cincinnati pitcher Dutch Reuther shut down the Chicago offense. In addition to going the distance while allowing just six hits, he went three for three from the plate with two triples and three runs batted in. Eddie Cicotte, Chicago's pitcher, did not perform as well. He started the game by hitting the first batter in the back with a pitch, and was pulled when he gave up five runs in the fourth inning.

Only later would the nation learn that Cicotte had accepted $10,000 in cash to throw the game by a gambler who bet heavily on Cincinnati (Cicotte was instructed to hit the first batter with a pitch if the game was being thrown). The rest of the White Sox had also made a deal to split $20,000 for each game they lost in the series. Despite losing the series five games to three, the White Sox team was never paid the amounts they were promised. The eight players who participated in the scandal were banned from baseball for life.

❧ ❧ ❧ ❧ ❧

The diplomatic receptions and public appearances continued at a hectic pace after Wilson's stoke. In addition, Lois continued to try to nurse Izzy towards health. Despite their best efforts, the child's condition did not seem to improve.

> *Never were we away from him, sick baby that he was, a single day without a message coming to tell us of his health. There was but one unending cry through all the days, and but one continuous dream of the nights: "Is it well with the child?"*

In February of 1920, the Vice President was in New England to deliver a speech when word came that Izzy's health was deteriorating. Lois left her husband to return to Washington – only the second night in their marriage that the two were separated. Lois found three-year-old Izzy critically ill from a blood condition. She summoned the manager of the Willard Hotel, who had often helped Lois in caring for the baby. The daughter of the hotel manager tells the rest of the story.

> *Mrs. Marshall, having no experience as a mother, would frequently call on my mother for information and assistance when their adopted child became sick, which he did very often. Once a call came in the middle of the night. Mother hastened to the Marshalls' rooms but it was too late. The child had died.*[352]

Though hardened by the stress of state and national governance, the realities of politics and the violence of war, Tom Marshall never recovered from the death of Izzy.

> *I cannot even speak of him for whom I grieve without a feeling that I ought not to do so. He was and is and ever will be so sacred to me that I much doubt whether his blessed memory should be used even for a holy purpose. For three years he spelled for me*

in every ripple of laughter and his every lisping word God and democracy.

Perhaps Izzy's death brought to the surface long-suppressed memories of the death of those he loved, including his fiancée Kate Hooper. Since Lois had come into his life he knew he could not speak of his first love who had died on the eve of their wedding. With Izzy, though, his grief was sincere and open for all to see.

> *He stayed with us until he was three years and a half old and then one morning, as the sun came up, his soul took flight upon the wings of light, into a land where there is no shadow. I have only hope and faith that there is a land of pure delight, which we call Heaven. I know not where it is, but this I do know – he is there! And I shall never see the glory of another and a fairer world, until I see his curly locks again and hear the music of his voice amid the angelic choir.*[353]

✿ ✿ ✿ ✿ ✿

Alfred Bernhard Nobel was born in Stockholm, Sweden on October 21, 1833. At an early age he developed an interest in science, particularly chemistry. At the age of thirty he began work as a chemist at his father's workshop. While there he began experimenting with mixtures which could create different types of explosives and he was eventually successful in developing a process to produce nitroglycerine. He obtained a patent on a special type of nitroglycerine, which he called "dynamite". His invention soon proved popular both for commercial use but also in warfare, as well. Concerned about the destructive use of his invention, Nobel was torn between his desire to be of service to mankind and the violent actions that for which dynamite was used.

Nobel became one of the wealthiest men in the world. He vowed, though, that he would use the profits from his invention to promote peace among the nations of the world. After his death in 1896, he created the Nobel Foundation. The income from his bequest would be used to annually honor the greatest achievements in various areas of human endeavor. According to his will, his gift would provide awards to "those who, during the preceding year, shall have conferred the greatest benefit on mankind." Beginning in 1901, Nobel Prizes would be awarded in literature, physics, chemistry and medicine. But, true to Nobel's intentions, the most coveted prize each year was the Nobel Peace Prize. To emphasize the importance of the award, the Nobel Prize is announced on November 10, the anniversary of Nobel's death in 1896.

The first Nobel Peace Prize in 1901 was split among Henri Dunant of Switzerland and Frederick Passy of France for their work in creating international peace organizations including, in Dunant's case, the International Red Cross. Subsequent prizes were awarded to President Theodore Roosevelt for his efforts to negotiate peace between Russia and Japan, and Elihu Root for his success in negotiating several arbitration agreements among nations.

But the outbreak of World War I created a dilemma for the selection committee from the Nobel Institute. How could they award a prize for peace, it was argued, when the entire world was consumed in war? The Institute chose not to make any award in 1914, 1915 or 1916. In 1917, to commemorate their efforts to relive suffering around the globe, the award was presented to the International Red Cross. But November 10, 1918 and 1919 passed without the announcement of any award.

Eventually, on December 10, 1920, the President of the Norwegian Parliament announced:

> *The Nobel Committee of the Norwegian Parliament has the honor of announcing herewith its decision to award the Nobel Peace Prize for 1919 to the President of the United States of America, Mr. Woodrow Wilson.*

The announcement in 1920, in fact, awarded the Nobel Peace Prize for both 1919 and 1920, with the second award going to Léon Bourgeois, president of the French Senate and president of the Council of the League of Nations. To underscore the importance of the League of Nations to world peace, the Nobel Peace Prize for two consecutive years was awarded to the author of the League of Nations, and to its first leader.

> *Today, Gentlemen, as the Norwegian Parliament meets to present the Nobel Peace Prize for the first time since the World War I, it is with the conviction that the great ideal of peace,*

so deeply rooted in the hopes for survival of the nations, will gain fresh ground in the minds of men as a result of the recent tragic events. As the name of President Wilson comes to the fore on this occasion as the recipient of the Peace Prize, I know that the award is accompanied by the thanks of the people of Norway, because in his celebrated Fourteen Points the President of the United States has succeeded in bringing a design for a fundamental law of humanity into present-day international politics. The basic concept of justice on which it is founded will never die, but will steadily grow in strength, keeping the name of President Wilson fresh in the minds of future generations.[354]

Wilson's illness prevented him from attending the award ceremony on December 10, 1920. Albert G. Schmedeman, the United States ambassador to Sweden, accepted the prize on the President's behalf. He delivered President Wilson's remarks to the Nobel Committee, stating, in part,

Mankind has not yet been rid of the unspeakable horror of war. I am convinced that our generation has, despite its wounds, made notable progress. It will be a continuing labor. In the indefinite course of the years before us there will be abundant opportunity for others to distinguish themselves in the crusade against hate and fear and war. Whatever has been accomplished in the past is petty compared to the glory and promise of the future.[355]

இ இ இ இ இ

Eventually, the day came when Marshall left the Capital for the last time as Vice President. He and Wilson had little contact the last few months of his presidency. By now, it was well known that Wilson's health was poor, and that impression was not contradicted when a feeble Wilson slowly moved from the car that brought him to the Capital to a waiting wheelchair.

President-elect Warren G. Harding, Vice President-elect Calvin Coolidge, Marshall and a small crowd of political leaders met Wilson. The President, in his last official acts, signed several dozen minor bills. By tradition, at this meeting representatives of both Houses report to the departing President that the work of the Sixty-sixth Congress was now over and they were ready to adjourn. Though feeble, Wilson met each man with a smile and cordial welcome.

Just after noon, the meeting was joined by Senator Henry Cabot Lodge. When his nemesis entered the room, Wilson's friendly demeanor disappeared. As was his duty, Lodge turned to Wilson and indicated that the work of Congress was complete. He asked if there was any final message that the President wished to communicate.

"I have no communication to make," Wilson answered icily, "I appreciate your courtesy; good morning, sir!"

Lodge glanced at his watch. "It's time we're moving."[356]

While Wilson was too ill to attend the inaugural ceremonies, it was Harding, not Wilson, who would die first. Harding would be dead just two years after taking office. Wilson spent his final years surrounded by his family. On a sunny Sunday morning, February 3, 1924, after whispering the word "Edith", Woodrow Wilson died.[357]

Soon after Wilson's death, Marshall wrote:

> *No man ever had a firmer faith in the good intentions of the people, than had Woodrow Wilson. His confidence in them is deserving of all praise. But, alas, he did not know the petty meanness of mankind and so, -- although worn by the nerve rack of the war and that larger nerve rack at Paris where, as it seems to me , he went down from Jerusalem to Jericho and fell among thieves—his faith in the people still being supreme, he took his life in his hand in an effort to appeal from Philip drunk to Philip sober. It was too much for mere humanity. He broke under the strain and for nearly eighteen months was a physical wreck. It is of no moment whether you were for or against the League of Nations; whether you were with him or against him; whether you liked him or hated him; you take off your hat to him for his courage, for his persistence in what he believed to be his line of duty.* [358]

Epilogue

(1921-1925)

At the end of his term in 1921, Marshall returned to private life and he and Lois moved to a home in Indianapolis. They had considered returning to Columbia City, where Tom could affiliate with a local law firm, but decided that the professional opportunities would be greater in the capital city of Indiana.

Marshall had put his name forward for President at the Democratic Convention in San Francisco in 1920. Tom Taggart agreed to send an uncommitted Indiana delegation to the gathering, and the Vice President had let it be known that he would not be opposed to having his name considered for the nomination. When Mark Thistlethwaite traveled to the convention, though, it was clear to him that the delegates wished to put any reminders of the Wilson administration behind them. Marshall received few votes beyond those of the Hoosier delegates. The Democrats eventually chose James Cox of Ohio, with young Franklin Roosevelt as his running mate. Republicans also chose a candidate from Ohio, Warren Harding, with Calvin Coolidge, the Governor of Massachusetts, for Vice President. After Coolidge was nominated, Marshall sent him a telegram which read, "Please accept my sincere sympathy".[359]

Four years later, when the Democrats gathered for their convention in New York, the meeting deadlocked and balloting went on for more than a week. As the tired delegates looked for anyone to break the stalemate, Marshall's name was put forward but failed to generate much interest. He received two votes on the ninety-seventh ballot, three on the ninety-third, and two on the ninety-fourth. Later, humorist Will Rogers claimed that he was responsible for the "swing to Marshall".[360]

❧ ❧ ❧ ❧ ❧

Despite the potential constitutional crisis that Wilson's illness had caused, it would be more than fifty years before Congress would take action to clarify the ambiguity of the presidential succession language in the Constitution. Led, perhaps appropriately, by a politician from Indiana – Democratic Senator Birch Bayh – the Senate and House both passed the Twenty-Fifth Amendment to the Constitution in 1965. In February, 1967, it received the necessary two-thirds ratification from the states and became law.

The Twenty-Fifth Amendment corrected several succession issues. As originally ratified, the United States Constitution stated that in the event the office of President became vacant, "the Same shall devolve upon the Vice President." Did this mean that the Vice President only has the duties of the President without the title? The amendment made it clear that if the President is disabled the Vice President succeeds to the office of the President.

In addition, until the passage of the Twenty-Fifth Amendment there was no method of filling a vacancy in the office of Vice President. President William Howard Taft considered appointing a new Vice President in 1912 upon the death of John Sherman, but the legality of such an action was unclear. With the new language, if there was a vacancy in the office of Vice President of the United States, the President nominates a successor, who is confirmed by the majority vote of both houses of Congress.

Probably most importantly, the new language provided a clear method for presidential succession. The president may invoke the Twenty-Fifth Amendment voluntarily by transmitting to the President pro tempore of the Senate and the Speaker of the House of Representatives a written declaration to declare himself or herself unable to discharge the powers and duties of the office. The Vice President would serve as Acting President until the President sends another written declaration declaring himself or herself able to resume the office.

In addition, an alternative method of succession is described should the president be unable or unwilling to step down. Under this involuntary withdrawal method, the Vice President, along with a majority of the Cabinet, can declare the President disabled. At this point, the President can resume his office by sending a written declaration sent to the President pro tempore and the Speaker. If the Vice President and Cabinet, however, continue to believe that the President is disabled, they may within four days of the President's declaration submit another declaration that the President is incapacitated. If this occurs, Congress decides the issue, and a two-thirds vote in each House is required to permit the Vice President to assume the Acting Presidency.

Shortly after the Twenty-Fifth Amendment was ratified, it was invoked to resolve several succession issues. After Vice President Spiro Agnew resigned in October of 1973, President Richard Nixon appointed Michigan congressman Gerald Ford as Vice President. Ford was quickly confirmed by Congress. Less than ten months later, after President Richard Nixon resigned on August 9, 1974, Vice President Gerald Ford succeeded to the presidency. He subsequently nominated former New York Governor Nelson Rockefeller to succeed him as Vice President, and Rockefeller was sworn into office in December, 1974.

In July of 1985, President Ronald Reagan underwent surgery and transferred the powers of the presidency to Vice President George H.W. Bush. Similarly, nearly seven years later when George H.W. Bush, now President, underwent a similar surgery he invoked the Twenty-Fifth amendment to transfer power to Vice President Dan Quayle.

∾ ∾ ∾ ∾ ∾

In his retirement, Thomas Marshall dabbled with some legal matters, but was still looking for projects to both use his experience and generate some income. He wrote articles for periodicals and made speeches across the country. He considered becoming the head of a life insurance company, but eventually declined the offer. He was approached by a businessman representing an oil company, but grew suspicious when offered a large sum for very little work. "I knew I was not worth that much to any firm," he later said, "so I thought I had better just come on back to Indiana."[361] Marshall's suspicions proved correct, as the country would soon be consumed by the Teapot Dome scandal.

Warren Harding helped Marshall find an outlet for his energies. In 1921, he appointed the former Vice President to the Lincoln Memorial Commission. The following year, Marshall was given a more lucrative position on the Federal Coal Commission, which also provided an annual salary of $7,500.

Around this time, Marshall also embarked on the culmination of many public lives – writing his memoirs. He chose the title, "A Hoosier Salad" for, as he noted at the beginning of the book,

> *To make a perfect salad there should be a spendthrift for oil,*
> *a miser for vinegar, a wise man for salt and a madcap to stir*
> *it up.*

Thomas's endearing personality was present even in his autobiography. As he noted in the forward:

> *This book is not intended to turn the tides of history nor to*
> *change the opinion of men as to the great things which took*
> *place when I was in public life. It has been written in the hope*
> *that the Tired Business Man, the Unsuccessful Golfer and the*
> *Lonely Husband whose wife is out reforming the world may find*
> *therein a half hour's surcease from sorrow.*

Unlike many biographies of today, the Vice President did not feel the need to fill his book with undisclosed secrets or after-the-fact venom. Instead, he wrote the book much as he lived his life: In a friendly, cordial and straightforward manner, praising those he respected and saying little or nothing about the fools and charlatans he had met in his career.

> *I fear I can not make this salad better by adding more ingredients.*
> *I prefer to watch its being served just as it is, and to take note of*
> *how the consumers like it. I have not touched upon controversial*
> *questions for they would have made it too sour; and I dared not*
> *speak of my intimate relations of life and the friends that I have*
> *grappled to my heart with hooks of steel lest it should have been*
> *so sweet as to be nauseating.* [362]

Marshall never lived to see his book published. It was substantially complete at the time of his death, and the Bobbs-Merrill publishing firm purchased the rights from Lois for the unprecedented sum of $50,000 – some of which might be considered an honor to Mrs. Marshall for her years of service to both the State of Indiana and the nation in her role as the Vice President's wife.

Marshall wrote soon before his death:

> *I have been a fairly contented and happy man. I have never risen to real greatness nor have I been cast down into the depths of despair. I have sounded most of the shoals and depths of human passion, and yet I venture to throw to myself this little bouquet gathered out of the garden of an interesting if not serviceable or profitable life: That I have learned, with the Apostle Paul, to be content in whatsoever station of life I am.*[363]

Thomas Marshall never embraced the philosophy that politics was a bitter fight waged with high emotion and guided by vindictiveness towards your political opponent. Unlike Wilson, he respected those with opposing viewpoints and felt that rational and friendly discourse was the most effective way of reaching an agreement.

> *I had found, long before I arrived in Washington, that the ability to drive men ended at Appomattox; that more things were accomplished by good humor and a spirit of fairness than ever had been brought about by an attempt to enforce what you conceived to be the right. It was not easy work, nor was it soon ended. But I have a feeling that when it was all over, the members of the Senate disagreeing with me, as many of them did, both along political lines and lines within political lines, saw me go with the conviction that there was no bitterness or resentment in my heart because a man did not agree with me; that he might dispute everything I said, disagree with every view I held and yet he might remain my personal friend. I do not know whether this attitude toward life is worth anything or not. It does not get a man very far, I know, but it does leave him with a sweet taste in his mouth.*[364]

Marshall's goals for his state and nation may not have been as lofty or as well-documented as Wilson's, but he had a political vision that transcended political squabbling.

> *The political dream of my life has been to educate our people in law, literature and religion so that they would become a self-governing body of men and women who, in the absence of all political leadership, would, in unbroken ranks, march in the vanguard of civilization to greet the millennial dawn.*[365]

In May of 1925, Tom Marshall agreed to return to northeast Indiana to deliver graduation speeches to the high schools in Columbia City, his hometown, and North Manchester, the city of his birth. His wit remained intact. "If you are expecting the usual thing in commencement addresses you are bound to be disappointed," he said.

> *That kind of address is delivered by a reputed wise man and attempts in forty or fifty minutes to give enough sound advice and philosophy to last a lifetime. Now that I am out of politics, I am old enough to tell the truth. The world never had, has not now, and never will have any great men save those who do something for their countries and for their God."*[366]

Thomas Riley Marshall died of a heart attack on June 1, 1925, at the Willard Hotel in Washington, D.C. The *Indianapolis News* reported that the former Vice President "was sitting up in bed reading the Bible when the fatal attack took him." Lois retired to Arizona, where she remained a widower for 33 years before she died in 1958.

Marshall's biographer, Charles Thomas, summarized his contradictions:

> *He was, prior to 1898, a most pronounced drinker and at the same time a leader in the church. He was inconsistent, yet he was trusted. He was a fundamentalist in religion, yet not (intolerant of other beliefs). He was enjoyed as the biggest wit in town, yet his judgment was respected by those who knew him, and his leadership was accepted. His political career proves*

that, despite his conflicting traits, there was something in his character which made people like him.[367]

Born into relative privilege and called at a young age into public service, Thomas Riley Marshall stumbled through the early years of adulthood. Rescued from personal and professional oblivion by a devoted soul mate, well past the age of fifty he started a meteoric political ascent that took him the width of an artery away from the presidency. Through tragedy and disappointment he kept his faith in his God, his love for his wife and his devotion to his country. History will remember him as a man who put his belief in the system of American democracy above his own personal ambition, and until the day he died he remained a genuine Hoosier from rural Indiana.

Bibliography

Angle, Paul M. Crossroads: 1913. Chicago: Rand McNally, 1963.

Barry, John M. The Great Influenza the Epic Story of the Deadliest
    Plague in History. New York: Penguin Books, 2005.

Blum, John Morton. Joe Tumulty and the Wilson Era.
    Boston: Houghton Mifflin, 1951.

Boomhower, Ray E. Jacob Piatt Dunn, Jr a Life in History and Politics,
    1855-1924. Indianapolis: Indiana Historical Society, 1997.

Brands, H. W. Woodrow Wilson. 1st Ed. ed. New York: Times Books, 2003.

Brown, John E. "Woodrow Wilson's Vice President: Thomas R. Marshall and
    the Wilson Administration, 1913-1920." Diss. Ball State Univ., 1970.

Chernow, Ron. The House of Morgan an American Banking Dynasty and the
    Rise of Modern Finance. 1st Ed. ed. New York: Atlantic Monthly P, 1990.

Columbia City Commercial Oct. 1878.

Cooper, John Milton. Breaking the Heart of the World Woodrow Wilson and
    the Fight for the League of Nations. New York: Cambridge UP, 2001.

Fadely, James P. Thomas Taggart Public Servant, Political Boss : 1856-
    1929. Indianapolis: Indiana Historical Society, 1997.

Fletcher, Stephen J. "The Business of Exposure: Lewis Hine and Child
    Labor Reform." Traces of Indiana and Midwestern History 4 (1992).

Heckscher, August. Woodrow Wilson. New York:
    Maxwell Macmillan International, 1991.

Houston, David Franklin. Eight Years with Wilson's Cabinet, 1913
    to 1920. St. Clair Shores, Mich.: Scholarly P, 1970.

Leuchtenburg, William Edward. The Perils of Prosperity, 1914-
    1932. 2nd Ed. ed. Chicago: University of Chicago P, 1993.

Levin, Phyllis Lee. Edith and Woodrow the Wilson
    White House. New York: Scribner, 2001.

Macmillan, Margaret. Paris 1919 Six Months That Changed the
    World. 1st U.S. Ed. ed. New York: Random House, 2002.

Marshall, Thomas R. <u>A Hoosier Salad: Recollections of Thomas</u>
<u>R. Marshall, Vice President and Hoosier Philosopher</u>.
Indianapolis: Bobbs-Merrill Company, 1925.

McAdoo, William Gibbs. <u>Crowded Years</u>. Port Washington, N.Y.: Kennikat P, 1971.

Miller, Nathan. <u>New World Coming the 1920s and the Making of Modern</u>
<u>America</u>. 1st Da Capo Press Ed. ed. Cambridge, MA: Da Capo P, 2004.

Montgomery, Keith S., *Marshall's Victory in the Election of 1908*,
<u>Indiana Magazine of History</u>, LII (1956), pp. 147-166.

Morison, Samuel Eliot. <u>The Oxford History of the American</u>
<u>People</u>. New York: Oxford UP, 1965.

Morris, Edmund, <u>The Rise of Theodore Roosevelt</u>. New
York: Coward, McCann & Geoghegan, 1979.

O'Toole, Patricia. <u>When Trumpets Call Theodore Roosevelt After</u>
<u>the White House</u>. New York: Simon & Schuster, 2005.

Phillips, Clinton J. <u>Indiana in Transition: the Emergence of an</u>
<u>Industrial Commonwealth</u>. Indianapolis: Indiana UP, 1968.

Roosevelt, Eleanor. <u>Autobiography</u>. 1st Ed. ed. New York: Harper, 1961.

Shachtman, Tom. <u>Edith & Woodrow a Presidential</u>
<u>Romance</u>. New York: Putnam, 1981

Thomas, Charles Marion. <u>Thomas Riley Marshall, Hoosier</u>
<u>Statesman</u>. Oxford, O.: The Mississippi Valley P, 1939.

Tuchman, Barbara Wertheim. <u>The Zimmermann Telegram</u>.
New Ed. ed. New York: Macmillan, 1966.

Tumulty, Joseph P. <u>Woodrow Wilson as I Know Him</u>. New York: AMS P, 1970.

Weisman, Steven R. <u>The Great Tax Wars Lincoln to Wilson, the</u>
<u>Fierce Battles Over Money and Power That Transformed</u>
<u>the Nation</u>. New York: Simon & Schuster, 2002.

Wolff, Leon. <u>In Flanders Fields</u>. New York: Viking P, 1958.

Zimmermann, Warren. <u>First Great Triumph How Five</u>
<u>Americans Made Their Country a World Power</u>. 1st Ed.
ed. New York: Farrar, Straus and Giroux, 2002.

Endnotes

1   Marshall, Thomas R. <u>A Hoosier Salad: Recollections of Thomas R.</u>
    <u>Marshall, Vice President and Hoosier Philosopher</u>, Bobbs-Merrill Company,
    Indianapolis, 1925, p. 363., hereinafter referred to as <u>Recollections</u>.

2   Levin, Phyllis Lee. <u>Edith and Woodrow the Wilson</u>
    <u>White House</u>. New York: Scribner, 2001, p. 14.

3   Thomas, Charles M., <u>Thomas Riley Marshall, Hoosier Statesman</u>,
    Mississippi Valley Press, Oxford, Ohio, 1939, p. 11.

4   <u>Recollections</u>, p. 19.

5   <u>Recollections</u>, p. 21.

6   <u>Recollections</u>, pp. 20-21.

7   Thomas, p. 12.

8   Brown, John Eugene, *Woodrow Wilson's Vice President: Thomas R.*
    Marshall and the Wilson Administration, 1913-1920., unpublished
    Ph.D. dissertation, Ball State University, 1970, p. 10.

9   Thomas, p. 12.

10 Morison, Samuel Eliot. <u>The Oxford History of the American</u>
    <u>People</u>. New York: Oxford UP, 1965, p. 591.

11 Morrison, p. 594.

12 Morrison, pp. 601-602.

13 Thomas, p. 13.

14 <u>Recollections</u>, p. 64.

15 Letter in Papers of Thomas Marshall, Indiana State Library.

16 <u>Recollections</u>, pp. 220-221.

17 Morrison, pp. 722-723.

18 <u>Recollections</u>, p. 79.

19 <u>Recollections</u>, p. 81.

20 Thomas, p. 15.

21 <u>Recollections</u>, p. 90.

22 <u>Recollections</u>, p. 91.

23 <u>Recollections</u>, p. 91.

24 <u>Recollections</u>, p. 129.

25 Thomas, p. 36.

26 <u>Recollections</u>, p. 88.

27 <u>Recollections</u>, pp. 137-138.

28 Morrison, p. 730.

29 Document in Marshall archives, Indiana State Library.

30 <u>Recollections</u>, p. 96.

31 <u>Recollections</u>, p. 95.

32 <u>Recollections</u>, p. 102.

33 Thomas, p. 19.

34 Thomas, p. 19.

35 <u>Recollections</u>, pp. 106-107.

36 <u>Recollections</u>, p. 347.

37 Thomas, p. 23.

38 Zimmermann, Warren. <u>First Great Triumph How Five Americans Made Their Country a World Power</u>. 1st Ed. ed. New York: Farrar, Straus and Giroux, 2002, p. 67.

39 <u>Recollections</u>, pp. 143-144.

40 <u>Recollections</u>, p. 144.

41 <u>Recollections</u>, p. 144.

42 Letter from Marshall to Dr. Charles E. Rice of Alliance, Ohio, July 27, 1912.

43 Columbia City *Commercial*, October, 1878.

44 Thomas, p. 27.

45 Thomas, p. 31.

46 Phillips, Clinton J. <u>Indiana in Transition: the Emergence of an Industrial Commonwealth</u>., Indianapolis: Indiana UP, 1968, , p. 10

47 Phillips, pp 12-13.

48 <u>Recollections</u>, pp. 144-145.

49 Thomas, p. 27.

50 Thomas, p. 29.

51 Thomas, p. 29.

52 Montgomery, Keith S., *Marshall's Victory in the Election of 1908*, <u>Indiana Magazine of History</u>, LII (1956), p. 149.

53 Montgomery, p. 149.

54 Hendricks to Marshall, October 28, 1884, as quoted in *Brown*, p. 25.

55 Phillips, p. 27.

56 Fishback, William P., *A Plea for Honest Elections: An Address Delivered to the Students of Indiana State University*, May, 1886 (Indianapolis: A.R. Baker, Printer, 1886), pp. 17-18, as quoted in Boomhower, Ray E. Jacob Piatt Dunn, Jr a Life in History and Politics, 1855-1924. Indianapolis: Indiana Historical Society, 1997.

57 Recollections, pp. 335-336.

58 Fadely, James P. Thomas Taggart Public Servant, Political Boss : 1856-1929. Indianapolis: Indiana Historical Society, 1997.

59 See, for example, *A Monetary History of the United States: 1867-1960*, by Milton Friedman and Anna Jacobson Schwartz, Princeton, New Jersey, 1963.

60 Chernow, Ron, The House of Morgan, New York, 1990, pp. 75-78.

61 Morrison, p. 798.

62 Weisman, Steven R. The Great Tax Wars Lincoln to Wilson, the Fierce Battles Over Money and Power That Transformed the Nation, New York: Simon & Schuster, 2002, pp. 123-130.

63 Weisman, p. 123.

64 Weisman, p. 127.

65 Fadely, pp. 13-58.

66 *Columbia City Post*, December 20, 1961.

67 Brown, p. 377.

68 Phillips, p. 44.

69 See www.agecon.purdue.edu

70 Recollections, p. 147.

71 Morris, Edmund, The Rise of Theodore Roosevelt. New York: Coward, McCann & Geoghegan, 1979, , p. 241.

72 Gray, p. 195.

73 Angle, Paul M., Crossroads: 1913, New York: Rand McNally, 1963, pp. 37-40.

74 Recollections, p. 150-151.

75 Thomas, P. 39.

76 Recollections, p. 159-160.

77 Recollections, p. 154.

78 Recollections, p. 156.

79 Recollections, p. 158.

80 Recollections, p. 159.

81 Brown, p. 30.

82　Fadely, p. 116.

83　Indianapolis Star, March 27, 1908, as quoted in *Montgomery*, p. 150.

84　<u>Recollections</u>, p. 161.

85　Montgomery, p. 151.

86　<u>Recollections</u>, p. 154.

87　Montgomery, p. 151.

88　<u>Recollections</u>, pp. 162-163.

89　Montgomery, pp. 163-164.

90　Montgomery, pp. 152-153.

91　Campaign handbill, as quoted in *Montgomery*, p. 163.

92　<u>Recollections</u>, p. 169-170.

93　Montgomery, p. 156.

94　Montgomery, p. 157.

95　Montgomery, p. 161.

96　Montgomery, p. 162.

97　Montgomery, p. 161.

98　Montgomery, p. 162.

99　<u>Recollections</u>, pp. 187-188.

100　Montgomery, pp. 152-153.

101　Phillips, p. 100.

102　Boomhower, p. 78.

103　<u>Recollections</u>, p. 166.

104　Montgomery, p. 158.

105　Montgomery, p. 154.

106　<u>Recollections</u>, p. 169.

107　Gray, p. 206.

108　Morris, p. 328.

109　Morris, p. 328.

110　O'Toole, Patricia, <u>When Trumpets Call: Theodore Roosevelt After The White House</u>; Simon & Shuster, New York, 2005, p. 93.

111　Brown, p. 35.

112　<u>Recollections</u>, p. 174.

113　Brown, p. 37.

114　Harlow Lindley (ed.), *The Indiana Centennial 1916* (Indiana Historical Commission, Indianapolis, 1919), pp. 330, 333.

115 For a discussion of Indiana agriculture at the time of
Marshall's term as governor, see Phillips, pp. 132-180.

116 Recollections, pp. 178-179.

117 *Indianapolis News*, January 6, 1909, as quoted in Brown, p. 35.

118 Speech by Marshall to Indiana General Assembly, January 1913.

119 Fletcher, Stephen J., *The Business of Exposure: Lewis Hine
and Child Labor Reform*, Traces of Indiana and Midwestern
History, Volume 4, Number 2, Spring 1992.

120 Phillips, pp. 334-335.

121 Recollections, p. 196.

122 Marshall letter, April 10, 1910, Indiana State Library Manuscript.

123 Recollections, p. 180.

124 Thomas, p. 81.

125 Recollections, pp. 180-181.

126 Recollections, pp. 207-208.

127 Recollections, pp. 199-200.

128 Recollections, p. 198.

129 Recollections, p. 201.

130 Recollections, p. 202.

131 "The Governors' Messages to the People, The World
Today, January, 1910, p.47, as quoted in *Brown*.

132 Recollections, p. 188-189.

133 Recollections, pp. 170-171.

134 Fadely, pp. 108-109.

135 Fadely, p. 118.

136 Thomas, p. 76.

137 Thomas, p. 77.

138 Thomas, p. 77.

139 Recollections, p. 183.

140 Recollections, pp. 193-194.

141 Recollections, pp. 194-195.

142 Boomhower, p. 73.

143 Recollections, p. 210.

144 Boomhower, pp. 84-85.

145 Thomas, pp. 150-151.

146 Boomhower, p. 90.

147 Boomhower, p. 88.

148 Boomhower, p. 83.

149 Boomhower, p. 80.

150 Boomhower, p. 80.

151 Recollections, p. 209.

152 Recollections, p. 213.

153 Recollections, p. 213.

154 Recollections, p. 214.

155 James B. Morrow, "Thomas R. Marshall Gives His Views on What the Democrats Should Do," Indianapolis Sunday Star, January 23, 1910, as quoted in Brown.

156 Recollections, p. 241.

157 "Marshall Fights Presidential Bee," Indianapolis Star, April 14, 1910, page 1, as quoted in Brown.

158 Hatfield, Mark O., at http://www.senate.gov.

159 Hatfield.

160 Hatfield.

161 Levin, p. 33.

162 Brands, H. W. Woodrow Wilson. 1st Ed. ed. New York: Times Books, 2003, p. 17.

163 Brands, page 18.

164 John B. Stoll, History of the Indiana Democracy, 1816-1916, (Indianapolis: Indiana Democratic Publishing Company, 1917, p. 1036, as quoted in Brown.

165 Brown, p. 103.

166 "Suggest Cabinet Members Advise Congress in Person", Washington Sunday Star, October 2, 1921, as quoted in Brown.

167 "Wilson Accepts the Nomination", Indianapolis News, August 7, 1912, pages 1 and 10, as quoted in Brown.

168 Brown, pp. 118-119.

169 Brown, pp. 119-120.

170 "Governor Marshall Talks on Tariff at Portland", Indianapolis News, August 27, 1912, page 9, as quoted in Brown.

171 "Mr. Marshall says Trusts are Happy", New York Herald, August 28, 1912, as quoted in Brown, p. 132.

172 Brown, p. 133.

173 "A Talk with Governor Marshall: Some Interesting Opinions Elicited
in an Interview with the Democratic Nominee for Vice President",
Harper's Weekly, July 13, 1912, pp. 10-11, as quoted in *Brown*.

174 Shipp, Thomas R., Thomas R. Marshall of Indiana: The Story of his Rise from
Country Lawyer to Governor, Then to Vice Presidential Candidate,", American
Review of Reviews, August, 1912, pp. 185-190, as quoted in *Brown*, p. 127.

175 "Exclude Asiatics, says Mr. Marshall", *New York Herald*,
October 23, 1912, as quoted in *Brown*.

176 Brown, p. 135.

177 Letter from Mark Thistlethwaite to Albert Burleson, October 16, 1912,
Albert S. Burleson papers, Library of Congress, as quoted in *Brown*, p. 137.

178 Hatfield.

179 *Brown*, p. 145.

180 "Mrs. Marshall Sure She is No Suffragist", *Indianapolis News*,
July 22, 1912, p. 7, as quoted in Brown, p. 147.

181 Theodore Roosevelt, "The Three Vice presidential Candidates and What They
Represent," *American Monthly Review of Reviews* 14 (September 1896): 289-97.

182 This and the preceding paragraphs from Brown, pp. 149-150.

183 Blum, John Morton. Joe Tumulty and the Wilson
Era. Boston: Houghton Mifflin, 1951, p. 1.

184 New York Times, March 5, 1913, as quoted in *Brown*, p. 165.

185 New York Times, March 6, 1913, as quoted in *Brown*, p. 168.

186 Tuchman, Barbara Wertheim. The Zimmermann Telegram.
New Ed. ed. New York: Macmillan, 1966, p. 72.

187 Recollections of W.N. Wishard, Marshall Collection, Indiana State Library.

188 "Crowd Overruns Marshall", New York Times, March
6, 1913, as quoted in *Brown*, p. 169.

189 Recollections, pp. 226-227.

190 Brown, p. 170.

191 Hatfield.

192 Both quotations from *Brown*, p. 173.

193 Recollections, p. 85.

194 Brands, p. 42.

195 Recollections, pp. 16-18.

196 New York Times, March 13, 1913, as quoted in *Brown*, page 210.

197 "Marshall, Carnegie Critic", *New York Times*, March
    24, 1913, as quoted in Thomas, p. 154.

198 Thomas, p. 146.

199 "Vice President Marshall Hints at Laws to Seize Large Private Fortunes",
    New York Herald, April 13, 1913, as quoted in *Brown*, pp. 197-198.

200 Brown, p. 197.

201 Thomas, p. 146.

202 Weisman, pp. 177-178.

203 Thomas, p. 199.

204 Harvey, George, "Thomas Riley Marshall", *North American Review*,
    October 1916, pp. 620-621, as quoted in *Brown*, pp. 206-207.

205 "Marshall Assails Lawyers", New York Sun, April
    21, 1913, as quoted in *Brown*, p. 200.

206 Brown, p. 224.

207 Weisman, p. 249.

208 "Marshall's Tariff Views", New York Times, January
    17, 1913, as quoted in *Brown*, p. 185.

209 Recollections, p. 321.

210 Recollections, pp. 321-322.

211 Recollections, pp. 322-323.

212 Brown, p. 186.

213 Chernow, pp. 121-130.

214 Recollections, pp. 244-245.

215 Recollections, p. 272.

216 Recollections, p. 293.

217 Recollections, p. 339.

218 Zimmerman, p. 33.

219 Brown, p. 230.

220 Brown, p. 230.

221 McAdoo, William Gibbs. Crowded Years. Port Washington, N.Y.:
    Kennikat P, 1971, p. 269, as quoted in Brown, p. 270.

222 Sulzberger, C.L., The Fall of Eagles, New York, 1977, pp. 229-242.

223 Levin, p. 48.

224 Brands. p. 30.

225 Recollections, pp. 256-247.

226 Brown, p. 233.

227 Wolff, Leon, In Flanders Fields: The 1917 Campaign, Time-Life Books, 1980.

228 Information available at www.worldwar1.com.

229 Brown, p. 255.

230 Brown, p. 257.

231 Brown, p. 260.

232 Brown, p. 262.

233 Recollections, pp. 261-262.

234 Chernow, pp. 192-195.

235 Brown, p. 252.

236 Brown, p. 239.

237 Roosevelt, Eleanor. Autobiography. 1st Ed. ed. New York: Harper, 1961, p. 80, as quoted in *Brown*.

238 Brown, p. 244.

239 Brown, p. 249.

240 Brown, pp. 250-251.

241 Brown, p. 268.

242 Brown, P. 270.

243 Levin, p. 52.

244 Macmillan, Margaret, Paris 1919 Six Months That Changed the World. 1st U.S. Ed. ed. New York: Random House, 2002, p. 9.

245 Brown, P. 264.

246 Brown, p. 295

247 "Marshall Ridicules Hughes' Hindsight", New York Times, October 28, 1916, page 3, as quoted in *Brown*.

248 Thomas, p. 231.

249 *Fort Wayne News Sentinel*, September 17, 1916, page 1.

250 *Fort Wayne News Sentinel*, September 19, 1916, page 6.

251 O'Toole, p. 293.

252 Brown, p. 307.

253 Brown, P. 206.

254 "50,000 See Wilson Inaugurated Again," New York Times, March 6, 1917.

255 Recollections, pp. 338-339.

256 Blum, pp. 131-132.

257 Recollections, p. 339.

258 *New York Times*, May 20, 1973.

259 Recollections, p. 335.

260 <u>Recollections</u>, p. 147.

261 <u>Recollections</u>, pp. 268-269.

262 Brown, p. 455.

263 Brown, pp. 456-457.

264 <u>Recollections</u>, p. 340.

265 Hatch, Alden, <u>Edith Boling Wilson: First Lady Extraordinairy</u> (New York: Dodd, Mead and Company, 1961), p. 106, as quoted in *Brown*, p. 319.

266 Weisman, pp. 327-337.

267 <u>Recollections</u>, p. 346.

268 Brown, p. 322.

269 Levin, pp. 107-108.

270 <u>Recollections</u>, p. 362.

271 <u>Recollections</u>, pp. 362-363.

272 See Barry, John M. <u>The Great Influenza the Epic Story of the Deadliest Plague in History</u>. New York: Penguin Books, 2005.

273 Brown, p. 344.

274 Brown, pp. 345-346.

275 Levin, pp. 217-218.

276 Levin, pp. 219-220.

277 <u>Recollections</u>, p. 363.

278 <u>Recollections</u>, p. 361.

279 Brown, pp. 355-356.

280 Luechtenberg, p. 52.

281 McCullough, p. 257.

282 Zimmerman, p. 426.

283 Zimmerman, p. 424.

284 Macmillan, p. 6.

285 Brown, p. 359.

286 Brown, p. 360.

287 Brands. p. 104.

288 Brands, p. 105.

289 <u>Recollections</u>, p. 253.

290 Brown, p. 372.

291 Brown, p. 375.

292 Brown, p. 375.

293 Brown, p. 375.

294 <u>Recollections</u>, p. 365.

295 Macmillan, page xxviii.

296 Cooper, John Milton. <u>Breaking the Heart of the World Woodrow Wilson and the Fight for the League of Nations</u>. New York: Cambridge UP, 2001, p. 51.

297 <u>Recollections</u>, p. 366.

298 <u>Recollections</u>, p. 267.

299 Macmillan, p. 175.

300 <u>Recollections</u>, p. 234.

301 <u>Recollections</u>, pp. 236-237.

302 <u>Recollections</u>, p. 237.

303 <u>Recollections</u>, p. 364.

304 Morrison, p. 414.

305 Undated document in Marshall manuscripts, Indiana State Library.

306 Macmillan, p. 97.

307 Barry, pp. 381-382.

308 Barry, pp. 383-385.

309 Macmillan, p. 495.

310 Macmillan, p. 417.

311 Macmillan, p. 422.

312 Brown, p. 389.

313 <u>Recollections</u>, p. 287.

314 Macmillan, p. 489.

315 <u>Recollections</u>, p. 364.

316 Cooper, p. 157.

317 Cooper, p. 187.

318 Cooper, p. 189.

319 Levin, p. 331.

320 Levin, p. 333.

321 Heckscher, August. <u>Woodrow Wilson</u>. New York: Maxwell Macmillan International, 1991, p. 609.

322 Schachtman, pp. 208-209.

323 Levin, p. 337.

324 Weinstein, p. 357.

325 Levin, p. 337.

326 *New York Times*, October 3, 1919, page 1.

327 Brown, p. 403.

328 Cooper, p. 202.

329 Heckscher, p. 613.

330 Levin, p. 341.

331 Houston, David Franklin. <u>Eight Years with Wilson's Cabinet, 1913 to 1920</u>. St. Clair Shores, Mich.: Scholarly P, 1970, p. 37.

332 Brown, pp. 418-419.

333 Brown, p. 407.

334 Cooper, pp. 209-210.

335 See http://www.historylearningsite.co.uk/adolf-hitler.htm.

336 Ibid

337 <u>Recollections</u>, p. 367.

338 Morison, pp. 882-883.

339 Levin, p. 14.

340 Cooper, p. 210.

341 <u>Recollections</u>, p. 368.

342 <u>Recollections</u>, p. 375.

343 <u>Recollections</u>, p. 375.

344 <u>Recollections</u>, pp. 380-381.

345 <u>Recollections</u>, p. 380.

346 See Lonsdale, Frances, <u>Edward VIII: The Road to Abdication</u>, Lippincott Williams & Wilkins, 1st American edition, 1984.

347 Macmillan, p. 491.

348 Cooper, pp. 258-259.

349 Cooper, p. 262.

350 Cooper, p. 287.

351 Brown, p. 420.

352 Brown, p. 421.

353 Recollections, pp. 379-380.

354 See http://nobelprize.org/nobel_prizes/peace/laureates/1919/speech.html.

355 Ibid

356 Miller, Nathan. <u>New World Coming the 1920s and the Making of Modern America</u>. 1st Da Capo Press Ed. ed. Cambridge, MA: Da Capo P, 2004, p. 10.

357 Shachtman, Tom. <u>Edith & Woodrow a Presidential Romance</u>. New York: Putnam, 1981, p. 271.

358 <u>Recollections</u>, p. 367.

359 Thomas, p. 240.

360 Thomas, p. 240.

361 Thomas, p. 243.

362 <u>Recollections</u>, p. 363.

363 <u>Recollections</u>, p. 80.

364 <u>Recollections</u>, pp. 223-224.

365 Handwritten notes found in Marshall's papers
   by the author, dated May 16, 1919.

366 Brown, Jeanette, "Thomas Marshall", Whitley County
   Historical Museum, December 2002, page 9.

367 Thomas, p. 35.

Printed in the United States
69391LVS00002B/205-399